The Health of Men
and Wome

The Health of Men and Women

SARAH PAYNE

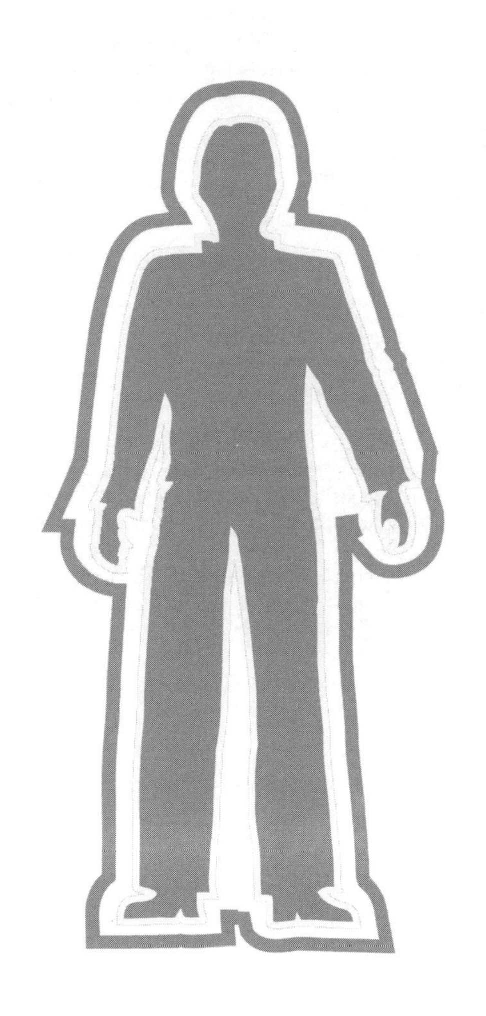

polity

First published in 2006 by Polity Press

Polity Press
65 Bridge Street
Cambridge CB2 1UR, UK.

Polity Press
350 Main Street
Malden, MA 02148, USA

ISBN-10: 0-7456-3453-2
ISBN-13: 978-07456-3453-1
ISBN-10: 0-7456-3454-0 (pb)
ISBN-13: 978-07456 (pb)

A catalogue record for this book is available from the British Library.

Typeset in 11 on 13 pt Scala
by Servis Filmsetting Ltd, Manchester
Printed and bound in Great Britain by
TJ International Ltd, Padstow, Cornwall

For further information on Polity, visit our website: www.polity.co.uk

Contents

List of Figure and Tables

Acknowledgements

Many people have helped in the writing of this book in various ways – in conversations, teaching, seminars and conferences. The structure and the content have both benefited in particular from input by Lesley Doyal, Veronica Pearson, and two anonymous reviewers who offered very helpful and constructive ideas on the first draft. More generally, I have received great support and encouragement over a number of years from colleagues in the School for Policy Studies, particularly those who work with me in the Centre for Health and Social Care Research, including Rachel Lart, Ailsa Cameron, Liz Lloyd, Sue Kilroe, Joan Langan, Marsha Henry, William Turner and Patricia Lucas. I should also like to thank the School for giving me study leave to complete this book, and Linda Price for her work supporting the Research Centre during this period. This book builds on funded research projects I have worked on, and I would like to take this opportunity to thank the World Health Organization, the Economic and Social Research Council, the Equal Opportunities Commission, the Department of Health and the Leverhulme Trust for their support. Emma Longstaff at Polity has been a great editor – positive and constructive; she has also prompted me nicely when necessary. And finally my thanks go to my family, Rob, Ella and Joe.

1 Sex, Gender and Health

Introduction

Global patterns of illness and health have changed in recent years. Life expectancy has increased in many countries, but the burden of chronic disease around the world is also increasing. More people than ever before now suffer from long-term health problems which limit their daily functioning and quality of life, and this poses particular difficulties for health care systems and for society, as well as for individuals themselves. One of the most significant changes in patterns of health around the world is the growing number of people with non-communicable diseases in both developed and less developed countries, where chronic conditions exist alongside the continuing threats to health posed by infectious diseases such as HIV/AIDS, malaria and tuberculosis (WHO, 2004e). Both men and women are affected by these shifting patterns of health, but there are important differences between them in how they are affected. Almost half of the increase in non-communicable disease relates to cardiovascular conditions, for example, which are experienced differently by women and men; the rapidly increasing global burden of tobacco-related illness is unequally distributed between women and men; HIV/AIDS in the parts of the world most affected is more prevalent among women; and the marked increase in mental health problems is also experienced differently by women and men (WHO, 2001, 2004e).

This book is about the relationship between sex, gender and health. It is about mortality and morbidity across the life course, and the role of sex and gender in explaining differences between women and men. Data about the health of women and men are more widely available in developed countries, and this shapes the discussion that follows; but the different experiences of women and men in less developed countries also add to our understanding of the relative importance of sex and gender as influences on health in different contexts. Similarly, the ways in which sex and gender interact with and are mediated by other forms of difference, particularly socio-economic status, ethnicity and sexuality, are relevant to an understanding of the influences on health and risks of death and will form part of our enquiry.

Why, then, do we need a book about the health of women and men, and the ways in which sex and gender affect health? Books about the specific health experience of women are not new, and there are a number of texts which cover issues relating to women's experiences of morbidity and mortality (e.g. Sargent and Brettell, 1996; Boswell and Poland, 2002; Pollard and Brin Hyatt, 1999; Lorber, 1997; Doyal, 1995) and women's experiences of the health care system (Foster, 1995; Doyal, 1998; Waller and McPherson, 2003; Hayes and Prior, 2003). An on-line search of medical and social science journals will produce a long list of papers on women's health across different disciplinary areas. For example, a search on Medline – one of the largest databases covering the major international medical and health policy journals – comes up with over 10,000 papers with the phrase 'women's health'. The vast majority of these papers were published in the last ten years or so, and over 1,000 of them also include the keyword 'gender'. Many focus on specifically female disorders – reproductive health in particular – but a number of them explore women's experiences of diseases which affect both sexes: HIV and AIDS, heart disease, mental illness and epilepsy, for example. In addition, there are papers which focus on service issues relating to women's experience of health care and treatment, and on gender in the medical curriculum.

A similar search specifically focusing on men's health is also interesting. In recent years the number of books and articles explicitly about men and health has increased (e.g. Sabo and Gordon, 1995; Griffiths, 1996; O'Dowd and Jewell, 1998; Watson, 2000). This represents a new dimension in health literature, although the earlier absence of texts specifically exploring the health of men does not mean that men's health was entirely neglected in the past. As many authors have remarked, there has been a tendency for medical research to focus on the health experiences of men as though this reflects the population as a whole (Doyal, 1995; Courtenay, 2000). However, a search on Medline for the phrase 'men's health' finds only a fraction of the number of papers on 'women's health'. Most of these are recent publications, and only a minority include the term 'gender' as well as 'men's health'.

The content of papers on 'men's health' differs too. A significant proportion of the writing on men's health deals with HIV infection and AIDS, particularly among men who have sex with men. Other papers focus specifically on conditions which are biologically defined as male – testicular cancer, prostate cancer and erectile dysfunction, for example – while relatively few take a wider view of what makes men healthy, or not. In comparison with the material on women's health, a smaller proportion of the papers focus on service issues in relation to men. There are also fewer journals dedicated to men's health in comparison to women's health, and those we have are recent additions – the *International Journal of Men's Health* was launched in 2002, for example, while the *Journal of Men's Health and Gender* was first published in 2004.

This explicit focus on men's health as a specific subject area, rather than as a synonym for the health of the whole population, is thus relatively new. However, until recently the subject has been conceived in rather narrow ways, looking at a restricted range of problems, and at specific subgroups of men with particular conditions. Initially there was less discussion in this literature of the social construction of men's health, or the way in which men are treated within the health care system by professionals. In the last decade there have been some changes – in particular with the publication of papers in medical rather than social science journals about masculinity and the cost to men's health of being a man ('Healthy masculinity starts in boyhood' (Biddulph, 1995); 'Men's health: their own worst enemy' (Williamson, 1995)) and about the ways in which men are treated by practitioners or how their health care needs might best be met ('Older men's health – overcoming barriers to their care' (Schotanus, 1998); 'Exploring men's health in a men-only group' (Rees et al., 1995)).

While both the women's health literature and work on men's health is valuable in terms of our understanding of factors influencing the health of women and men, this separate discussion of men's health and women's health leaves a critical gap in the analysis of the relationship between health, gender and sex. This book explores the influences of sex and gender on health for both men and women, in order to understand the differences and the similarities between them, the relative importance of biological and socially constructed differences, and the way these intersect with each other and with other factors affecting the health of men and women.

There are, then, two specific reasons for this book. The first is that there is a tension between women's health and the emerging field of men's health, and this tension is in need of resolution, most obviously in debates over gender equity and health policy. The second is that it has become increasingly clear that men's and women's health experiences are complex, and that we need to review existing 'truisms' about the gaps between men and women. Without a systematic approach to sex and gender, our theorizing about health inequalities between women and men, and about inequalities more generally, will remain incomplete (Macintyre and Hunt, 1997).

Men's health, women's health and gender equity

From the 1980s onwards there has been a debate in national and global health policy, and in the media, about the need for services to target men's health. This debate has opened up the question of inequalities in health provision in relation to men and women as users of health care, as well as the question of health behaviour and ways in which unhealthy practices of men and women might be changed.

In academic writing, much of the recent interest in men's health has developed from men's studies and work on masculinity and masculinities. The late 1980s and the 1990s in particular were a time when increasing numbers of writers were working on the meaning of masculinity, and the implications of masculinity for aspects of men's lives, including fatherhood, power, sexuality and health (Connell, 2000; Seidler, 1997). The study of masculinity and health has largely meant the study of gendered influences on men's health. While medical research has tended to focus on sex-specific male health problems such as prostate disease and testicular cancer (Griffiths, 1996), social scientists have explored the dangers of masculinity for men's health, and in particular their risk of early death (Sabo and Gordon, 1995; Waldron, 1995; Helgeson, 1995).

Explanations of men's mortality have emphasized male behaviour, including smoking, alcohol use, risk taking and men's use of health care, for example (Waldron, 1995; Cameron and Bernardes, 1998; Moynihan, 1998; Denton and Walters, 1999; Courtenay, 2000; Banks, 2001). This literature has also largely focused on the health costs to men themselves of male behaviour, despite the fact that masculinity also carries significant implications for the health of women. This is most obvious in the physical and mental health costs to women of male violence (Abbott and Williamson, 1999; Lorber, 1997; Ganju et al., 2004a), but masculinity has other consequences for women's health. The association between masculinity, heterosexual sexuality and penetrative sex, for example, increases women's risks of poor health through sexually transmitted diseases, the risk of pregnancy, and the risks associated with female forms of contraception (Doyal, 1995; Lorber, 1997).

The growing interest in the problem of men's health can also be seen in public health debates in a number of developed countries, including England, the USA and Australia (Zinn, 1996; Thom, 2003; Lloyd, 2002). These debates have led to proposals for specific health interventions and health targets for men. In the USA, men's health centres have been increasing in number in the last few years (Shelton, 1999). In England, men's health entered the public health agenda in the early 1990s with Department of Health initiatives on the delivery of health care to men (Griffiths, 1996; Cameron and Bernardes, 1998). Recent health promotion programmes in the UK have targeted men and male conditions – the 'Keep your eye on the ball' campaign to increase awareness of prostate cancer, for example (Griffiths, 1996). This focus has been reinforced by a number of 'Men's Health' conferences, Men's Health Weeks, the development of a Men's Health Forum, and the creation in 2001 of an All Party Parliamentary Group on Men's Health, which aims to raise awareness of the issue at policy level (Cameron and Bernardes, 1998; Men's Health Forum, 2002). In developed countries this interest in men's health has also been reflected in the popular media, with widespread reports on a 'crisis' in male health – a study of men's health behaviour in the UK which revealed that men were more likely to tolerate symptoms or self-medicate than seek medical advice, for example, was widely discussed by the British press.

For many, this growing interest from medicine and policy makers in the health of men raises a dilemma. Feminist writers in particular have argued that in health, the delivery of health care, medical research and the orientation of Western medicine, women remain at a disadvantage to men. For Doyal (2000a), for example, women are disadvantaged in terms of their access to those resources which promote health. This is most obvious in the health of women in developing countries, where women have less food and less access to the economic and social capital of the household; but it is also true in more developed countries, where women are also more likely to experience poverty, deprivation and social exclusion than men (Graham, 1984, 2000). Secondly, women are particularly at risk where their reproductive health is concerned, especially in developing countries

(Sundari, 1994; Doyal, 1995). Thirdly, medical research continues to study major life-threatening conditions using solely or largely male samples, and this puts women further at risk (Doyal, 1995; Krieger and Zierler, 1995; CIHR, 2000).

For example, until the early 1990s the US Federal Food and Drug Administration restricted the participation of women in research studies, on the grounds that research trials might endanger women's health or that of an unborn child (Bird and Rieker, 1999). Although National Institute of Health Guidelines then required that women and ethnic minority groups should be included in medical research, reviews have found little change in the inclusion and reporting of data on women in general empirical studies since 1993 (Vidaver et al., 2000; Ramasubbu et al., 2001). In the area of cardiac research, for example, where the gender gap in research was pronounced, more trials have included women, and there have been more single sex, women-only studies, but specific aspects of women's cardiovascular health – including responses to medication – are relatively unexplored, and many studies continue to report aggregate rather than sex-specific data (Blake et al., 2005). Other countries, including the UK, have not yet made participation of women in research studies a requirement of government funding (Epstein, 2004). In addition, the continued use of male bodies in medical textbooks, except where reproductive systems are the focus, suggests that men's health is still the norm against which deviations – including the female body – are measured (Lawrence and Bendixen, 1992; Mendelsohn et al., 1994; Scully, 2003; Ussher, 2003).

These observations have led to a demand from some that gender equity in health should mean equity in the provision of health care resources, not equity of outcome (Doyal, 2000a; Broom, 1999). Policy should not aim to reduce the health gap between men and women, but to ensure that both have equal opportunities to maximize their health chances. Doyal (2000a) argues that women's health continues to be damaged by men, and that what men gain overall from the gender system outweighs the dangers attached to masculinity. Others, however, stress that the health of men is also adversely affected by gender and constructions of masculinity. As Watson observes, if 'masculinity is treated as an undifferentiated construct, it is presumed that all men benefit equally from being male in a patriarchal system' (Watson, 2000: 41) – and this may obscure the very real costs endured by some men, particularly those from lower socio-economic groups, from minority ethnic groups, and those with disabilities.

A central aim of this book, then, is to draw together the evidence about differences and similarities in the health of women and men, while also recognizing the part played by other forms of difference.

The complexity of men's health and women's health

The second reason for this book is that it is increasingly apparent that patterns of men's and women's health are complex, and that in both mortality and morbidity the gap between women and men is far from straightforward (Hunt and Annandale, 1999). Although differences between men and women in terms of their prospects of longevity are fairly well known, there are variations in the gap between women and men in mortality which reflect the complexities of underlying patterns of health. It is true that women live longer than men in virtually every country, and that, globally, female children have a better life expectancy than male children at birth (WHO, 2004e). In 2002 male life expectancy at birth was higher than female life expectancy in only one of the 192 World Health Organisation member states (Qatar), and even here the extent of male advantage was narrow. In a small number of other countries there is little difference between women and men in life expectancy – in Bangladesh women and men have equal life expectancy, while in Botswana, Niger, Pakistan and Zambia female life expectancy is only slightly higher than that of men. Although female life expectancy overall is greater than male life expectancy, the fact that the gap between women and men varies widely – from around eight years' advantage in Europe to two years in Africa and the Eastern Mediterranean, for example – suggests that a range of social factors are at work shaping the mortality risk of women and men (WHO, 2004e).

The gap between men and women in terms of mortality has also changed over time. At the start of the last century, while life expectancy in more developed countries favoured women, the female advantage over men was relatively narrow, compared with the middle years of the twentieth century, when the gap widened (Waldron, 1995). In countries such as the USA and the UK, however, the gap between female and male life expectancy narrowed again towards the end of the last century, as men's life expectancy increased faster than women's (Waldron, 1995; WHO, 2004e).

Differences between women and men in patterns of mortality also vary over the life course and in relation to specific causes of death. In the developed world, for example, the mortality gap between men and women is particularly marked in early adulthood, when men are more at risk of dying from violent accidental and non-accidental injury (Waldron, 1995; Watson, 2000). In less developed countries the gap in mortality at this age is narrower, reflecting women's reproductive health risks. The risk of dying very young also differs for boys and girls, but again this is not consistent across all countries. In most of the WHO member states boys have a greater risk of dying before the age of 5 than girls. However, in Pakistan, India, Bangladesh, Botswana and China the risk of death under the age of 5 is greater for female children, not because of biological differences in mortality risk but because of gendered differences in access to nutrition and health care and the increased risk of infanticide for girls, reflecting the low status of girl children in these countries (Murphy, 2003; Pearson, 2005).

There are further variations between women and men in what they die from, but this has also changed over time in relation to changes in gendered risk factors rather than biological ones, reflecting shifting patterns of behaviour. The sex ratio for lung cancer mortality, for example, has narrowed in most developed countries, following an increase in smoking among women (Wynder and Muscat, 1995; Jemal et al., 2003). In contrast, the gap between men and women in suicide mortality throughout the developed world has increased in the past 20 years due to particularly marked increases in suicide among men (Canetto and Sakinofsky, 1998).

Mortality rates also vary in other ways. Non-white ethnic groups in the UK, Australia and the USA have shorter life expectancy and higher mortality rates than white populations, and the cause of mortality varies, with some diseases playing a more significant part in the risk of death for different minority groups. Cancer mortality, for example, is higher among black Americans than white (NCHS, 2004), while diabetes-related mortality is higher among South Asians in the UK compared with the white population (Mather et al., 1998). Although the gap between women and men remains when we look at different minority ethnic groups, the size of the gap in mortality varies between groups and with different conditions, which also adds to the complexity of the picture.

In addition, mortality differs by social class throughout the world. In the UK, for example, life expectancy at birth for males in the highest social class is more than seven years greater than life expectancy in the lowest class, while women from the highest social class have an advantage of nearly six years over women in the lowest class (ONS, 2005b). In the USA, life expectancy is better for both men and women in higher-income groups, although the gap between high- and low-income women is narrower than the gap between men from different classes (Pamuk et al., 1998).

If we turn to patterns of ill health or morbidity, men and women's experiences again vary in complex ways (Emslie et al., 1999). In the past, research has suggested that women are more likely to suffer illness during the life course. One study in particular proved remarkably influential in constructing a conventional wisdom that 'women get sicker but men die quicker' (Nathanson, 1977), and the apparent paradox of women's longevity combined with poor health dominated feminist health writing in the 1980s and 1990s (Verbrugge, 1989; Lorber, 1997). Nathanson's research in the USA showed that women had higher rates of self-reported ill health and incapacity compared with men, and these findings were replicated in subsequent research in a number of Western countries (e.g. Popay et al., 1993; Lorber, 1997). Women's poorer health was particularly noticeable in self-reported health status and figures for mental health problems in the USA and the UK (Dunnell et al., 1999).

More recently, this conventional wisdom has been challenged by research which suggests that variations in patterns of ill health between men and women are rather more complex (Emslie et al., 1999; Annandale and Hunt, 2000). Studies exploring the health of men and women have reported a narrower gap than before, with little evidence that women suffer more health problems overall during their lives (Kandrack et al., 1991). A study in Scotland by Macintyre et al. (1996), for example, found similar levels of health problems for men and women, apart from psychological illness, which was greater among women, while the gap between men and women in morbidity varied by age. A later study of men's and women's answers to questions about chronic illness by Macintyre et al. (1999) found no significant differences between men and women either in their likelihood of reporting health conditions or in the number of symptoms they reported.

One explanation for this apparent convergence in health status between men and women is that the earlier research over-reported the difference, partly as a result of the measurements used (Macintyre et al., 1999). In addition, as a number of writers have pointed out, research which reports variations, rather than similarities, is more likely to be selected for publication in journals, and this also emphasizes difference (Emslie et al., 1999; Kandrack et al., 1991). The binary divisions used in research – men/women, male/female – also encourage a focus on variance rather than similarity (Emslie et al., 1999).

Other studies carried out at the same time as that of Nathanson (1977) found few differences in symptoms between men and women – but these were less often cited in subsequent studies of men and women's health (Macintyre et al., 1999).

It is also possible that patterns of morbidity have changed, reflecting shifts in the factors influencing men's and women's health, variations across the life course, and a 'cohort effect'. Younger generations of women have different experiences of both health and gender in comparison with women born earlier, and these variations may have contributed to reductions in the health gap between women and men over the past 30 years. For example, research suggests that participation in paid work can bring positive health benefits for women, depending on the context and the combination of other roles that women are performing. More women in younger age groups have continued with paid employment after having children, and this may be significant in explanations of differences in the gender gap between older and younger cohorts (Hunt, 2002; Emslie et al., 1999; Denton and Walters, 1999; Bartley et al., 1999).

Again, it is important to point out the wide variation globally in this health gap between men and women. In many developing countries girls' and women's health expectancy – as opposed to life expectancy – remains limited by their social position and underlying inequalities between women and men (Doyal, 1995; Vlassoff, 1999). This may be linked to oppressive gendered practices which directly impinge on girl's and women's health – female genital mutilation and early marriage, for example – or to socially constructed differences which deny girls and women access to health-promoting resources or medical care (Doyal, 1998) or which may put women at risk of sexually transmitted disease (Lorber, 1997). Gender also affects men's health in developing countries, and men's healthy life expectancy is poorer than that of women in most countries (WHO, 2004e). Men's health is affected by gender-linked factors both positively, through access to resources which improve health and the high premium attached to male children which is associated with additional food and health care, and negatively, through behaviour which is sanctioned for men but not women – the use of tobacco and alcohol, for example (Tomlinson, 1997; Pandey et al., 1999).

These complexities in health differences between men and women mean that we need a way of understanding health which reflects the wide range of influences involved, at different points in time, for different groups of men and women. In order to make sense of women's and men's health risks and opportunities, the connections between sex or biology and those related to gender or socially constructed differences need to be fully addressed.

Sex and gender for both men and women

Given that patterns of men's and women's health are so intricate, explanations of health and illness which focus only on either men or women are likely to be inadequate. Brod and Kaufman (1994) suggest that theories of gender which are built on the experience of men or women alone cannot effectively explain differences in power or in the effects of such differences on women and men: we need to explore the interrelationships between women's and men's experience. This is particularly true when seeking to explain the sum of factors which add up to health chances for men and women (Emslie et al., 1999; Hunt and Annandale, 1999; CIHR, 2000). Feminist analyses of women's health in the 1970s and 1980s have been central to the development of explanations of gendered differences in health in so far as these relate to women. Explanations of women's apparently higher rates of morbidity highlighted the health impact of poverty, for example, in particular the mental health impact of deprivation (Graham, 1984, 2000). Studies also explored the costs to women's health of parenting – either alone or in two-parent households; the costs of women's social and caring responsibilities (Bird and Rieker, 1999; Popay et al., 1993; Baker et al., 1999) and the issue of women's health in later life (Arber and Cooper, 1999).

While this work has been influential in the development of men's studies and interest in men's health, less explicit attention has been paid in men's health studies to the impact of sex and gender on health and of interactions between these influences. For example, there is little research on the ways in which men's experiences of parenting impact on their health. A large part of the work on men's health has instead focused on men's behaviour and masculinity (Connell, 2000; Courtenay, 2000). This difference between women's health writing and men's health writing is interesting, as each approach highlights different kinds of health costs, rather than different sources of health benefit. If we want to explore ways in which health might be improved for men or for women, it might be useful to consider these explanations in reverse – men's access to economic resources and their relative lack of caring and domestic responsibilities may help to explain some of the good health they enjoy, while the gendered construction of femininity – as opposed to masculinity – shapes women's health behaviour in ways which positively affect their health.

There is therefore a need to put sex and gender together for both men and women, in order to build an understanding of health which reflects physical differences, socially constructed differences including gender, and the interactions between these.

What do we mean by 'sex' and 'gender'?

'Sex' and 'gender' are not without problems as concepts. While they describe two kinds of differences between men and women, with 'sex' referring to biological differences and 'gender' referring to socially constructed differences, the way in which they are used in practice varies. Oakley's (1972) distinction between sex differences based on physical features and gender differences based on the way in which society defines the physical characteristics belonging to each sex was an intervention which many feminist writers found useful. In an exploration of health differences between women and men, in particular, this idea of the influences which relate to biological factors linked with hormones and the reproductive organs and those which arise from gender-linked factors, such as behaviour and access to health-promoting goods, was extremely important.

However, there are a number of difficulties with the idea of biological difference. Some writers have argued that 'biological facts' are to a greater or lesser extent socially constructed, and that the relative prominence given to different facts, particularly in explanations of the health of men and women, is similarly shaped by culture (Emslie et al., 1999: 35). At different times, for example, different aspects of biology will be seen as crucial to women's and men's vulnerability to particular diseases. In addition, some of the differences between men and women which in the past have been thought of as biological in origin have since been established as socially or culturally specific – from physical skills to nurturing abilities.

Thus both sex and gender may be seen as socially constructed to some extent, rather than objectively defined and constant. The terms 'sex' and 'gender' have also been blurred in practice, and at times the words are used almost interchangeably (Emslie et al., 1999). In particular, the word 'gender' has often been used in medical research to mean women – so that the phrase 'gender and health' has frequently meant, in reality, writing and research about women's health, not the health of both men and women. And as Emslie et al. point out, while writers may highlight gender as being socially constructed, and argue that we cannot map gender on to sex differences, research often then compares two groups, males and females, who are differentiated by their biological characteristics alone, without going back to the distinction between sex and gender (Emslie et al., 1999).

A model of sex and gender as separate and opposite is problematic, therefore, when it presents men and women as homogeneous groups, and so obscures differences within the categories 'men' and 'women'. The presentation of data by 'sex' – that is, for men and women as two distinct groups – implicitly suggests that these groups are internally consistent, or that differences within the groups are of less relevance than the differences between them. This also reinforces the idea that the biological basis of difference is more important than gender – as respondents or cases are allocated to one group or another on the basis of biological sex, not gendered attributes.

In much of the writing on gender, and in particular on masculinity, gender is seen as being discursively constructed, something that is performed. But again this raises important questions about the ways in which assumptions about 'doing' gender are tied to biological sex. Discursive constructions of masculinity and femininity do not always reflect what men and women actually do or how they act in real life, and we need to be able to recognize instances where women also 'do' various forms of masculinity, to varying degrees (and with different impacts on their health), and where men do 'femininity' (Lee and Owens, 2002).

A further problem arises in that most diseases are not the result of either biological causes or social differences, but interactions between the two (Wizeman and Pardue, 2000; Krieger, 2003). Even differences in health between men and women which relate to the reproductive system, for example, are mediated by socially constructed factors, including the way in which such differences are viewed, diagnosed and treated.

But what, then, can we do with research findings? In the relationship between gender and health, what are important are the ways in which the economic, social, cultural and psychic construction of being a man or being a woman add together to impact on health, alongside the impact of other experiences and other aspects of difference. Sex and gender may be socially constructed categories, but they continue to have significant effects on the health of both women and men, and these effects need further elaboration (Emslie et al., 1999). So here we use the terms 'sex' and 'gender', and data collected on the basis of this difference, in order to explore the health experiences and expectations of women and men, while recognizing the need to remain aware of the difficulties inherent in these categories.

Sex and health

The term 'sex' when it is used in relation to men and women refers to those differences which are the result of, or can be traced back to, the biological differences between them: 'Sex; a biologic category, defined by biologic characteristics pertaining to the ability to reproduce' (Krieger and Zierler, 1995: 253). The physical bodies of men and women are different, reflecting fundamental differences in reproductive systems. However, only part of men's health and women's health is explained by these reproductive variations. The fact that women conceive and bear children – a biological fact – is distinct from the social construction of women as caring and nurturing, which in turn impacts on women's economic and social subordination and their opportunities for health. Similarly, the male role in reproduction through the insemination by sperm is a biological detail which is distinct from the social construction of men as breadwinners and secondary carers.

Despite the limits of biology in explaining the health of men and women, recent work, particularly around the human genome, has increased awareness of the importance of the role played by sex in shaping health. This biological differentiation is of more or less importance, depending on the condition we want to explore: 'Sex can determine differential propensities for certain health conditions or diseases, different risk factors or treatment requirements' (CIHR, 2000: 1). For example, male sex opens up the possibility of prostate disease and testicular cancer; female sex establishes the risk of similarly biologically differentiated disease such as cervical cancer and cancer of the womb.

With this in mind, the sex-specific focus of some health research is justified in so far as certain conditions are risks only for men or only for women, not both (Griffiths, 1996). However, other diseases which may appear to be similarly the result of biological difference are less straightforward. Research shows that women have an advantage over men in certain respects in relation to the immune system and blood pressure, a result of their biological capacity to conceive, where a depressed immune reaction and lower blood pressure are valuable for a healthy pregnancy (Bird and Rieker, 1999). Such advantages may reduce coronary heart disease, for example, particularly during reproductive years.

There are other diseases where biological risk factors may act to increase women's vulnerability: women may be more at risk of lung cancer, for instance, at the same level of smoking as men, and a greater proportion of non-smokers with lung cancer are women than men. These differences are related in part to sex-specific genetic factors (S. Payne, 2001, 2004). But the actual impact of such biologically shaped advantages will be mediated by gender-related factors – such as health behaviours, access to social and economic capital, which can affect stress, or the availability of health-promoting resources, and the medical profession's ability to recognize and offer appropriate treatment to women and men.

Gender and health

The term 'gender' describes those differences between men and women which stem from social causes: 'a social construct regarding culture-bound conventions, roles, and behaviours for, as well as relations between, women and men and boys and girls' (Krieger and Zierler, 1995: 253). Gender differences help shape the health of men and women by influencing their exposure to various health risks, their access to health-promoting resources, and how they are treated by health services (CIHR, 2000). However, gender can be conceptualized in various ways. Field et al. (1997), for example, suggest that the body is mapped through culturally specific gendered knowledges, and that as gender is performed by men and women, we can separate this performance, or the construction of gendered identity, from biological sex. In this way gender is not driven by biology, but discursively constructed, and masculinity and femininity do not attach to one or other sex – masculinity can be enacted or performed by either men or women. This allows for a viewpoint in which gender does not necessarily map on to biological difference.

> [T]erms often used to capture a crude dichotomy of gender are *masculine* and *feminine*. These terms, however, are restrictive, because they assume biologic sex determines gender. Additionally they imply gender is only about male–female interactions. But gender differentiation and gendered interactions also occur among people of the same sex. (Krieger and Zierler, 1995: 252)

It is particularly important to view gender outside a simple male/female, masculine/feminine dichotomy, in order to understand the relationship between sex, gender and health for both men and women.

It allows recognition, for example, of the dangers of what has been described as 'masculine' behaviour, regardless of whether it is women or men adopting such behaviour, and thus extends arguments that masculinity is a health risk for men to focus more clearly on health lifestyles.

What is the relationship between sex and gender?

If sex and gender are emerging as concepts which are less than straightforward, there are further complications in the ways in which sex-linked factors and those related to gender combine to influence health. These interrelationships focus on the ways in which gender might impact on the body and performance to bring about physiological change, and the ways in which the biological body impacts on gendered prescriptions of behaviour and being. The term '*gendered expression of biology*' is used by Krieger and Zierler (1995) to describe the ways in which biological differences influence social constructions of gender. For example, in most societies women's ability to conceive (a biological fact) is associated with economic subordination (a gendered outcome) through limits placed on women's employment and expectations of caring roles (Krieger and Zierler, 1995). Similarly, biological differences have been used to justify exclusion of women from medical research on the grounds that hormonal differences, the working of the menstrual cycle, or changes associated with pregnancy if this occurred during a trial period, would invalidate the results (Doyal, 1995; CIHR, 2000).

Krieger and Zierler (1995) use the phrase, the '*biologic expression of gender*', to refer to the manner in which gender, as a social construction, is incorporated into the body and expressed physically 'in ways that may or may not be associated with biologic sex' (Krieger and Zierler, 1995: 253). This allows understanding of men doing femininity and women doing masculinity, and uses notions of embodiment to explore the impact of socially constructed differences on the body itself. For example, the failure of the medical profession to identify some health problems in women – due to gendered constructions of health difference – then become 'incorporated' in the woman's body, having a physical effect on the body. If a health professional views coronary heart disease as a problem affecting men, as a result of gendered stereotypes about health risk, the failure to recognize this in women affects their bodily health. Similarly, gendered differences in emotional behaviour which result in men being less likely to admit to mental health problems may result in bodily differences – most obviously when difficulties in identifying and sharing mental distress may lead to suicidal behaviour.

In these two additional aspects of sex and gender we can find space to observe the ways in which interactions between biology and gender relations also impact on health.

Sex, gender and diversity

Other forms of differences also intervene in health and death. Not all women are the same or share the same exposure to health-related risks, and equally not all men are the same. We need, therefore, to consider ways in which sex-related and gender-related factors are affected by other influences.

One of the most significant of these other influences, in terms of health experience, is that of ethnicity, itself a complex and contested term. Just as the concepts of sex and gender distinguish between biological and social differences between men and women, so there are two terms which have been used in the study of differences between racial or ethnic groups. 'Race' has been used to suggest populations which differ biologically or genetically from other populations, while ethnicity has developed as a term referring to socially constructed differences. However, whereas there is agreement on the value of both sex and gender, 'race' is increasingly seen as an invalid term which overstates differences between populations and which misrepresents the causes of poor health of different ethnic groups (Jones and Williams, 2004; Krieger and Fee, 1994).

Criticisms of the term 'race' focus on the limited evidence of significant biological or physical differences between different 'races' (McBeth, 2001; Bhopal, 2001). Explanations of health inequalities between ethnic groups highlight instead structural factors and disadvantage, the failure of health care systems to provide adequate or appropriate treatment for minority ethnic groups, and lifestyle factors which have their origins in poverty and discrimination. In many countries both men and women from minority ethnic groups have poorer health by comparison with the ethnic majority, while also suffering a greater risk of poverty, poor-quality housing, unemployment, exclusion and discrimination (Griffiths, 1996; Nunez and Robertson, 2003; Schiller and Bernadel, 2004).

It can be useful, as with sex and gender, to explore interactions between race and ethnicity. Stereotypical ideas about physical characteristics (attached to 'race') have been used to justify social differences, which then impact on health – for example, beliefs about higher pain thresholds of black and Asian women can mean that they are offered inadequate pain relief when in labour (Vangen et al., 1996). Similarly, socially constructed differences between ethnic groups may be seen as being 'embodied' by these groups, with adverse consequences for their health – the stress produced by experiences of discrimination and racism leading to poorer cardiovascular health, hypertension and so on. We could interpret the description by Staples (1995) of the young black urban American male as an 'endangered species' as the embodiment of structural factors such as poverty, lack of access to good health care, and of discrimination and a particularly dangerous expression of masculinity.

In the USA, there has been considerable debate over the meaning of both race and ethnicity, and official data are now presented in two ways – by race, including white, black, American Indian and other groups, and by origin, with two separate groups: Hispanic/Latino and Non-Hispanic/Latino. Writers in the USA often use the term 'race/ethnicity' to describe differences reflecting minority status and discrimination, rather than either 'race' or 'ethnicity'. However, others have argued that the term 'ethnicity' is now in danger of being used in the same way as 'gender' has substituted for 'sex' – as a more acceptable term to refer to different populations while maintaining an implicit acceptance of biological origins in health inequalities.

Social class is also a significant influence on the health of women and men, but here too there are difficulties in the terms used. There is a large volume of research which demonstrates that experiences of inequality, measured in various ways, increase the risk of premature death and poorer lifetime health (Wilkinson, 1997; Davey Smith et al., 1999). Class-based inequalities may restrict access to health-promoting resources, such as a healthy diet, and increase the likelihood of living in poor-quality or overcrowded housing and in deprived neighbourhoods with high levels of pollution and poor resources. Inequality can also mean restricted access to health care, both where access depends on financial means – insurance or the money to pay user fees – and where there are indirect costs, including loss of wages for the time taken up in consultation or transport costs. Occupational inequalities are also associated with poorer health, both because of workplace hazards and the health costs of some forms of labour, and because some jobs are more insecure and poorly paid than others, and have lower status, which brings other health consequences.

Social class interacts with health in other ways beyond the impact of material resources, however, particularly when inequality and class discrimination are quite literally embodied, or incorporated by the body of the individual man or woman through complex, multi-level pathways – including diet, stress, environment, behaviour and exposure to risks at work, for example (Krieger, 2005).

Social class is often based on occupational status, ranked from professional and managerial classes through to manual labourers, and is used as an indicator of a range of factors which may influence health, including both material resources and status. In the USA socio-economic data are largely absent from national statistics on mortality and morbidity (Krieger et al., 2003), but in other countries – particularly the UK – data are routinely presented in relation to social class. However, measuring class is problematic, particularly when studies use household measures of class based on the occupation of the male head of household, or determine married women's social class by their husband's job. In recent years the problems inherent in this approach – especially difficulties disentangling psychosocial and material effects of class on women's health – have led to wider use of other indicators, often combining education with household income or a proxy measure of occupational status. However, it remains true that social class is interpreted differently in various research studies, and this presents difficulties for comparisons.

Age, cohort differences, sexuality and disability also affect the interplay of sex and gender. Research shows that gender shifts in meaning and impact across the life course (Charles and Walters, 1998; Annandale and Hunt, 2000), so that gendered health effects in early adulthood may be very unlike gendered health effects at the end of life, while the experiences of one group of women or men at a particular point in the life course will not be the same as the experiences of an earlier or later group of women or men at the same point of their life course.

Sexuality also affects health, and is again difficult to define. Much of the research literature on health and sexuality refers to women and men in relatively simplistic ways in terms of sexual preference – lesbians and gay men, for example – but such terms deny the reality and complexity of sexual behaviour, and again impose a false dichotomy, by creating homosexual or heterosexual subjects. Terms such as 'men who have sex with men' and 'women who have sex with women' allow recognition of changing sexualities, but still define people by who they have sex with. An alternative which focuses on sexual acts, rather than the people engaged in those acts, is better in the sense that it does not attempt to construct identities out of sex; but most research is not reported in this way, and throughout the book where I discuss sexuality as an influence on health, the descriptors used in the original research or data are necessarily those used here.

Similarly, disability is an important aspect of health experience, as well as an important influence on health, and is also hard to define. Again there is a problematic division between disabled and able-bodied/normal bodies in much of the research on chronic health, disability and limiting illness, which often operates with normative understandings of ordinary bodies rather than subjective experience.

Conclusion: towards a model

Krieger (2003) suggests three frameworks for explanations of inequalities: psychosocial frameworks, which highlight endogenous biological responses to human interaction and stress; the political economy approach, which highlights the economic and political determinants of disease; and ecosocial frameworks, which draw together biological, social and ecological models of disease production into a more dynamic and fluid understanding of the diversity of factors affecting individual and population health. This last approach builds on a number of different perspectives, including those relating to sex-linked factors and gender relations, social and cultural relations, economic factors and individual history. It also incorporates ideas about embodiment and the role of 'the body' in understanding health processes, something which many other perspectives cannot.

An ecosocial model of the health of women and men includes biology, for example, in the relative risk of some diseases, and the influence of genetic factors on vulnerability to some causes of ill health and mortality (Wizeman and Pardue, 2000). In addition, gender-linked factors in health behaviour, access to material resources, use of health care, and the ways in which services are delivered, are important. Other aspects of social, economic and cultural relations reflecting sexuality, ethnicity, disability, class and development also form part of the explanation of the health of women and men. The mechanisms through which such influences affect health relate to the ways in which the body takes on different meanings, and the ways in which gender is enacted as well as experienced. At the end of the day, what we find using such an approach is that our health is affected by a wide range of factors, and that sex and gender are both significant elements within a larger framework.

The chapters which follow discuss the health of women and men in more detail, focusing on different aspects of morbidity and mortality. Differences reflecting social class and ethnicity need to be kept in mind in this discussion, as both have a substantial impact on sex and gender differences in health – at times class and ethnicity are more important in an individual's health than whether they are male or female, and the intersections between gender, class and ethnicity are also relevant.

Chapter 2 discusses the main ways in which health differences between women and men might be explained, and sets the scene for the rest of the book. Chapter 3 looks in more detail at patterns of health across the life course for men and women, and illustrates these differences with a detailed look at two chronic health conditions. Chapter 4 focuses on one aspect of women and men's health experience relating to psychosocial health, with more detailed case studies of eating disorders, depression and suicide, while chapter 5 looks at sexual and reproductive health. In chapter 6 we explore death and the differences and similarities between women and men in mortality, using violent death as a case study to illustrate the influences of sex and gender. The final chapter returns to the question of sex, gender and explanations of men and women's health and, in particular, the ways in which it might be possible to develop a model which reflects these various influences while recognizing the complexities of how they operate.

2 Explaining the Health of Women and Men

Introduction

The last chapter suggested that differences and similarities in the health of men and women might be explained in various ways. In this chapter we explore these different explanations in more detail, focusing on sex and gender as influences on mortality and morbidity. We begin with the part played by sex in shaping health experience, and then go on to consider three different aspects of gender: factors relating to structural inequalities, including poverty, disadvantage, employment and caring roles; factors relating to gendered differences in health lifestyles; and factors relating to gendered aspects of the delivery of health care and health systems. The main point to be taken from this chapter is that explanations of men's and women's health, and of differences or similarities between men and women, do not rely on sex or gender alone, but on both, as well as on the ways in which they come together at the level of the individual in the context of other influences.

Sex, biology and health

While biological factors play a key part in health experience for both women and men, the impact of sex-linked factors on health varies, being greater for some conditions than for others. There are relatively few conditions which affect the health of men and women which are not influenced by biology in some way, even if this influence is minor. In recent years, particularly with advances in understandings of human genetics, medical research has revealed new aspects of biological influences on women and men's health. This recognition of the importance of biology in shaping differences between women and men, however, should not be confused with biologically deterministic explanations of health – particularly women's health – which have formed part of medical discourse in the past.

Medical literature has previously regarded women in particular as being at the mercy of their hormones. Scully and Bart's (1978) research on the presentation of women in gynaecology textbooks, for example, revealed a biological explanation of women's gynaecological and sexual health. The early women's health movement was highly critical of medicine's focus on reproductive difference, the stereotypical portrayals of women in medical literature and in clinical practice, and the failure of health care providers to offer gender-sensitive treatment (Ruzek, 1978; Barrett and Roberts, 1978); and this critique helped to construct a discourse of women's health which emphasized the importance of gender relations, sometimes to the point where biological factors were obscured or lost. More recently, however, medical knowledge has integrated psychosocial and biological factors in explanations of health, while in the social sciences there has been increasing acceptance of the part played by sex-linked factors in health experiences.

Biological factors in human health, including not only reproductive and hormonal differences, but also genetic influences, have been known for some time, particularly those related to X and Y chromosomes. However, the full impact of these factors on health is only now being understood. Differences in the health of women and men reflecting reproductive variations are perhaps the most apparent. Women's health is affected by their capacity to conceive, not only in terms of the consequences for their health of pregnancy and childbirth, but also because they are at risk of disorders associated with reproductive organs – cancer of the ovary or breast, for example, or infections of the reproductive tract. Men, on the other hand, are at risk of conditions specifically associated with male reproductive organs – testicular cancer, prostate cancer, or an enlarged prostate gland, for example. These differences are biological in origin, although social factors can affect the risk of a condition and how it is treated.

In addition to reproductive health differences, recent research on the human genome has revealed unexpected variations between males and females in genetic make-up, which influence vulnerability to specific conditions. While this is related to X and Y chromosomes, it is also linked to variations in the activity of male and female cells, which can affect health in complex ways (Wizeman and Pardue, 2000). Differences in genetic make-up begin in the womb, and these are significant in explaining why the male foetus is less likely to survive prenatally, as well as why male children are more at risk of mortality in the first year of life (Wizeman and Pardue, 2000). One of the key ways in which genes influence health appears to be through their expression, which is the process through which the information carried by the gene is converted into a cell – sometimes described as whether a particular gene will come into play or not. For example, differences between women and men in gene expression are associated with added vulnerability to some forms of cancer, particularly women's greater risk of lung cancer at the same level of smoking, in comparison with male smokers (Haugen, 2002; Shriver et al., 2000).

The health of women and men is also affected by hormonal factors related to genetic make-up. Although hormones are often referred to as either female or male, this can be misleading, and offers an example where biological differences are not clear-cut. Both women and men have the 'male' hormone testosterone, although it is present in greater quantities in men. Testosterone is used in some cases to treat breast cancer in women, and is also sometimes used to increase libido among women. Similarly, the 'female' hormone oestrogen is found in both women and men, although the amount of oestrogen is normally low in men.

Much of the research on hormonal influences on health has focused on female hormones and women's health, and rather less looks at male hormones. Female hormones appear to protect women from certain conditions which can lead to both illness and death, particularly during the 'reproductive' years. For example, women have lower risk of cardiovascular disease until after the menopause, partly as a result of the protective effects of oestrogen on arterial walls, serum lipid profile and cholesterol (Legato, 1997; Lee and Owens, 2002; Wizeman and Pardue, 2000; Fodor and Tzerovska, 2004). Declining levels of oestrogen during and after the menopause also contribute to osteoporosis, a leading cause of poor health among older women.

Far less is known about how male hormones change through the life course or in response to different triggers, or how these changes affect health. There is some evidence that reductions in male hormones as men age may be associated with increased osteoporosis, although the risk of osteoporosis remains lower for men overall (Wizeman and Pardue, 2000). Research also suggests that while oestrogen stimulates the immune system, testosterone acts to reduce immunity, increasing men's risks of some diseases, including viruses and parasitic infections (Legato, 1997).

Male hormones, collectively known as the androgens, are responsible for characteristics such as body build and shape, voice, hair growth, the development of male sexual characteristics, including the penis and the production of sperm. Testosterone in particular has been associated with aggression, and some studies have reported raised levels of testosterone among men acting in violent and aggressive ways (Courtenay, 2000). Testosterone is central to masculinity discourses in which biology is used to explain male behaviour: 'the He hormone . . . has become a metaphor of manhood . . . it affects every aspect of our society, from high divorce rates and adolescent violence to exploding cults of body-building' (Sullivan, cited in Zitzmann and Nieschlag, 2001: 183). This connection between male hormones and gendered performance is as biologically reductionist as the association between female hormones and nurturing behaviour in women, however, and research suggests that the association between testosterone and aggression is in fact rather more complex.

This is partly because testosterone levels are difficult to measure, and vary over periods of time, as well as between men. As a result, evidence relating to the relationship between testosterone and emotion is inconclusive. Studies of the hormone levels of men taking part in sporting competition, for example, have shown that testosterone levels increase after the event compared with levels of the hormone beforehand, indicating that it may be manufactured in response to aggressive or competitive performance rather than inciting that performance (Zitzmann and Nieschlag, 2001). Testosterone does play a key role in metabolic rate, however, and also in the synthesis of protein and the manufacture of red blood cells, which can mean that men recover more quickly from injury and illness (Wizeman and Pardue, 2000). Very little research has been carried out on women's testosterone and associations with emotions or behaviour, although this would be helpful in explorations of the relative importance of biology and gender in aggressive behaviour. Also many of the studies carried out on men have focused on male prison populations, which creates particular difficulties in distinguishing between biological and social factors in hormone production, as well as contributing to masculine discourses around criminality.

Gender is also implicated in complex ways in other areas of biological difference. Research demonstrating an association between the surge in testosterone levels in adolescent boys and increased aggression suggests that sex-linked factors might affect behaviour, but these hormonal changes need to be set in the context of social constructions of adolescent masculinity. Such constructions include the ways in which young men are themselves affected by masculine discourse, and how this affects their behaviour, and the ways in which the reactions of others are also shaped by assumptions about the behaviour of young men. Similarly, girls experience rapid increases in oestrogen levels at puberty, and these physical changes have been associated with the more developed linguistic skills of girls at this age. But again, social factors such as the ways in which others interact with girls affect both the development of language and the observation or measurement of language skills (Wizeman and Pardue, 2000).

The relationship between sex, or biology, and pain is also important. Research shows that women suffer more often from chronic painful conditions such as fibromyalgia, irritable bowel syndrome, carpal tunnel syndrome and some forms of migraine and headaches, while men suffer more often from other painful conditions, including duodenal ulcers, pancreatic disease and cluster headaches (Wizeman and Pardue, 2000). Women and men also respond differently to analgesics, in terms of how well pain relief reduces symptoms and which forms of pain relief work best. Women are often more sensitive to pain than men with the same condition, and some women report variations in sensitivity to pain relating to the menstrual cycle. The pain responses of women and men are shaped both by genetic differences and by hormonal factors, particularly the influence of oestrogen on pain receptors in some women. These variations between women and men are not found consistently, however – not all women experience changes in their sensitivity to pain at different points in the menstrual cycle, for example, and women do not always report more pain than men with the same condition (Wizeman and Pardue, 2000; Fillingim, 1999). While this is likely to reflect the complexity of biological influences on pain, and on health more generally, it also reflects difficulties distinguishing between the impact of biology and that of gender. For example, in most societies it is more acceptable for women to report pain, in comparison with men, who must present themselves as strong and stoical, and the medical profession may also have a tendency to see men as having higher pain thresholds than women.

Other physical differences between women and men have also been reported which suggest the role of sex-linked factors in health variations. For example, the average size and weight of the brain differs for women and men, and women's brains have more neurons and more connections, which may be why women are more likely to recover their speech after a stroke, and may explain differences between men and women in the development of language skills in early life (Legato, 1997).

Overall, then, biological influences, including differences in genetic make-up and hormones, as well as reproductive factors, are important in the health experience of women and men. However, biology has to be seen as interacting with socially constructed factors including gender.

Gender and health

We turn now to explore the ways in which gender affects health, focusing on three aspects of gender relations: resources, health behaviour and health care.

Gender, resources and roles

One of the key influences on anyone's health is the resources they have at their disposal and the environment in which they live. Structural factors which may impact on health include, for example, paid employment, caring responsibilities, income, the availability of social support and access to housing. All of these help explain inequalities in health between different social and economic groups, between people living in different parts of the world, in different cultures and so on. The key questions are whether health inequalities between women and men reflect inequalities between them in such resources, whether these inequalities are the result of gender relations, and how far interactions between gender and class explain women's and men's health. Research by Emslie et al. (1999), for example, suggests that health differences between men and women, particularly those associated with minor morbidity, are strongly associated with occupational and socio-economic inequalities. Differences in health across the life course and the risk of poor health in later years reflect the cumulative effects of socio-economic disadvantage, including paid work, over a lifetime (Macintyre et al., 1996). Women are more likely than men to work in occupations which are low-paid, have few benefits and which offer less in terms of self-esteem, and these factors contribute to explanations of differences between women and men in mental and psychological well-being in particular (Pugliesi, 1999). Class disadvantage also affects health through the embodiment of discrimination, and for women and for some ethnic groups this combines with the embodiment of other forms of inequality to the detriment of both physical and mental health.

Some of the differences between women and men in health experience relate to the sexual division of labour still found in most countries, in which some jobs with specific health risks are more likely to be carried out by men or by women. The health consequences of traditional male employment – in construction, manufacturing and engineering, for example – increase their risk of injury and mortality, as well as disorders associated with the specific environment in which they work. Men suffer higher risks of work-related mortality, including increased numbers of circulatory conditions, some cancers, respiratory disease, as well as accidental injury (Nurminen and Karjalainen, 2001). Women suffer health risks associated with their work in clerical occupations and in the service industry – for example, women experience upper limb musculo-skeletal disorders more frequently than men (Bammer and Strazdins, 2004; Treaster and Burr, 2004). These occupational hazards help to explain different patterns of health experienced by men and women, particularly variations in the likelihood of mortality and chronic ill health, for example. The risks posed by the ergonomic design of the workplace and the repetitive nature of some jobs where women predominate, including data processing, clerical labour and packing, for example, increase their chances of chronic ill health rather than mortality. For women these health risks are added to by a gendered division of labour in the home, which, in most countries, means that women carry out more household work and have more caring responsibilities. Domestic responsibilities also reduce women's opportunities for leisure and relaxation, and are stressful both in themselves and in the way women have to juggle various tasks and expectations (Bird and Rieker, 1999). In addition, women are more at risk of harm to their health from the conditions in which they work at home – damp housing, for example, has more adverse effects for women's respiratory health partly because women spend longer at home than men (Rennie et al., 2005).

Work-related stresses are also important, and both women and men experience adverse health effects due to the stresses of employment, including anxiety about job security, boredom, repetitive work and harassment. Women's paid work, however, may contain different kinds of stress which impact particularly on mental rather than physical well-being (Pugliesi, 1999). For example, both women and men 'do gender' in the workplace, and women take on responsibility for emotional labour, both where it forms part of the job in caring work and also in smoothing working relationships in other settings (Henson and Krasas-Rogers, 2001). Women are also more at risk of sexual harassment in the workplace in both developed and developing countries. In some parts of the world – particularly in Free Trade Zones in low income countries – women workers in manufacturing plants have little protection or job security, and sexual harassment combined with the fear of losing their job if they complain add considerably to the pressures and adverse health effects of paid work (Prieto Carron, 2004).

There is also extensive research which shows a relationship between health and the experience of poverty and disadvantage (Davey Smith et al., 1999). People in low income groups, those who suffer various forms of deprivation and those who are socially excluded, around the world, are more likely to report both physical and mental health problems, to use health care, particularly accident and emergency services, and are more likely to die at an early age (Davey Smith et al., 1999; Leon and Walt, 2001). Poverty restricts opportunities to improve health, and people who are poor are more likely to have poor-quality diets, to live in damp, unsafe or overcrowded housing, to live in areas with environmental pollution, and to have less access to those resources that might promote health (Davey Smith et al., 1999). In addition, people living in poverty are less able to access health care, particularly in countries where there are out-of-pocket expenses or where transport is unavailable or expensive, and this adds to the risk of long-term health problems and premature mortality.

These experiences are also gendered. In developed and developing countries more women than men live in deprived circumstances, which increases their exposure to ill health (Graham, 2000; Oxaal and Cook, 1998). Women are particularly vulnerable to poverty when responsible for children, and also in later life (Benzeval, 1998; Arber and Cooper, 1999). Where households are poor, female members of the household suffer greater deprivation than male members when they are denied equal access to resources, when they are unable to attend health care because they do not make the financial decisions and when they carry the main responsibility for domestic and caring work in conditions which make this work more difficult (Stafford et al., 2005). When men experience poverty and deprivation, the impact of this on their health also relates to gender, and their primary construction as the breadwinner in most societies creates particular stresses for them when employment is unavailable, when lack of work means that they must leave the family home to find employment, and when they work in dangerous or unhealthy conditions in order to provide for the household (Patel and Kleinman, 2003).

Food is an important aspect of poverty, and food scarcity is also gendered. The health consequences of a poor diet include increased risks of obesity, diabetes, cancer, bowel disease, osteoporosis and dental disease (WHO, 2002b). Food scarcity is found in both high- and low-income countries, when people do not have the food they need or cannot obtain good food, due to lack of availability or transport barriers (Sayers, 2002: 151). Food poverty has been described as, 'a worse diet, worse access, worse health, a higher percentage of income going on food, and less choice from a restricted range of foods. Above all food poverty is about less or almost no consumption of fruit and vegetables' (Lang, 2001).

In developed countries food poverty has been explored in terms of 'food deserts' – the geographical distribution of retail outlets which means that in areas of disadvantage and low income there are fewer food shops, and those which are accessible sell largely high-fat, high-sugar, pre-packaged food. Food deserts in developed countries make it more difficult for those already disadvantaged by their income to eat healthily, but the impact of this falls differently on men and women – while both are adversely affected by such scarcity, women more often have responsibility for food preparation, and so carry the burden of additional travel to find good food, or stress associated with being unable to provide well for their families.

In less developed countries large parts of the population do not consume recommended levels of nutrients, particularly from fresh fruit and vegetables, and there are signs that increasing numbers of people are not able to eat healthily. Again, gender differences in access to food mean that women's diet is more likely to be inadequate in absolute terms relative to that of men: women consume less animal protein; more of the food they eat is made up of vegetable protein, and women are more likely to have a diet deficient in vitamins and minerals (Sayers, 2002; Vlassoff and Bonilla, 1994; Siefert et al., 2001). Around the world, women's diet tends to be poorer in the lowest-income and most disadvantaged households, and, critically, the differences in nutritional status between women and men are at their widest in poorest households (Sayers, 2002). Differences between women and men begin early on with infant feeding practices, which mean that girls get less food overall and poorer-quality food. Men in circumstances of food insecurity may have more to eat, and more access to animal protein, but many men in developing countries, particularly those in transition to urban economies, will also suffer inadequate and unhealthy diets due to the growth of processed food and fast-food outlets. Gender differences in the contributions made to household food where women play a major role in food cultivation and production, while increasing the burden of work and stress, may also offer more food security for women than would cash income, particularly in developing countries (Oxaal and Cook, 1998; Standing, 1997).

Overall, then, differences between men and women in their exposure to health risks due to structural inequalities and the roles that men and women occupy play an important part in explanations of gender inequalities in health.

Gender and health-related behaviour

One of the most important aspects of health difference between women and men is behaviour – both health-promoting behaviour and behaviour which adversely affects health. In particular, behavioural factors have been shown to be powerful predictors of health status for men, while social structural and psychosocial determinants of health are generally more important for women (Denton and Walters, 1999; Denton et al., 2004).

In the sections that follow we explore different aspects of health behaviour. The concept of health lifestyles refers to patterns of health-related behaviour, reflecting the multi-causal nature of many diseases and the ways in which health behaviour is often 'clustered' – that is, the same individual is likely to engage in a number of behaviours which affect health either in an adverse or a favourable way (Liang et al., 1999). Health lifestyles have been defined in various ways in the context of specific studies and specific health conditions, but primarily focus on smoking, alcohol use, diet and exercise to explore ways in which these behaviours vary across socio-demographic groups.

There are important gender differences in health lifestyles. More men than women, for example, combine smoking, drinking high levels of alcohol, a poor diet and no exercise, while women's behaviour clusters tend to be more positive – healthy eating, the use of screening services, sunscreen and exercise, for example (Hagoel et al., 2002; Berrigan et al., 2003; Thom, 2003; Bajekal et al., 2003). This 'clustering' of some behaviours may increase health risks beyond the behaviour itself, and this will also affect the gap between women and men. Both low levels of physical activity and a diet lacking in fresh fruit and vegetables, for example, are associated with an increased risk of cancer, and smoking may be a greater threat to health when combined with other behaviours (Cummings and Bingham, 1998; Shephard and Shek, 1998).

The sections that follow break down health lifestyles into different kinds of behaviour, focusing particularly on diet, obesity and body image; exercise, including body-building; smoking, alcohol use and illicit substance use.

Diet

While enforced food scarcity affects the health of many people worldwide, there are also differences in diet within advantaged populations that reflect preferences and food beliefs as well as access to resources. Women in developed countries are more likely to consume recommended levels of fruit and vegetables, and women consume less fat and sugar than men (Courtenay, 2000; Aliaga, 2002). Men's diets tend to be higher in saturated fat, salt and sugar, and lower in fibre and fresh fruit and vegetables throughout the world (WHO, 2002b; NZMOH, 2004; AusStats, 2002; Schiller and Bernadel, 2004). In France, women eat more fruit and vegetables than men, and pay more attention to their diet and restrict calories more frequently than men (Aliaga, 2002). In England, young women tend to have healthier diets than men and are more likely to eat recommended amounts of fruit and vegetables (Sproston et al., 2002). Diets vary by class with reduced consumption of fruit and vegetables in lower social classes, but even in these groups women are more likely than men to consume recommended levels (Sproston et al., 2002).

There are also variations between different ethnic groups in many countries, with poorer-quality diets among minority populations than among white or majority populations. In New Zealand, for example, Maori and other minority groups consume fewer vegetables, and Maori men have the lowest consumption of fruit and vegetables compared with European men or Maori women (NZMOH, 2004). In England, diets rich in fruit and vegetables are more common among Chinese men and women than other ethnic groups, but in all groups more women than men consume the recommended levels (Erens et al., 1999).

The practice of dieting, as a means of reducing weight and changing body shape, is also gendered. In the last few years increasing emphasis has been placed by a number of national governments, as well as the media, the medical profession and global health organizations, on the importance of consuming a healthy diet as a key means through which both men and women can enhance their well-being and life expectancy. Government policy which urges us to eat more fruit, more vegetables, less fat, and less sugar and starch coincides with a period when global consumption of fat, sugar and starch are higher than ever before. In 2004 the UK government published a public health White Paper, *Choosing Health: Making Healthier Choices Easier* (DOH, 2004) which highlighted the health costs of obesity. However, such policy documents tend not to discuss differences between women and men in food intake and weight control, despite evidence suggesting that men and women eat differently, view their bodies differently, and show different degrees of interest and success when it comes to dieting.

Dieting is more common among women than men, to the point where in the developed world dieting has become normal practice for the female population (Neumark-Stzainer et al., 2002). Women are also more likely than men to engage in what are described as extreme or unhealthy weight loss practices – severe calorie restriction, for example – and this has implications both for the risk that weight lost will be regained and also for long-term health (Neumark-Stzainer et al., 2002). Alongside dieting, there are also gender differences in eating disorders, with more women reporting disordered eating and more women than men diagnosed with anorexia and bulimia.

Obesity

Obesity is not a health behaviour as such, but it is associated with both diet and physical activity. Globally, 'obesity' has increased dramatically in recent years, and an estimated 1 billion people around the world are overweight, with 30 million defined as obese (WHO, 2003b). Obesity is largely defined in relation to excess body fat or by a ratio of weight to height. It is often measured using a tool called the Body Mass Index (BMI), which is calculated from an adult's metric weight divided by their squared metric height. A BMI of more than 30 for an adult is generally seen as obese; a BMI of between 25 and 30 is described as overweight; while under 18.5 is seen as underweight. A woman who is 1.65 metres tall (5 feet, 5 inches), for example, could weigh anywhere between 55 and 68 kilos (between 112 and 154 pounds), and her weight would be considered normal.

However, the BMI is of limited value in comparisons between men and women, as it does not take into account body frame, muscularity, or the distribution of fat, all of which affect both weight and whether weight constitutes a health risk. For example, abdominal weight, which is not measured by the BMI, is a risk factor for cardiovascular disease for men in particular. This suggests that a combination of indicators reflecting body shape may be more useful in assessing health risks for women and men (Haslam, 2004). Further difficulties are created when using BMI for different age groups, as the percentage of body fat which is normal increases with age, and figures for overweight and obesity among older populations based on the BMI cut-off used for younger people are less accurate. There are also race/ethnicity differences in body mass and height, which may mean that it is less accurate as a measure of morbid weight problems for minority groups than it is for the white population (Erens et al., 1999). Some writers have also raised questions over the accuracy of research demonstrating that BMI correlates with health risk. Campos (2004), for example, argues that there is a weak correlation between obesity and health risk, in the absence of information about physical activity.

Although these are important concerns, BMI and other measures of obesity can be used as approximate indicators of health risks. BMI statistics suggest that obesity is becoming more common in developed countries, and also in less developed countries, particularly those undergoing rapid urbanization, where obesity and malnutrition are found together (WHO, 2002b, 2003b). The prevalence of obesity in some African countries is as low as 5 per cent, compared with over 20 per cent in the USA, for example; but in some urban areas in China it is estimated that 20 per cent of the population is obese (WHO, 2003b; NCHS, 2004).

Obesity has been associated with an increased risk of type 2 diabetes, cardiovascular disease, stroke, hypertension and some forms of cancer, including breast, colon and prostate (WHO, 2002b). Obesity among children is also growing rapidly, and this is associated with an increased risk of obesity in adulthood, as well as health complications such as childhood diabetes.

Differences in weight between women and men are not consistent between countries, but in general men are more likely to be classed as overweight, while women are either as likely or more likely than men to be classed as obese (Sproston et al., 2002; NCHS, 2004; ASSO, 2005). Overweight and obesity also vary across the life course, and more men than women are overweight in younger age groups, while in later life obesity is more common among women (WHO, 2003b).

Obesity rates vary by ethnic group for both women and men, which reflects socio-economic factors as well as cultural dimensions of food, diet and body image. In the USA, for example, more of the black and

American Indian/Alaska Native population are defined as overweight or obese than the white population, but rates of obesity among the Asian population are low (NCHS, 2004). In England a recent national survey found higher levels of obesity in the black Caribbean and Irish population (Erens et al., 1999), and in Australia and New Zealand obesity is more common among the Maori and Pacific populations (ASSO, 2005).

Women from minority groups are, however, more likely to be defined as obese than their male counterparts. In England, women of black Caribbean origin are the most likely of all groups to be obese (Erens et al., 1999). In New Zealand, the highest rates of obesity are found among Pacific women, nearly half of whom are classified as obese (ASSO, 2005). In South Africa levels of obesity are similar for white women and men, but African and black women are four times as likely to be obese as African and black men, and three times as many Coloured women as men are also defined as obese (Health Systems Trust, 2004). Similarly, black American women are more likely to be obese than black American men (Schiller and Bernadel, 2004).

The 'obesity epidemic' is also associated with social class: poorer populations are more likely to be obese, and in higher-income countries there is an inverse association between overweight and obesity and socio-economic status. Again, however, there are gendered differences, and among those living in poverty more women than men are obese in both the USA and the UK (Wang and Zhang, 2004; Sproston et al., 2002).

Weight cycling – repeated weight loss and gain – may be particularly harmful to health, although this is an area of obesity which is still relatively under-researched (Campos, 2004). Women are more likely than men to engage in weight cycling, perhaps because of gendered differences in the pressure to be slim combined with the difficulty of maintaining weight loss (NZMOH, 2004), and this may add to the adverse health consequences associated with overweight and obesity for women.

Obesity in the developing world has been described as another form of malnutrition, which has arisen through a switch to the consumption of high-fat, high-energy and high-sugar foods rather than traditional foods which are high in vegetable fibre and fruit and which have relatively less fat and animal protein (WHO, 2002b; IASO, 2004). This shift in eating habits relates to the move to an urban population who must buy rather than grow food, combined with long hours of work and exposure to media campaigns by global food corporations aiming to increase sales of such foods (WHO, 2002b; Lang and Heaseman, 2004). In addition, HIV/AIDS discourse in many African countries, and the use of the word 'slim' for the disease because of the wasting which accompanies HIV/AIDS, adds further value to the fat body, and reduces the desirability of losing weight in some parts of the world.

Obesity and body image

The term 'obesity' is a social and subjective construct, and anti-fat stigma in the popular media, public health policy, and among health professionals helps to construct a discourse in which obese bodies and their owners are constructed as immoral, unacceptable and responsible for their own health problems, while also being a source of disgusted fascination (Schwartz and Brownell, 2004). Anti-fat bias or discrimination appears to be more acceptable than bias against other minority groups, reflecting the individualization of obesity as a problem (Schwartz and Brownell, 2004). Campos (2004), for example, suggests that anti-fat bias has replaced other forms of discrimination that are now prohibited in civil society – racism and class bias in particular. Higher rates of obesity among ethnic minority and poorer populations means that the same groups in society are discriminated against and reviled, but this is legitimated by the 'war on fat', and the apparent neutrality of the obese body.

Obesity and anti-fat discourses are also gendered, however. Research suggests that women are more likely than men to feel stigmatized by obesity, and are more likely to be perceived negatively, with white women reporting the most stigma (Schwartz and Brownell, 2004; Palinkas et al., 1996).

The causes of obesity are complex. Obesity relates to stress and psychological difficulties, which may in part stem from bias against body weight above socially accepted 'norms'. While stress can increase eating and also affect weight gain through biological changes – in the release of cortisol, for example – poor mental health can also be a consequence of unhappiness with the body. This body dissatisfaction affects women and men differently, however: more women are unhappy with their bodies, and throughout the life course women are more likely to describe themselves as overweight or obese even when they are not. Women are also more likely to take steps to change their bodies due to this dissatisfaction (Schwartz and Brownell, 2004; Paquette and Raine, 2004). These frequently include severe restrictions in food intake and the adoption of unhealthy weight loss practices, increasing women's risks of experiencing eating disorders and reduced self-esteem (Schwartz and Brownell, 2004). Men's bodily discontents may also lead them to unhealthy eating practices, but men are more likely to try to change their bodies by increasing their levels of exercise and fitness, by body-building, and in some cases by using steroids to increase the impact of body-building practices on muscle size (Paquette and Raine, 2004). Differences in concern with weight and size between women and men mean that body discontent impacts on health in a gendered way. However, most of the research on body dissatisfaction has been carried out on women, and much less is known about the relationship between body size, discontent and bodily practice among men (Schwartz and Brownell, 2004; de Casanova, 2004).

There are also differences in levels of body satisfaction between gay and heterosexual men and women. Gay men, for example, are more likely than heterosexual men to express dissatisfaction with their bodies, while there are fewer differences between lesbians and heterosexual women in body image and reported discontent (Schwartz and Brownell, 2004; Lakkis et al., 1999).

Body satisfaction is also related to ethnicity and cultural differences in body image and desirability. However, bodily discourses reflect complex cultural and ethnic differences. Hill Collins (1990), for example, suggests that discursive constructions of normal white (female) bodies require the 'other' to exist – that is, black bodies, with different characteristics, signify the opposite from which the white body can be constructed as normal or right. This 'white/other' dichotomy is also reflected in representations of body types – particularly that of the white thin body, compared with the stereotype of the overweight black woman (Lovejoy, 2001). Black women's resistance to the negativity of this discourse and their rejection of the white ideal have led to models of beauty which include strong images of women with curves, and a positive valuation of the mature, fleshy body (Lovejoy, 2001).

This positive ideal is in part associated with cultural constructions of black femininity, in which motherhood is particularly important and the role of black women in the family is valued, as well as with constructions of gender in which 'masculine' traits such as confidence and self-esteem are available for women (Lovejoy, 2001). Research among young black and Latino women also suggests that their ideal of beauty is more flexible than that of young white women, and that it is an ideal which is accommodating of different physiques, emphasizing personal style rather than the body underneath (de Casanova, 2004). However, this positive body image is also problematic, partly in the assertion of femininity as being fulfilled in the context of familial roles and motherhood, but also because eating problems experienced by black and minority women may be obscured. Logio (2003) also points out that a further tension is experienced by black women between the ideals of feminine beauty expressed by their families and those expressed by a media which reflects white ideals, a tension which is embodied by black women in their struggle with weight and eating problems.

One potential outcome of a larger body image is that while white women are more likely to experience eating disorders associated with the desire for thin bodies – anorexia, bulimia and purging – black women suffer from over-eating and are more at risk of compulsive eating behaviours (Lovejoy, 2001; Beauboeuf-Lafontant, 2003). A number of writers suggest that this behaviour is associated with the trauma and pain of racism, and experiences of sexism and sexual abuse, where women are using food to cope with their psychic distress (Lovejoy, 2001; Beauboeuf-Lafontant, 2003). Black women are described as literally 'embodying' their oppression, 'carrying the weight of the world on their bodies' (Beauboeuf-Lafontant, 2003: 115). To some extent, the risk of compulsive eating is compounded by a construction of black women as strong mothers, which increases pressures on them to absorb not only their own pain but also that of the family, while simultaneously coping with the work and demands of domestic life:

> [M]any Black women find it hard to admit they are overworked, overwhelmed, underloved and depressed . . . So instead of complaining or asking for help, many black women try to keep on while they medicate their pain in self-destructive ways, by over-eating, drinking or using drugs. (Mitchell and Herring, 1998: 67)

The cost of these pressures to women's health may be disguised in the discursive construction of black women's bodies as 'naturally' and appropriately large, which means that their over-eating is not recognized as a problem. Certainly eating disorders are stereotyped as 'white women's' problems: black women's problems are less often recognized by themselves or by health professionals, and obesity among minority women is more likely to be individualized as a personal failure of self-control (Lovejoy, 2001; Beauboeuf-Lafontant, 2003).

What about the male body among minority groups? As with men in general, far less has been written about body image and satisfaction among minority men, although there is evidence that some minority ethnic men experience more dissatisfaction with their size in comparison with white men, including concern about being overweight and concern among some Asian men who see themselves as too small in comparison with the white 'standard' (Neumark-Sztainer et al., 2002; Davis and Katzman, 1998).

Exercise and activity

Physical activity is an important part of health (WHO, 2002c). The World Health Organisation estimates that in 2001 physical inactivity resulted in nearly 2 million deaths and 19 million disability-adjusted life years (DALYS), including 20 per cent of ischaemic heart disease (WHO, 2002c). Exercise is a means of increasing energy expenditure, which helps to maintain healthy body weight, and exercise also affects body mass and composition by altering bone tissue and the ratio of fat to muscle (WHO, 2003e). In addition, exercise may improve cardiovascular health, reduce the risk of stroke and diabetes, and also improve mental well-being. There are further potential health benefits from exercise in relation to reductions in the risk of certain cancers, including breast and colon cancer, but research remains inconclusive about these. Lung cancer risk, for example, may be reduced among those who take part in regular vigorous activity, after controlling for smoking and other factors (Thune and Lund, 1996). As with other behaviours, overall health lifestyle is also important in explaining health risks – people who engage in exercise are less likely to smoke or to be very overweight.

Levels of physical activity are difficult to compare between women and men because of differences in what counts as activity. Activity may be broken down into four types: work-related activity, domestic labour activity, exercise related to transport (cycling or walking, for example), and leisure-based activity (WHO, 2002c). Where figures include all activity, as in the WHO figures above, then the health risks of *in*activity are greatest. The health impact also varies in association with the intensity of the activity and the context in which it is carried out – leisure-based cycling in a pleasant environment, for example, offers different kinds of benefit to cycling to and from work in an urban area with poor air quality.

When we look at gender and exercise, there are important differences in both the amount and the kind of activity that women and men engage in. In contrast to other kinds of health behaviour, where women have healthier lifestyles, men are more likely than women to participate in exercise (Courtenay, 2000; O'Brien Cousins and Gillis, 2005), although measurements designed around typically male activities may mean women's total activity rates are underestimated (Shephard and Shek, 1998; Thune and Lund, 1996).

Figures suggest that there are differences around the world in the amount of physical activity carried out by men or women and in the proportion of this activity which is leisure-based. Work-based physical activity is generally greater among men than women, mainly due to differences in occupation and the continuing sexual division of labour in the workplace, though it also reflects a failure to record women's work in the home (O'Brien Cousins and Gillis, 2005). The extent of physical activity required in the workplace is associated with occupational class, and higher-status men will have lower levels of occupational activity, while some women will have more activity in their jobs than some men.

Figures for leisure-based physical activity routinely show more men than women engaged in these forms of exercise, throughout the life course (GHS, 2004; Sandman et al., 2000; Courtenay, 2000; Sproston et al., 2002). In the USA, for example, around 60 per cent of the population participate in physical activity, but men are more likely than women to engage in regular physical activity and in activities described as vigorous (Lethbridge-Cejku et al., 2004). The US Commonwealth Fund surveys in the mid-1990s found that over half of men exercised three or more days a week, compared with two-fifths of women, and more women than men never exercised (Sandman et al., 2000). In Australia, New Zealand and the UK, more men than women participate in vigorous activity, and men spend more time in such activity (NZMOH, 2004; GHS, 2004). Similarly, in France more men than women report exercising, particularly in sports activities (Aliaga, 2002). When activity includes walking, however, participation for women is often higher than for men, reflecting the way in which this form of activity is associated with other responsibilities, such as shopping or taking children to and from school, the fact that women have less access to cars, and also the fact that walking is cheap and easier to fit around other activities, compared with organized sport or exercise which requires specialist equipment.

Men and women also give different reasons for exercise: while women exercise to improve their health, men exercise to get stronger, build muscle or because they enjoy competing (Saltonstall, 1993). This partly reflects differences between women and men in embodied health – men highlighting function and capacity rather than appearance, for example, saying things like 'being able to go through my day and accomplish things' and 'being in shape physically so I can do things' (Saltonstall, 1993).

These differences affect the kinds of activity men and women engage in, how easy it is to sustain over time, the health risks associated with the exercise, and also the benefits. In Britain and in the USA, more men than women participate in activities where there is a greater risk of injury, including weight training, rugby, football or soccer, and climbing, for example, while women are more likely to participate in yoga and keep-fit (GHS, 2004; Courtenay, 2000). These differences in choice of sport mean that women more often take part in physical activities which contribute to long-term health, while men's morbidity risk is increased by their choice of competitive sports, and this affects differences in health between women and men.

While physical leisure-based activity is less common in lower socioeconomic groups and poorer populations, reflecting the time and cost of many kinds of activity, differences between women and men persist across social classes (GHS, 2004; NZMOH, 2004; Sandman et al., 2000; Collins et al., 1999). In addition, people in minority ethnic groups in the USA, the UK and other countries are less likely to take part in physical exercise than people in the white population, and though this is true for both women and men, women from minority groups are particularly unlikely to participate in exercise (GHS, 2004; Sandman et al., 2000; Collins et al., 1999; Lethbridge-Cejku et al., 2004; NZMOH, 2004). In South Africa, for example, figures for vigorous activity among younger people show higher rates of activity among young men than young women, but more white men and women participate in these activities than other ethnic groups (Health Systems Trust, 2004).

There are further differences between gay men, lesbians, and heterosexual men and women in exercise activity. Research suggests that lesbians are more likely than heterosexual women to take part in regular physical exercise (Moran, 1996; Roberts et al., 2003). However, competitive sport has been constructed around heterosexual identity, and homophobia is widespread particularly in male sports. While sporting prowess is a key component of masculinity, this is less available for openly gay men. In recent years gay men have increased their participation in individual exercise, especially body-building work, and there are also gay football teams, but few of the players at national and international level in football, rugby, cricket, baseball or tennis are openly gay (<http://www.iglfa.org/ index1.htm>).

Data on physical activity for leisure are less widely available for developing and low-income countries. The 2002 World Health Report

(WHO, 2002e) reported more inactivity in developed countries, but these figures conceal decreasing levels of activity in some parts of the less developed world, particularly in rapidly urbanizing populations, where employment has become less active, populations have less time and space for leisure-based exercise, and public transport has replaced walking. In São Paulo in Brazil, for example, an estimated 70 per cent of the population is now physically inactive (WHO, 2002b).

Exercise and body image

Exercise is now used more than diet by both women and men as a means of controlling weight (Neumark-Stzainer et al., 2002). Public health promotion leaflets do not advise us to take up exercise in order to look better, but in order to feel better. Exercise is also seen as something that is morally valuable, and taking care of oneself is constructed as a virtuous activity (Sassatelli, 2002). 'A lot of days I don't feel like working out, but I do anyway, I push a little harder because I know that when I get through my workout, I'll feel better' (man cited in Saltonstall, 1993: 10).

Exercise can take different forms, and while those involved in various activities associate their participation with increased well-being and health benefits, some activities are particularly linked with the desire to reshape the body rather than improve general health status. Different sports and activities do different things to our bodies, increasing or defining specific groups of muscles, or increasing tone and flexibility. Aerobics, for example, is an activity mainly engaged in by women to get fit and maintain their weight, and the exercises which make up a typical aerobics session are designed to build women's bodies along stereotypical lines, with repeated movements to narrow waists, tighten buttocks and reduce thighs (Sassatelli, 2002).

A particular form of exercise which has taken on more importance in recent years is body-building, an activity which is gendered as well as racialized and located in class discourse. Body-building – the practice of training with weights and exercises to increase muscle mass and definition – is also about changing the appearance of the body towards a particular ideal form. Fitness and exercise are posited as good for every body, but the body-builder goes further, to build muscles and bulk, in a particularly defined or prescribed way:

> The bodybuilder functions to expand a capitalist morality of hard work, meritocracy, discipline, competition and progress defined through quantifiable and empirically confirmable results. The bodybuilder also functions

> symbolically to propagate a sexed division of labour strengthening the discursive links between biologically ascribed gender traits and labour roles. (Saltman 2003: 49)

A number of writers have questioned the meaning of the gym, and the bodywork that goes on there. Saltman (2003), for example, describes body-building as a war in which 'the bodybuilder is embattled against other bodies and against his or her own body' (p. 49). Body-building is contradictory – this 'perfect' body can only be achieved through the consumption of specific resources – gym time, high-protein foods, often from specialist shops, clothing associated with the activity, and fake tan when in competition – combined with denial – of food, alcohol, leisure time, and of pain, fatigue and boredom when working out.

However, the exercised body is also gendered. While gender is neutral in the space of the gym itself, and women's and men's bodies tend be treated as equivalent in terms of exercise potential and abilities, outside the gym, gender differences and their importance are reasserted (Sassatelli, 2002). Changing rooms are divided into male and female, and beyond these spaces the exercised body in popular discourse – in media and advertising, in particular – is recognizably either male or female, and reflects gendered ideals of beauty and form. Although body-builders have traditionally been male, there has been a rapid growth in women's participation in this activity in recent years. Women body-builders describe body-building as empowering, and as challenging the equations of masculinity as muscularity and femininity as soft yielding fleshiness (Grogan et al., 2004). However, while the female body-builders' ideal shape is muscular, these women are engaged in a difficult 'balancing act' in which the body must not be too muscular or too lacking in feminine characteristics (Grogan et al., 2004). In body-building practices, women labour to produce bodies that emphasize feminine and in particular reproductive bodies – big breasts and narrow waists which accentuate the hips, for example. This might be seen as ironic, in that steroid use and extreme levels of physical activity reduce reproductive capacity – stopping menstruation, for example. But it also illustrates the tension for women who body-build between consumption and denial in that the loss of one discursive option – the role of the mother – relates to the production of another – the desirable (reproductively immature) female body.

For men, body-building means enlarging and reinforcing the masculine body – making the body even more male (Richardson, 2004). Male body-building may also be sexually subversive, either as an explicit part of gay masculinity, or as a practice in which body fetishism, the promotion of the hairless and tanned physique, reflects gay practice and ideals, whether or not the body-builder declares himself to be gay.

Class is also important. Among heterosexual men body-building might be read as oppositional to aspects of hegemonic masculinity which emphasize white middle-class concepts of achievement, particularly finance and economic power rather than physique and physical power. One body-building website describing a training session put it this way:

> What is, to an 'outsider,' hard and gruelling labor to be parceled out for minimum wage is the essence of their endeavor; their craving, to be deliciously satisfied; the rock-ribbed passage to unknown strength. Discipline is not a gift. (<http://davedraper.com/article69-getting-ripped.html accessed 13/3/2005>)

Body-building can have adverse health effects, however, including biological changes, particularly for women's reproductive health, and the dangers of the very low-fat diet followed to promote thinner skin and better definition of veins – a feature known as being ripped, shredded or cut (Richardson, 2004). There are also risks of injury, but these vary in relation to individual body-builder's knowledge and practices. One of the most significant health risk arises from steroids, which are used to enhance bulk and muscles, and which are associated with increased violence and aggression, male impotence, poor mental health, suicidal thoughts, sexual risk taking and higher levels of body dissatisfaction (Courtenay 2000; McCabe and Ricciardelli, 2004). Steroid use is most common among younger populations of men, who are also most at risk of suicide, violence and poor mental health (Peixoto Labre, 2002). In addition, the majority of the anabolic steroids used by men to gain muscle or size are bought illegally, which further increases the health risk of taking these drugs.

However, 'roid rage' has also been described as an outsider view by those who question medical evidence on the dangers of steroids, and who suggest that body-builders are aware of the risks involved and use steroids selectively, following the advice of body-building websites which promote 'responsible' steroid use (Monaghan, 2001).

Illicit drug use

There are also important differences between women and men in their use of illicit drugs. This can impact on health in various ways, including the effects of the drug itself on physical and mental health, the risks associated with unclean equipment and sharing needles in the case of injecting drug-users, and increased risks of homelessness, poverty, unprotected sex, reckless behaviour and imprisonment (Thom, 2003). In addition, substance-users have a high risk of other health conditions, particularly psychiatric disorders, while accessing health services may be more difficult for those using illicit drugs (Singleton et al., 2001).

The risks to health of illegal drug use clearly vary with the kind of substance used, the frequency of use, and the ways in which the drug is obtained. For example, marijuana use increases the risk of respiratory and cardiovascular disease and lung cancer, particularly when combined with tobacco, while cocaine increases risk of psychosis, cardiovascular disease and gastric disorders (WHO, 2004c).

Figures on the use of illegal substances – whether collected through self-report surveys or measures based on use of health care services – are likely to underestimate the number of people using such drugs. Gender bias in this data is also possible, particularly where services are more accessible to men or are gender-insensitive, as when women are not asked about use of drugs in medical consultations (Brems et al., 1998).

In Britain, more men than women report using illicit drugs, and the ratio between men and women varies with the type of drug and also over the life course. Younger age groups report the highest use of illicit drugs, with similar numbers of men and women engaged in substance use, while in older age groups more men are involved (Singleton et al., 2001). In the USA, substance abuse and substance dependence are both greater among men, and men start using substances at a younger age in comparison with women (Courtenay, 2000). Young American men report more use of all illegal substances apart from MDMA (Ecstasy), which is used by similar numbers of young women and men (Schiller and Bernadel, 2004). In New Zealand and Australia, illicit drug use is more widespread among men than women (NZMOH, 2004). Illicit drug use is also higher among both lesbians and gay men in comparison with heterosexual men and women (King et al., 2003; Solarz, 1999).

In addition, illicit drug use is reported more often by women and men from minority ethnic groups. In New Zealand, for example, a fifth of Maori men and a tenth of Maori women are regular users of marijuana, compared with fewer than 10 per cent of European men and 3 per cent of European women (NZMOH, 2004). In the USA, ethnic minority men report more drug use, particularly African American men. Staples (1995) suggests that this is partly due to greater availability of illicit drugs for these men, but also that the use of illegal drugs can be seen as a response to the stress of racism, poverty and disadvantage: African American men are described as using drugs as a coping mechanism, albeit one which impairs their health: 'simply to become so narcotized that their subjugation under Euro-American rule is tolerable' (p. 132).

Smoking

The health effects of smoking are well known, and include increased risks, of lung cancer, chronic respiratory disease, stroke and cardiovascular disease (WHO, 1997). While these are often seen as mortality risks, the risk of morbidity is also greater among smokers, both for the diseases listed above and also for other health conditions (Ashley, 1997).

Smoking also affects the health of women and men differently, and this relates to gendered differences in smoking behaviour (for example, type of cigarette) as well as biological risk factors including hormonal differences (S. Payne, 2004). Smoking appears to increase the risk of myocardial infarction more for women than for men, for example (Fodor and Tzerovska, 2004; Prescott et al., 1998), and more women who smoke are diagnosed with Crohn's disease, although the condition is more evenly distributed among non-smokers (Ashley, 1997).

Overall more men smoke worldwide. In countries where the 'smoking epidemic' is relatively advanced, the sex ratio has narrowed in recent years, but in countries where smoking is still on the increase, men are significantly more likely to smoke than women (WHO, 2002d). In England, for example, the proportion of women and men who smoke is very similar. Around a quarter of all men and women smoke, but among younger age groups women are more likely to smoke than men (GHS, 2004; Thom, 2003). Fewer women than men smoke heavily, however, and more women smoke 'low tar' cigarettes. Among current smokers men are more likely to have started before the age of 16, but this reflects the greater number of male smokers in the past, and may be changing, given increases in smoking among younger women. In the USA, smoking is still more common among men than women, and men are less likely to quit or attempt to quit (Courtenay, 2000; Schiller and Bernadel, 2004; Collins et al., 1999; Sandman et al., 2000). In Sweden and Norway, however, women smoke as much as men (WHO, 2002d).

Smoking is another health behaviour where there are variations by social class as well as gender. In developed countries, smoking is more frequent in lower-income and occupational groups (Thom, 2003; GHS, 2004; AIHW, 2004). In the USA, smoking is highest among those with least education, and men in this group are more likely to smoke than women (NCHS, 2004). In comparison, in England and Wales more young women from the lowest-income groups smoke (Sproston et al., 2002).

Smoking also varies by ethnic group in complex ways which reflect cultural factors as well as socio-economic differences. In New Zealand, for example, more Maori men and women smoke than their white counterparts, while in the USA smoking is higher among African American men in comparison with white men, but lower among Hispanic men. Among American women, however, white women are more likely to smoke than other women (NZMOH, 2004; NCHS, 2004). In England, cigarette smoking is much higher among Bangladeshi, Irish and black Caribbean men than white men, but for women smoking is generally lower among minority groups than among white women (Erens et al., 1999).

There are also differences in relation to sexuality, with higher levels of smoking among gay men and lesbian and bisexual women compared with heterosexual men and women (Tang et al., 2004; Hughes and Evans, 2003). The higher prevalence of smoking among lesbians and gay men may reflect factors which are associated with tobacco use in general: in particular, smoking in response to stress, including experiences of homophobia and poor mental health. It may also relate to health lifestyles, especially the use of alcohol, as well as the failure of health promotion campaigns to address gay men and women specifically (Ryan et al., 2001).

The impact of smoking on health is related in part to smoking behaviour, including depth of inhalation, frequency of puffs on a cigarette or pipe, and the type of tobacco product consumed. Men appear to inhale more deeply, and are more likely to smoke unfiltered cigarettes and brands with higher tar and nicotine yields, all of which affect the health consequences of tobacco use (Courtenay, 2000; GHS, 2004). However, people who smoke low-tar cigarettes – the majority of whom are women – often adjust their behaviour to compensate for lower yields, by covering over the holes in the filter (Shields, 2002; Wynder and Muscat, 1995). Tobacco companies have a long history of gender-specific marketing, partly by the sponsorship of events such as beauty pageants, partly by advertising, and partly by package design.

These have been quite deliberate strategies which have drawn explicitly on both biology and gender to capture the female market:

> [The] smoking behaviour of women differs from that of men . . . more highly motivated to smoke . . . they find it harder to stop smoking . . . women are more neurotic than men . . . there may be a case for launching a female-oriented cigarette with relatively high deliveries of nicotine. (British Associated Tobacco research report 1976, cited in WHO, 2002d)

Alcohol

Alcohol consumption can affect health in a number of ways. Recent research has suggested that moderate consumption of alcohol may have a protective effect for heart disease and some cancers (Thom, 2003). However, high levels of alcohol consumption are associated with a number of morbid and fatal conditions, including colorectal cancer, cancers of the oral cavity and pharynx, bladder, oesophagus and larynx, as well as liver disease and mental health problems (Bagnardi et al., 2001; DeCosse et al., 1993; Levi et al., 1999). In addition, there are more immediate risks to health from behaviour following the consumption of excess alcohol, including unsafe sex, violence, road traffic and other accidents, and occupational injuries (Griffiths, 1996; Courtenay, 2000).

The risks attached to problem drinking are different for women and men. For example, heavy drinking may be more hazardous for women, and women's health seems to be more quickly compromised than men's at the same level of consumption (Redgrave et al., 2003). These increased risks are partly biological in origin, relating to body mass, percentage water, gastric activity and metabolism. Women who consume high levels of alcohol are more at risk of cancers of the reproductive system, liver disease, brain damage and psychiatric problems, and women who misuse alcohol also experience more short-term memory loss than men (Redgrave et al., 2003; Alcohol Alert, 1999; Prendergast, 2004). However, women with alcohol problems are often not identified by health professionals as needing treatment, and services for alcohol misuse are less widely available for women, reflecting gender stereotypes about alcohol use. Men's problems with alcohol often take different forms: men are more likely to be violent when drinking, and more often drink while at work, which increases their risk of occupational injury (Friedman, 1998).

Women's health is also at risk from men who drink to excess. Domestic intimate partner violence associated with men's use of alcohol obviously damages women's physical and mental health, but it can also lead to increased alcohol consumption by women suffering such violence (Abbott and Williamson, 1999; Redgrave et al., 2003).

In all countries men are more likely than women to drink above recommended levels. In Britain, around twice as many men as women report drinking on five or more days in the previous week, and twice as many report drinking over the recommended daily level, in every age group, although the gap between men and women is widest among older people (GHS, 2004; Singleton et al., 2001). In the USA, twice as many men as women are moderate or heavy drinkers, while more women are abstainers (NCHS, 2004), and similar differences between men and women are found in other countries (e.g. AusStats, 2002; NZMOH, 2004).

Alcohol consumption among young people is increasing in many countries. In England these increases are most marked for young women, although young men are still more likely than young women to drink more often and to drink more than the recommended levels (Sproston et al., 2002). More men than women also combine alcohol misuse with substance misuse, which further compromises their health and increases the risk of accidental and non-accidental injury (Waldron, 1995; Berrigan et al., 2003).

Unlike other health behaviours, alcohol consumption is greater among higher socio-economic groups and lower among deprived populations, reflecting the cost of alcohol. Despite this, hazardous levels of drinking are slightly more common among lower socio-economic groups for both women and men in a number of countries (NZMOH, 2004; Singleton et al., 2001).

The use of alcohol varies across different ethnic groups, but largely suggests that ethnic minority groups, especially men, are more at risk of alcohol-related harm. In New Zealand, for example, both men and women in European or white populations are more likely to consume alcohol than other groups, but hazardous drinking is more common among Maori men and women (NZMOH, 2004). In the USA, alcohol consumption is higher among men than women in all ethnic groups, but there are particularly high levels of consumption among American Indian and Alaska Native men, half of whom report hazardous levels of drinking (NCHS, 2004).

Sexuality may also be important in understanding drinking behaviour. Lesbians, gay men and bisexual men and women all report higher levels of alcohol consumption than heterosexual men and women, and levels of drinking among these groups tend not to reduce with age, as in other populations (Roberts and Sorenson, 1999; Hughes and Evans, 2003; King et al., 2003).

Explaining gender differences in health behaviour

Overall, then, men and women demonstrate differences in health behaviour which are associated with both morbidity and mortality, and women's health lifestyles tend to be better than those of men. In general, throughout the world, men are more likely than women to engage in activities which threaten their health, while women are more likely to avoid damaging behaviours. Among men, it is those who are poor, from low socio-economic groups and from minority ethnic groups who more often adopt behaviours which adversely affect their health, and some behaviours are also more marked among gay men. With women there is the same increased likelihood of damaging health lifestyles among those who are poor, marginalized, low status and from minority groups, and also among non-heterosexual women. Explanations of differences in health behaviour drawing on gender have to start from these findings. Some of the variation can be explained in the context of gendered expectations of behaviour, while gender differences in exposure to stress and in ways of dealing with stress are also significant. With both expectations of behaviour and stress response, gendered factors interact with other expectations or other sources of stress.

Exercise behaviour, for example, relates partly to differences between women and men in work and domestic responsibilities, including time available, opportunities and the resources needed to engage in leisure-based physical activity. There are also gendered expectations of behaviour which influence levels of participation in different activities and choice of activity (Saltonstall, 1993). Men may have more time and resources to pursue leisure-based exercise than women, while discourses of masculinity endorse different activities for different groups of men along class and ethnicity divides – rugby, tennis or golf for some men, compared with boxing or body-building for others.

Smoking behaviour also reflects access to resources, levels of stress, and gendered norms about appropriate behaviour. Women and men smoke in response to different triggers, and have different rates of success when they try to give up. Men appear to smoke more when relaxing, whereas women smoke more than men in response to stressful situations (Gritz et al., 1996). Both women and men also smoke more during periods of inactivity and boredom, and parents who smoke increase their smoking after children have gone to bed (Bancroft et al., 2003). However, gendered divisions of labour where smoking signifies 'time out' from responsibility for child care and domestic work also increase women's smoking compared with that of men, particularly among those with few material resources (Graham and Der, 1999). Gendered 'norms' have shifted over time, partly in response to tobacco marketing aimed at women, and in developed countries smoking is no longer a gender-specific behaviour. In a number of developing countries, more women now smoke, particularly in higher-income groups, again reflecting the way in which smoking has been sold to women as a sign of independence, modernity and fashion (Mackay, 1996).

Similarly, drinking behaviour can be both a response to stress and a way of enacting gender, particularly masculinity, while differences in alcohol consumption between women and men also reflect men's higher income. In younger age groups masculinity may be performed in various ways, but it is particularly associated with high levels of alcohol consumption (Capraro, 2000; Davies et al., 2000). Young men describe using alcohol as a means of building confidence, especially with women, and as a way of coping with stress and anxiety (Davies et al., 2000). Discursive constructions of masculinity support the association between masculine performance and drinking, and unlike women's magazines, men's magazines contain contradictory messages which both promote the consumption of large quantities of alcohol and draw attention to the danger of over-consumption (Stibbe, 2004).

A key element in understanding gendered behaviour and health relates to the masculinization of risk. On the sports field men are taught that mental and physical strength includes the denial of pain, and the performance of masculinity includes willingness to risk injury to win at all costs (Jefferson, 1998; Stibbe, 2004). Risks are constructed in a gender-specific way – both adults and children, for example, are able to identify risks as being either 'male' or 'female', and there are differences between women and men in expectations of their own and others' risk-taking behaviour (Lupton, 1999; Green, 1997; Thom, 2003; Lee and Owens, 2002).

Some of women's unhealthy behaviour may also be explained with reference to masculinity. Heavy drinking is common among women in the military, for example, as well as among men, and this reflects the ways in which women inside a heavily masculinized institution may adopt 'male' behaviour in order to survive or get on (Fertig and Allen, 1996). Increasing levels of drinking among young women in the UK, particularly binge drinking, similarly relate to masculinity through the idea of the 'ladette', in which women are constructed as copying male patterns of behaviour. Media reports of this culture of young women drinking to excess attribute the cause to women's increased disposable income and delayed marriage and child bearing, which give them the opportunity to behave like men (for example, Marsh, 2004).

There are other ways in which the health behaviour of men and women varies, particularly in relation to ethnicity, and these differences can also be related to stress, resources and gendered constructions of risk and identity. Performance, for example, is not only masculinized but also 'racialized', and different discourses of masculinity are associated with different kinds of behaviour which shape the risk of poor health and mortality for white and minority men (Jefferson, 1998). The very high levels of substance use, including both illicit drugs and alcohol, for example, among Maori men in Australia and American-Indian men in the USA, relate to specific constructions of masculinity within societies in which these groups suffer discrimination and disadvantage, and where other routes of masculine performance are not open to them. Similarly, while the social construction of femininity excludes many risky behaviours and encourages a presentation of the self constructed around health and attractiveness, different feminine discourses encourage different aspects of performance, so that lesbian discourse, for example, includes smoking and heavy alcohol consumption as well as physical activity.

What we see, then, when we look at the relationship between gender and health, is that differences between women and men reflect gender as well other factors in quite complex ways. A recent study by Denton et al. (2004) illustrates this complexity well, particularly the relative contributions made to women's and men's health by lifestyle, occupational class and material resources, employment and stress factors. First, they note that lifestyle factors, stressful experiences and material resources need to be seen as 'rooted in the social structural context of people's lives' (Denton et al., 2004: 2587). While class differences in 'health lifestyles', including smoking, diet and exercise, for example, play a part in explanations of health difference, we need also to ask how class differences in health behaviour can themselves be explained. Secondly, Denton et al. (2004) draw attention to the ways in which men and women embody stress differently. Their research suggests that women experience stressful life events more often than men, but also that the impact of stress differs for men and women – financial and personal problems are more strongly associated with chronic illness for women, for example, and environmental problems are also associated with poorer physical and mental health for women. Men, however, appear to have poorer health when experiencing difficulties in their personal relationships. Thirdly, health is affected by social circumstances, and women's economic and material deprivation partly accounts for their poorer self-reported health and their experience of chronic health conditions. Fourthly, some lifestyle factors seem to have more effect on the health of men than women – for example, male smokers had poorer functional health compared with women who smoked, and male drinkers had worse health than men who didn't drink, while women who drank moderate amounts of alcohol had better health than other women. On the other hand, women who were overweight had poorer physical health than men, and women who were underweight were more likely to suffer from poor mental health. Finally, having social support is generally associated with better health – but appears to be more important in shaping women's health than men's. This complex piece of research, which explored a range of social determinants of health for both men and women, and which looked at mental health and different measures of physical health, concluded that while there are common factors at work for both men and women – particularly those related to class, occupation and material inequalities – there are also important gender differences both in what affects health and the nature of that effect.

Gender and health care

Health care factors, including women and men's access to health care, how they use services and the appropriateness of health services, also affect patterns of health and disease, while variations between women and men in their use of informal health care reflect gendered differences in whether formal care is available and who is expected to provide this care. We start the exploration of gender and health care by looking at differences between women and men in health care-seeking behaviour.

Gender differences in health care-seeking behaviour – 'I don't go to the doctor unless something scares the hell out of me' (Stibbe, 2004: 36)

There are some important differences between women and men when it comes to the decision to consult a health care practitioner, to use screening services, or to follow health promotion advice. Although men are widely perceived as being more reluctant to use health care and as being difficult to reach in terms of preventive health care and health promotion (Glasgow et al., 1993; White, 2001), there is relatively little research which demonstrates this in a conclusive way. In particular, while there is evidence that women use services more than men, less has been written about how this use might relate to need.

In more developed countries, men consult health care practitioners less often than women at all levels of the system (Liang et al., 1999; Wyke et al., 1998; AusStats, 2002; Courtenay, 2000). Men visit doctors less often, use significantly fewer health care services, are less likely to have a regular doctor or be registered with a health practice, and in countries such as the USA are less likely to have insurance cover, and have fewer check-ups (Courtenay, 2000; Sandman et al., 2000). Women consult their general practitioners more often, make more use of out-patient medical care than men, even after visits for reproductive events have been excluded, and women consult more for preventive care (Malterud and Okkes, 1998; Wyke et al., 1998; Alt, 2002; O'Brien et al., 2005). Men are more difficult to engage in health-promotion activity, and those working in public health have devised a range of strategies to try and draw men into health-promotion activities, including placing clinics and information in workplaces and bars (Aoun and Johnson, 2002; Lloyd, 2002). Similarly, men make less use of preventive dental services (Kelley et al., 2000). Men are also more likely than women to delay help-seeking, and when they visit a doctor, it is some time after first noticing symptoms (Alt, 2002; Sandman et al., 2000; Banks, 2001).

In a series of focus groups in Scotland, a diverse group of men including those working in traditionally male occupations and men with chronic health conditions talked about how they tended to put up with minor symptoms, fearing that they would be seen as wasting the doctor's time or failing as men. They used expressions like 'You don't like to make a fuss' even when describing serious problems: 'I broke my thumb and it took me two days before I went to see a doctor . . . It was going septic, going green and purple and black and I was like "I'm not going to bother them"' (O'Brien et al., 2005: 508). This reluctance to consult included not only quite severe symptoms – one man described his shock when he eventually did seek help, on being told he needed a quadruple bypass operation – but also symptoms of depression and mental health problems which were similarly seen as not something a man could admit to.

Men are also less likely than women to carry out self-examinations – for example, men are less likely to examine themselves for prostate or testicular cancer than women are to conduct breast self-exams (Courtenay, 2000). Other forms of self-care are more common among women than men: men take fewer vitamin and mineral supplements, are less likely to stay in bed when ill, and are less likely to use sun cream to protect against skin cancer (Courtenay, 2000; Lee and Owens, 2002).

However, men's apparent reluctance to use health care compared with women is complex. Two large-scale studies in the USA, looking at the health and health behaviour of women and men, found that while a quarter of men would wait as long as possible before seeking medical treatment, a similar proportion of women also said they would delay seeking treatment (Sandman et al., 2000; Collins et al., 1999). The gap between women and men in how they might respond to symptoms changed with age. Younger men were more likely than women to say that they would wait, but over the age of 65, women were more likely than men to delay seeking help (Sandman et al., 2000; Collins et al., 1999). This may relate to gender differences in insurance cover, in expectations of health at different ages, or the role of others in the decision to get help. But it is likely that health care-seeking behaviour is affected by a range of factors.

Income is a significant factor in health care use, particularly in countries where care is available on the basis of private insurance or on a fee basis. In the USA, around a third of both low-income women and men report difficulties accessing the health care they need (Sandman et al., 2000). While low-income men and those with no health insurance are more likely than higher-income men to delay seeking treatment, low-income women also do not receive care, including breast exams, pap smears and cholesterol tests (Sandman et al., 2000; Collins et al., 1999). In the USA, women are more likely to be affected by financial barriers to health care because of gender disparities in income, while men say they are put off by lack of time – for example, having to wait more than 30 minutes for treatment significantly reduces the likelihood that men will consult a doctor (Xu and Borders, 2003).

Further differences in use of health care related to ethnicity are also associated with income and accessibility of services, as well as the actual and perceived appropriateness of care. Again, these factors affect both women and men. For example, over half of the Asian American women in the US Commonwealth Fund survey had not had a physical examination in the past year, and a third had not received preventive care, compared with only a sixth of white women

(Collins et al., 1999). Similarly, African American women are twice as likely as white women to have no health insurance (Nunez and Robertson, 2003). However, in the US Commonwealth Fund study, African American men and Hispanic men were more likely than white men to seek care as soon as possible when ill (Sandman et al., 2000).

There are also differences in health care use between gay men, lesbians and heterosexual men and women. Relatively little research looks at health consultations of gay or bisexual men apart from work on HIV and AIDs care, genito-urinary clinics and mental health services (Pearson, 2003). However, gay and bisexual men report a similar reluctance to heterosexual men in their use of both general and specialist health services (Davies et al., 2000). This reluctance may be associated with anxieties about pressures to disclose their sexuality, and actual and perceived homophobia in service delivery, as well as factors shared with other men (Scarce, 1999). In one study in the USA, for example, gay men who had disclosed their sexuality to health care providers felt unhappy with being treated as promiscuous and as an AIDS threat simply because they were gay:

> 'I disclosed that I had same-sex partners . . . although I had not put myself at risk and was not HIV positive . . . the chief resident, he wouldn't even come across the room. He didn't want to get too close to a fag.'
>
> '(I) find it frustrating that when I identify as gay, my doctor immediately implies "AIDS" issues and assumes promiscuity.'
> (Eliason and Schope, 2001: 130)

For lesbians there are similar issues in relation to health service use, although again this is an under-researched area (Solarz, 1999). In most countries, lesbians make less use of health care services in general, and are less likely to use health screening than heterosexual women (McNair, 2003; Hughes and Evans, 2003; Bailey et al., 2000). These differences follow both from the failure of health providers to provide care which is sensitive to the needs of lesbians and also from misperceptions by some medical providers and sometimes lesbians themselves regarding the need for some kinds of preventive care – particularly cervical screening (Ferris et al., 1996; Price et al., 1996). One US study found that nearly a quarter of lesbians reported either delaying seeking care until symptoms were at their worst or never seeking help, and the women expressed fears over health care which included difficulties in talking with the health care provider about their health and their sexuality (White and Dull, 1997). Similarly, in another study in the USA (Eliason and Schope, 2001), lesbians were critical both of the heterosexist assumptions of health care providers and of the ways in which lesbians were dealt with in health care encounters:

> 'I disclosed to my lesbian ob/gyn and after five years, she still asks what kind of birth control I use.'
>
> 'I work in a health care setting and have observed negative behaviours from health care professionals. I don't want information about my sexual identity in my medical record and risk being the subject of their jokes.' (Eliason and Schope, 2001: 130–1)

These findings about differences between women and men relate to the use of health care in high-income or developed countries. In low-income countries, where access to health care is dependent on financial resources for out-of-pocket expenses, women use health care less than men, partly due to their lack of access to household resources, and partly due to social and cultural factors which limit women's access to care in other ways (Akbar Zaidi, 1996; Hanson, 1999). In Bangladesh, for example, women use more self-care, more unqualified practitioners, and take more unlicensed medicines than men, who use the formal health care system more frequently than women (Ahmed et al., 2003). Gendered cultural and social constraints make access to medicines and services more difficult for women when they need permission from male members of the household to seek treatment (Baghadi, 2005). Women may also delay both self-care and help-seeking as a result of caring responsibilities and the need to put others first. In some countries women may be unable to use public transport on their own, and if no one is able or willing to accompany them, they cannot attend health care appointments (Tanner and Vlassoff, 1998). Men, on the other hand, may fail to consult as a result of other pressures on their time – particularly occupational status (Rumm and Johnson, 2002).

The social and economic consequences of some infectious diseases may also be greater for women. For example, some conditions are attributed to sexual behaviour which is seen as unacceptable for women and which means women receiving treatment are stigmatized (Tolhurst and Nyonator, 2002). Concerns about confidentiality may also be more significant for women in communities where a disease carries particular meanings and the knowledge that a woman is suffering from a condition might carry serious implications for her position in the household. Women in many developing countries also report feelings of stigma and discrimination from health care workers, and this further discourages them from using formal health care (Vlassoff and Bonilla, 1994).

Other explanations of the differences between women and men in their use of health care relate to health knowledge: men may have, or may see themselves as having, less understanding of symptoms, the way their bodies work, and risks to their health, while women are seen as better informed about the meaning and importance of their own symptoms as well as having a better understanding than men of the male body (White, 2001; O'Brien et al., 2005). Women's awareness of symptoms reflects gender differences in embodiment, and particularly women's greater familiarity with both physical and mental changes (Thom, 2003; Francome, 2000; Sandman et al., 2000; Alt, 2002). However, this does not mean that men are unaware of their bodies or that women always get it right. For example, women are less likely to recognize heart attack symptoms, and are surprised when they are told they have had a heart attack, partly due to stereotypes about masculinity and heart disease (Martin et al., 2004). Conversely, masculine discourses do not mean that men are not embodied, but that their embodiment takes specific forms. Men are concerned with particular aspects of their physicality – with strength, with muscle, and with the body as the outward signifier or representation of a particular form of masculinity (Jefferson, 1998) – rather than with symptoms of health or illness. And men are also concerned with the body in terms of comparisons with others – particularly when it comes to sexuality and physique. Male bodily concerns are not absent, then, and men are not indifferent to their bodies, but their concerns do not relate primarily to health care, and do not prompt health care behaviour. Instead, taking care of one's health is seen as a feminine thing rather than masculine or neutral (Lee and Owens, 2002). Moynihan (1998) suggests that both men and women with more masculine traits are less concerned about their health and use health care less than men and women with feminine traits. Masculine performance demands the act of invulnerability in the face of threats to health and remaining stoic and silent when the health threat becomes real, and this helps to explain lack of consultation for symptoms of both physical and mental problems (Lee and Owens, 2002).

Overall, then, women's and men's use of health care relates to gender in various ways, including access and control over economic resources, the availability of health care, gender roles and activities, decision-making power, and gender norms and identities (Tolhurst and Nyonator, 2002). Although little research has explored the use of health care by women and men in relation to need, epidemiological evidence does not consistently demonstrate that men's lower health care use reflects lower morbidity (Rumm and Johnson, 2002). In studies of people with specific health conditions, for example, men are significantly less likely than women to use health care (Courtenay, 2000).

Gender differences in health treatment

The ways in which health care is provided to men and women may also affect gendered experiences of health. As before, much of the research on this relates to the experiences of men and women in high-income countries, and less is known about differences in treatment in less developed countries. A number of factors are relevant to understanding treatment: in particular, differences relating to socio-economic status and class, ethnicity, age, sexuality and disability.

We saw earlier that women's and men's decisions to consult are in part associated with access factors – the cost of care and financial barriers to treatment, the availability of transport, caring responsibilities and paid employment, and the extent to which care is gender-sensitive (Doyal, 2000b, 2004). In addition, there may be gendered differences in the way services detect or treat health problems of men and women. For example, in the USA more women attend an annual physical examination which, while focusing on reproductive health, means that there are increased opportunities for screening for other problems and more likelihood that other problems will be discussed (Alt, 2002). But, more men than women receive health care including check-ups through employment, particularly in less developed countries (Chun et al., 2005).

One aspect of health care delivery which affects take-up and consultation is the sex of the physician. A number of studies have found that women prefer a female doctor, particularly women from South Asian ethnic groups and particularly for some conditions connected with reproductive health (Ahmed et al., 2003; Phillips and Brooks, 1998; Chapple et al., 1998; Vandenbrinkmuinen et al., 1994). However, this preference is not always met. Although there are fewer studies about men's preferences for female or male doctors, it seems that they are less likely to express a preference, and when they do (for example, in consultations which require intimate physical examination), they will also often prefer a female doctor (Fidler et al., 2000).

There are other ways in which the health care on offer may be more or less able to meet the health needs of women and men. In coronary heart care, for example, some diagnostic tests are less able to identify women with heart disease, while treatment may also be less effective for women (Shaw et al., 2000). Women with ischaemic heart disease in general practice are less carefully monitored than men – fewer have their body mass index, smoking status or blood pressure recorded in their notes; fewer women are tested for fasting cholesterol concentration; and fewer are prescribed lipid-lowering drugs, despite the fact that women with this condition are more likely than men to have high blood pressure, raised serum cholesterol concentration, and to be obese (Hippisley-Cox et al., 2001). Women with heart disease have been described as being treated 'less aggressively' than men: they receive less revascularization than men after admission with coronary heart disease; women with hypertension are less likely than men to get rehabilitation after acute cardiac admission; and women are less often referred for full evaluation for heart disease after symptoms such as pain after exercise (Wenger, 1997; Shaw et al., 2000; Raine et al., 2003). Women are also more likely than men to die after myocardial infarction, coronary artery bypass and angioplasty, which reflects both the older average age of women with coronary disease and also gaps in services (Wenger, 1997). However, there are other differences in coronary care affecting men. Courtenay (2000) suggests that in the USA men with hypertension are less likely to be picked up by screening than women, and, as a result, fewer men than women are on medication to control hypertension, one of the main risk factors in heart disease.

Some of the gaps between women and men in coronary treatment relate to differences in the symptoms of heart disease and in the value of diagnostic tests, due to sex differences in how the disease manifests itself in men and women. Younger women suffer symptoms similar to those of heart disease due to hormonal factors, and the concern that this might lead to false positives in diagnosis tends to reduce their chances of referral for specialist investigation. In addition, more women than men suffer from 'silent' myocardial infarctions or heart attacks, which leads to delay in treatment (McKinley, 1996; Meischke et al., 1998). As women with heart disease are on average older than men with the condition, women may also be less able to carry out exercise-based diagnostic tests at sufficient intensity (Wenger, 1997). These differences are partly biological in origin, but the relatively poorer understanding of women's heart disease reflects the exclusion of women in heart research over many years (Wenger, 1997).

Similarly, there is concern that men with depression are overlooked, particularly in general practice, due to stereotypes about mental health and about women's vulnerability to minor mental health problems (Blair-West et al., 1999). Gender stereotypes also affect the delivery of alcohol abuse services. Women who abuse alcohol tend to be invisible, because the majority of those with this problem are men, and women more often report feeling stigmatized by services, or being seen by health professionals as having low morals, being sexually promiscuous, and as being problematic or out-of-control patients compared with men who abuse alcohol (Redgrave et al., 2003). Women are also more likely than men to fear losing their children if they seek treatment, and this, combined with the failure of services to meet the needs of women, can lead to a lack of treatment for women with alcohol problems (Padayachee, 1998; Thom, 2003; Redgrave et al., 2003).

Gender sensitivity in the design of diagnostic tests may also be important. A study of tuberculosis in Vietnam, for example, found that women experience more delays in obtaining results and starting treatment, possibly due to gendered behaviour norms: coughing is less acceptable for women, which means that they produce less sputum in a TB test, and results are more difficult to detect (Tolhurst and Nyonator, 2002). Gender-sensitive tests would aim to overcome such difficulties for women, perhaps by allowing them greater privacy. Tuberculosis treatment is also problematic for women. TB is the greatest cause of infectious deaths among women, and particularly affects women of reproductive age. The recommended therapy – directly observed treatment short-course, or DOTS – can be more difficult for women, because TB is a stigmatized disease in many parts of the world, and DOTS is a very obvious treatment. Women fear discrimination if they are known to be suffering from TB, and may be reluctant to finish a course of treatment as a result (Amazigo, 1998).

Services also vary in how well they meet the needs of ethnic minority men and women. A national survey of minority health care in the USA, for example, concluded that both women and men from minority groups receive less up-to-date care, less expensive care, poorer-quality care, and that they have less choice over their care than the white population (National Comparative Survey of Minority Health Care, 1997). These gaps persist even when insurance status is accounted for (Williams and Tucker, 2000). Black women in the USA also receive less medical advice during pregnancy than white women, and of course this has serious implications for both their own health and that of their children (Kogan et al., 1994).

Health care needs to be sensitive not only to biology and gender, but also to sexuality. Lesbians, for example, are under-served in terms of screening, and clinicians often fail to take a full reproductive history, which leads to poor care and advice (Marrazzo and Stine, 2004; Hughes and Evans, 2003; McNair, 2003). Cervical screening in particular is a problem – although a significant proportion of women defining themselves as lesbians will have had sexual intercourse with a man at some point in their lives, and women who have not had sexual intercourse with a man may suffer cervical abnormalities, lesbians are less often referred for cervical smears than women defining themselves as heterosexual (Phillips-Angeles et al., 2004; Solarz, 1999; Hughes and Evans, 2003).

Gay men's reluctance to use health care stems in part from feelings that services are not sensitive to their needs (Davies et al., 2000). Increased sensitivity to specific health care issues for gay men would include the question of how to support disclosure of sexual preference. There are other important service needs, however. For example, sexually transmitted infections, particularly the anal human papilloma virus (HPV), are important risk factors in anal cancer, and screening might be a valuable means of reducing the risk of cancer mortality of gay men. But to be effective, such screening would need to be offered to gay men who engage in anal sex (as well as women who do so), and this requires a degree of communication and trust between patient and health care provider that is unlikely in the context of homophobia and fear of disclosure. Medical research on the link with HPV has also contributed to a discourse of risk which emphasizes promiscuity and individual blame, mirroring the association between cervical cancer and promiscuity among women. Ideas of moral contagion help to maintain the notion of 'gay' disease while reducing the likelihood that gay and bisexual men will receive care which is sensitive to their needs (Scarce, 1999).

Finally, there is gender bias in medical research and the medical curriculum which impacts on the delivery of health care for both women and men. Despite significant changes in medical understanding of biopsychosocial factors affecting health, representations of the body in medical textbooks continue to suggest that the male body is the standard, while the female body is other, relevant only in the study of reproductive health (Peterson, 1998; Clarke, 2003; Inhorn and Whittle, 2001). In the USA, for example, in the late 1990s men made up 85 per cent of research participants, while in Canada the figure is 95 per cent (Rogers, 2004). This includes heart disease trials, where women were less than a quarter of participants, and research on HIV and AIDS, where women made up less than 6 per cent of participants between 1995 and 1998. Although there has been a growth in research on HIV/AIDS among women, the focus of this research has largely been on aspects of transmission of the virus from mother to child (Rogers, 2004).

In addition, research which judges the success of interventions with reference to clinically observed outcome measures, rather than the value of particular outcomes to women and men, is problematic. For example, noreshisterone is a drug which can be used to treat menorraghia or excessive blood loss during menstruation. It is seen as ineffective by medical researchers, due to the relatively minor changes it produces in the volume of total blood loss, but women who have used the drug report high levels of satisfaction with the changes it produces and the way it helps them manage their lives (Rogers, 2004).

The problems of gender-blind research are made more significant by the use of systematic reviews which pool results from a number of studies. Such reviews are carried out increasingly in medicine to support evidence-based practice and to make better use of the existing research. However, the value of systematic reviews is greatly reduced when not enough women are included in the original studies, and when findings are not reported separately for men and women (Rogers, 2004).

Research on the health needs of lesbians and gay men is also inconclusive, inadequate, and often constructed simplistically around specific conditions and narrow concepts of sexuality (Solarz, 1999; Scarce, 1999). Some research suggests that lesbians have a higher risk of breast cancer, for example, associated with lower birth rates, but other studies suggest that cancer incidence among lesbians and gay men is the same as among the population in general (Frisch et al., 2003; Dibble et al., 2004). The Solarz committee on the health of lesbians in the USA concluded that lesbians are not at greater risk of specific health problems due to their sexual orientation, but that specific risk factors may be experienced differently by lesbians, including access to health services, which is affected by difficulties disclosing sexual identity when services and providers are perceived as homophobic (Klitzman and Greenberg, 2002).

Research informs medical knowledge and feeds into insensitivity in medical education as well as services, and as a result the health needs of lesbians and gay men are similarly underdeveloped in the curriculum of most medical schools (Robinson and Cohen, 1996; McNair, 2003).

Conclusion

This chapter has explored key explanations of differences in health experience and the risk of morbidity and mortality for women and men, focusing on the effects of biological factors and gender in the context of other kinds of difference. While men are more likely to engage in unhealthy lifestyles, they also have more access to resources which might promote health, fewer caring responsibilities, and health care services will often meet their needs more effectively. Women, on the other hand, are largely less likely to adopt unhealthy lifestyles, less likely to take risks, and are more likely to consult practitioners. However, their health is adversely affected by poorer resources, difficulties accessing health care, and gender-blind services which may fail to meet their needs. Sex and gender interact with other kinds of difference, including, in particular, social class, ethnicity and sexuality, and these also affect the health of women and men. The following chapters explore in more detail the evidence relating to health outcomes which follow from these differences, looking at data on general health status, mental illness, reproductive and sexual health and mortality, beginning in chapter 3 with an exploration of the ways in which patterns of morbidity or illness vary.

3 Illness and Health: Sex, Gender and Morbidity

Introduction

The last chapter explored explanations for the differences in women's and men's health, and how such explanations relate to sex and gender. Now we look at how well these explanations fit the data – when we look at the ways in which women and men experience health, how well do sex and gender explain the patterns we find? This chapter focuses on health and illness during the life course. While the focus is still on sex and gender as health influences, we continue to explore these in the context of other differences, including socio-economic status, ethnicity and age. The chapter begins by looking at generalized measures of the health of men and women, before going on to explore the ways in which men and women vary in terms of self-reported health status. We then look at measurements of ill health based on the use of health care by men and women.

With each of these sets of data we need to remain aware of what is being measured – in particular, whether we are looking at figures on health or the lack of health – and how gender affects the different measures used. We saw in the last chapter that men and women behave differently in terms of perceptions of health, recognition of symptoms, and health care use, and these differences affect estimates of morbidity and health. If gender is relevant in the delivery of health care, for example, it will also be relevant in how we interpret data based on general practice consultations, or in-patient treatment. Because of differences in concepts of health, health indicators developed for Western populations are also likely to be inappropriate for populations in developing countries (Knodel and Ofstedal, 2003), and this means that cross-country comparisons may not reflect the full extent of variations in health.

Many of the factors which affect health also affect mortality, and many of the differences between women and men in life expectancy draw on the same set of explanations as differences in morbidity. Coronary heart disease, for example, plays a part in both morbidity and life expectancy. Some of the risks of illness discussed here are also significant in understanding the mortality gap between men and women, which we return to later in the book. However, there are also differences between women and men in conditions which are not life-threatening but which cause chronic illness, ongoing pain or difficulty, and which affect quality of life. Osteoarthritis, for example, is a serious chronic condition which is more prevalent among women at all ages. Similarly, more women than men suffer from irritable bowel syndrome, a condition which produces painful and disruptive symptoms, while men are more likely to suffer from ankylosing spondylitis, another chronic long-term illness which seriously impairs quality of life (Heitkemper et al., 2003).

The direction and magnitude of the health gap between women and men varies, then, for different conditions and also in relation to other factors, including in particular age, ethnicity and social class. The gap between women and men in terms of health experience can also vary across generations (Macintyre et al., 1996; Liang et al., 1999; Hunt, 2002, Annandale and Hunt, 2000). This means that, in order to assess differences between women and men, more general descriptions of health need to be supplemented with detailed considerations of specific diseases. We explore variations in mental health, reproductive and sexual health, and mortality, in the following chapters. Here, we look at sex and gender as influences on health more generally, using population studies and survey data. At the end of the chapter we explore the role of sex and gender in two chronic non-life-threatening conditions to illustrate differences between women and men in vulnerability to disease and in the way in which ill health is experienced.

Gender differences in healthy life expectancy (HALE)

One way of assessing the health of men and women is through what has been described as 'healthy life expectancy', in contrast to life expectancy. One of the reasons for an approach which is not based simply on mortality is that death is a singular event. What people die of, and when, may not reflect their health during their lifetime, and when we are interested in the distribution of health across different populations – men and women, for example – we need a measure which reflects more than simply the end of life. There are a number of different ways in which this idea of healthy life has been conceptualized, reflecting the difficulties inherent in such an approach. The major problem with these measures, which include 'disability-free life expectancy', 'disability-adjusted life expectancy', and 'quality-adjusted life expectancy', is that while they are better than life expectancy as an indication of health status through the life course, the measures are normative. That is to say, these concepts and the tools used to measure them are based on generalized assumptions about the impact of illness or disability on quality of life and about the value of life without disability – assumptions which are questionable. Research looking at how people judge their own health shows that this is highly subjective, relating to individual expectations based on prior health experience and to comparisons with others (Saltonstall, 1993; Blaxter, 1990). Having a health condition which is defined as chronic by the medical profession, for example, does not preclude self-reported health status as being excellent or good (Blaxter, 1990). Judgements based on disability-free years also implicitly define life with disability as of poorer quality – something that many disabled people would challenge.

This criticism needs to be retained when we look at differences between women and men, as both the risk of disability and how disability is experienced will vary in relation to gender and other factors. However, bearing these limits in mind, figures based on healthy life expectancy go some way towards indicating the gap between women and men. The *World Health Report* (WHO, 2004e) uses measures of 'healthy life expectancy' (HALE) based on the idea of the proportion of the full-life span that an individual might expect to live in good health, without illness or disability. The HALE data begin with life expectancy at birth, which is then adjusted for estimates of time spent in poor health, based on indicators of health at country level. HALE is therefore 'the equivalent number of years in full health that a new born can expect to live based on current rates of ill-health and mortality' (WHO, 2004e: 96). The basis of these estimates is a multi-country survey study (MCSS) carried out in 2000–1, which used a measure of health status based on international classifications of functioning, diversity and health. The survey attempted to compensate for variations in self-reported health between countries and populations within countries by using performance tests and vignettes (WHO, 2004e).

Using this methodology, HALE figures suggest that in nine out of ten countries women have a higher healthy life expectancy than men, including 32 countries where the female advantage is five years or more. In the Russian Federation, for example, women have more than 11 years advantage over men. In more than a third of countries, women have between three and five years longer healthy life expectancy than men – and this includes countries as diverse as the USA, Belgium, Sri Lanka, the Democratic Republic of Congo and Rwanda. In a further third of WHO member states, including the UK, Sweden and South Africa, the female advantage is between one and three years. The gap between female and male HALE is narrow or non-existent in one in ten countries, including Nigeria, Zambia, India and Afghanistan, and in a few member states, including Qatar, Bangladesh, Pakistan and Botswana, male healthy life expectancy at birth is greater than female.

Thus, as figure 3.1 illustrates, although most women are likely to live longer in full health than most men, this is not universal, and in some parts of the world men have better expectations of health than women. The factors which explain health differences between women and men are likely, therefore, to reflect sex differences and gender relations – if biology alone explained men's and women's health, then differences between women and men in healthy life expectancy would be largely the same around the world. Instead, we must explore other, gender-linked factors, to explain these differences further. However, figure 3.1 also shows that the size of the gap between women and men is not simply related to a country's level of development – for example,

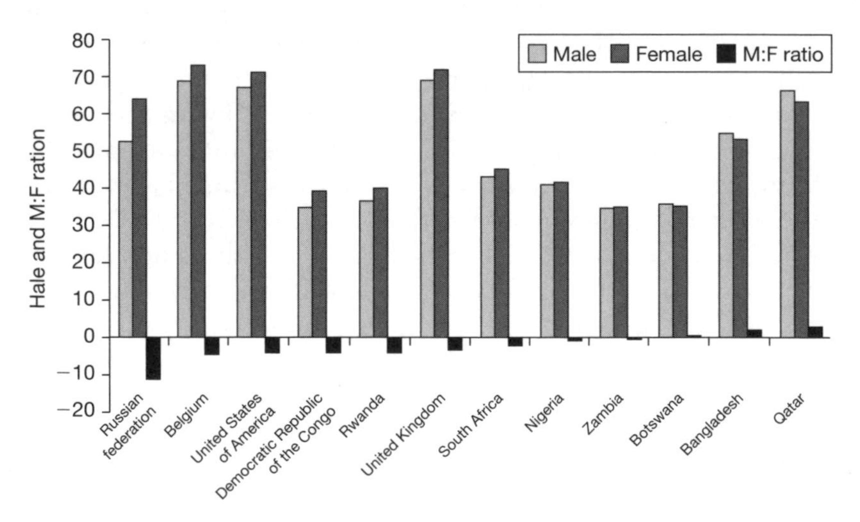

Source: Data drawn from WHO, 2004a.

Figure 3.1 HALE and male to female HALE ratio, selected countries, 2004

the ratio of male healthy life expectancy to female life expectancy is similar for the USA and the Democratic Republic of Congo, but both women and men in the USA have a high healthy life expectancy, while women and men in the Democratic Republic of Congo do not. The factors which affect healthy life expectancy for women and men vary in these countries. In the USA, healthy life expectancy is reduced for both men and women because of health lifestyle, and men's poorer health expectancy reflects differences in smoking and diet and their greater risk of accidental injury and occupational ill health, for example. In the Democratic Republic of Congo the key factors influencing healthy life expectancy of women and men are those of civil conflict, enforced migration, economic crises, poverty, famine and malnutrition, and lack of health care, together with infectious diseases, including malaria, cholera, tuberculosis, and HIV and AIDS (WHO, 2004a). As in many conflict situations, women and young people are particularly at risk of sexual violence and mental health problems, while men's poorer healthy life expectancy also reflects their health risks resulting from conflict and injury.

The variations in the gap between women and men in healthy life expectancy argue against a gender paradox description of health which suggests that women live longer than men but suffer poorer health during the life course. In the vast majority of countries, women have both longer life expectancy and spend a greater proportion of their lives in full health. We need to remain cautious about these data, given the difficulties involved in cross-national comparisons of something as difficult to measure as 'health', gendered differences in how health is defined, and the problem of measuring the impact of disability and illness on health status in this generalized way. However, the HALE figures are perhaps surprising, in that other studies have suggested that women have poorer health than men. We need to look in more detail, therefore, at how individuals themselves view their health status, to see how this varies between women and men.

Self-reported health among men and women

There are a number of ways in which morbidity can be measured at the individual level, including survey questions on how someone rates their own general health, whether they are suffering from a particular condition, and data which look at use of health care and screening tests. One of the most commonly used general health measurements is self-reported health status – essentially asking people how good their health is. Self-reported health measures often focus more explicitly on health rather than illness, and as such fit within the WHO definition of health as a positive sense of well-being, rather than simply the absence of illness.

Questions on self-reported health status appear in national surveys in many countries, including, for example, the National Health Interview (NIH) in the USA, the Household Survey component of the National Medical Expenditure survey also in the USA, the National Population Health Survey in Canada and the British Household Census in 2001. In addition, many sample surveys and longitudinal studies also use self-report measures of health status, and these different sources offer an opportunity to make comparisons across time and place.

Self-reported health status has been shown to be a good predictor of mortality risk, particularly for men, with those who report their health as poor having a greater risk of mortality than those who report their health as excellent (Benjamins et al., 2004; Benyamini and Idler, 1999). This may be because people take into account not only how they feel and health problems they know about, but also health behaviours or 'health lifestyle' factors, including whether they smoke, how much alcohol they drink, and their diet, for example. In addition, individual knowledge about family health histories and family longevity may be significant. In any case, the close association – which is equal to, if not better than, physician assessment in many studies – may be a useful indicator of health need (Ferraro and Farmer, 1999).

However, as self-reported data rely on the way in which individuals perceive their health and their willingness to report ill health, these figures are problematic if there are gendered differences in the interpretation of health conditions, symptoms and so on, or differences in the willingness of women and men to admit illness. As we saw in the previous chapter, constructions of masculinity mean that men may be less likely than women to recognize symptoms of illness, to consult a health care practitioner, or attend for screening. On the other hand, for minor conditions which do not require treatment, men may report their symptoms as more serious than women (Macintyre and Pritchard, 1989). Questions which are based on the extent to which health problems limit activities are also likely to be subject to gender bias, which relates to differences in expected activities – domestic and caring responsibilities, for example, are mainly carried out by women, who may be less able to see themselves as restricted because they cannot withdraw from these tasks when ill. Research in older age groups has found that men are more likely than women to report their health as poor at the same level of disability, and this may reflect gendered differences in role expectations as well as differences in the experience of symptoms (Arber and Cooper, 1999). Similarly, paid employment can influence health-related restrictions on activity, as income and job security may suffer as the result of time away from work. However, differences between women and men in responsibilities might also mean that limitations are more likely to be reported if the restrictions are more obvious – women after retirement age may report more limiting health conditions because they continue with domestic work, for example, and notice when this is affected.

These concerns suggests that morbidity measures based on self-report may not be strictly comparable for men and women. In addition, other kinds of difference may also affect self-reported health status – age, for example (Knodel and Ofstedal, 2003), or differences in health expectations and responsibilities between minority ethnic groups (Cooper and Arber, 2002). Qualitative research with African Caribbean men and women in London found that generalized self-report measures of health did not reflect the ways in which men and women viewed their health experience (Curtis and Lawson, 2000). There are also problems in making global comparisons of self-assessed health, partly because this kind of survey data is less often available in developing countries, but also because ideas about health may not readily translate across cultures, while issues around limiting health conditions are again affected by differences in responsibilities and the ability to withdraw from these (Knodel and Ofstedal, 2003).

Bearing these difficulties in mind, what do the data tell us? The HALE figures above might suggest that men would be more likely, in most countries, to report poor health. In fact, when we look across different countries, we find that figures for self-reported health for women and men are inconsistent: some studies report women as having slightly poorer self-reported health, but others have not found this difference between men and women (McCullough and Laurenceau, 2004). Self-reported health does not fit the HALE data, but also does not readily support the 'gender paradox'. The self-reported health of women and men also varies in relation to age and ethnicity, and differences between women and men are revealed as complex once we explore health status in more detail.

In the UK, the 2001 Census asked respondents to rate their general health over the past year as either 'good', 'fairly good' or 'not good'. Overall, women were only slightly more likely than men to rate their health as 'not good' (the age-standardized rates were 8.1 per cent for women and 7.8 per cent for men) (ONS, 2004).

In the USA, similar proportions of women and men report health as poor or fair, while men are slightly more likely than women to assess their health as excellent (Schiller and Bernadel, 2004). Among adults aged 18–64 for example, 10 per cent of women and 9.4 per cent of men said that their health was fair or poor in a national survey, while among those over 65, 20 per cent of both men and women gave this answer (HRSA, 2004).

Similarities between women and men in self-reported health are found elsewhere. In Australia in 2002, for example, just under a fifth of both women and men reported their health as excellent, 5 per cent of both women and men reported their health as poor, and women and men were as likely as each other to say that their health had remained the same in the past 12 months (AIHW, 2004). In older age groups, men were less likely than women to report their health as excellent or very good (AIHW, 2004).

A survey of Swedish men and women reported a slightly bigger gap between women and men – 6 per cent of men and 9 per cent of women said that their health was rather or very poor (Eriksson and Undén, 2001) – but researchers in Italy and Finland have found no substantial difference between women and men (Jylhä et al., 1998).

While data on self-reported health are more available in developed countries such as the USA, where figures have been collected in middle- and low-income countries the pattern revealed is also complex. In South Korea, for example, self-reported ill health is higher than in the USA or UK for both men and women, but more women report their health as poor or fair, while more men assess their health as excellent (Chun et al., 2005). A study of men and women in rural Bangladesh found that women were significantly more likely to report poorer health, and this was reflected in women's assessments of their daily activities and functional impairments as well (Rahman and Barsky, 2003). Sadana et al. (2000), in a comparative analysis of self-reported health among older people in a number of countries, reveal a wide variation in the male to female ratio – in Tanzania, Portugal and Egypt, for example, considerably more older women than men report poor health, while in Malaysia, Morocco, Côte d'Ivoire and Jordan men are more likely to report poor health than women.

How can we explain these apparently inconsistent findings between countries? Why would there be a narrower gap between women and men in the UK or Australia? One issue relates to the comparability of different measures – differences in the phrasing, the number of points on the scale between good and bad health, for example – and there are also differences across age groups which affect comparisons if measures are not age-standardized, both because self-reported poor health increases with age but also because studies suggest that the gap between women and men narrows over the life course (McCullough and Laurenceau, 2004). In addition, there are differences in relation to race and ethnicity and social class, and as with other measures of health, the intersection between these dimensions is significant.

In the USA, the Commonwealth Studies found that more men and women in the lowest-income groups rated their health as fair or poor compared with men and women in higher socio-economic groups (Collins et al., 1999; Sandman et al., 2000). National data on social class are less routinely collected in the USA, but data on poverty also show that self-reported health is worse for those who are poor (NCHS, 2004).

In the UK, both men and women in lower social classes report poorer health than those in the highest social classes, although in the 'intermediate' classes more men than women report their health as not good (Drever et al., 2004). The widest gap between women and men is found in the highest social class, where 25 per cent more women than men say that their health is poor.

Self-reported health also varies by ethnicity. In the USA, while the self-reported health of women and men is similar overall, there are differences between ethnic groups. For example, Hispanic and Latino men, and black and African American men, are more likely to assess their health as excellent or good than their female counterparts (Schiller and Bernadel, 2004).

In England, a study of self-reported health among minority ethnic groups found that in general such groups report poorer health than the white population, and that their reported health was associated with objective measures of morbidity (Chandola and Jenkinson, 2000). In the 2001 Census self-reported health among the white population was similar for men and women, but among the Asian population, including Indian, Pakistani, Bangladeshi and Chinese groups, and also among black British groups, women were more likely than men to view their health as being not good. Among white Irish people, on the other hand, more men reported poor health (ONS, 2004).

A second measure of health status which also relies on self-report, but which is more specific in terms of health conditions, asks individuals whether they suffer from a long-standing health condition which limits their daily activities. In Britain in 2002, just over a third of both women and men reported suffering from a long-standing illness – that is, an illness or condition which does not necessarily affect their day-to-day activities – while a fifth of both men and women reported suffering from a 'limiting long-standing illness' (GHS, 2004). The GHS also measures acute ill health – short-term illness that affects activities for a few days or weeks, rather than over a long period of time. Again levels of acute ill health among British women and men were very similar – in 2002 one in seven men and one in six women reported restricted activity in the previous fortnight, and women and men reported a similar number of days of acute ill health in the previous year (GHS, 2004). Figures for self-reported health vary, not surprisingly, across the life course, with more people in older age groups reporting poor health. However, the male to female ratios are largely similar for all groups over the age of 15 (GHS, 2004; Sproston et al., 2002).

In the USA, age-adjusted figures show that similar proportions of men and women report a chronic or limiting long-standing health condition, although more women describe themselves as suffering limitations in daily activities (Schiller and Bernadel, 2004), and over the age of 65, women are more likely than men to report chronic illness (NCHS, 2004).

Again, there are differences associated with social class for both women and men, which reflect differences in mortality data. In Britain self-reported chronic and acute ill health are both more common among both women and men in lower socio-economic groups (GHS, 2004; Sproston et al., 2002). Similarly, in the USA, self-reported health status is worse for those living in deprived areas and for those living in poverty (McCullough and Laurenceau, 2004).

And again there are further variations with ethnicity. In England, for example, women from black Caribbean and African, Indian, Bangladeshi and other Asian groups are more likely than men in these groups to report limiting long-standing illness, while white Irish men report more limiting long-standing illness than white Irish women (ONS, 2004; Erens et al., 1999; Cooper and Arber, 2002).

These figures for different measures of self-reported health add to the picture we are beginning to construct of women's and men's health. When we look at how people judge their health status, men often report better health than women, although the gap between women and men is narrow. In particular, it is interesting that although there is an association between poor self-reported health and mortality at the level of the individual, particularly for men, the gap between men and women in self-reported health status does not reflect mortality patterns. That is, men from most groups in both the USA and the UK see their health as better than, or as good as, that of women in the same group, but their mortality rates are higher. While some of this excess mortality relates to men's greater risk of injury, men are also more at risk of mortality from conditions which adversely affect health and which might be expected to show up in self-reported health. There are some variations in this pattern – the poorer self-reported health of white Irish men in Britain, for example, does reflect their poorer life expectancy – but overall the picture of health for men and women is of a relatively narrow gap between them in terms of how they see their own health, with men having a slight advantage. How does this relate to health as measured by use of health care services?

Consultation and use of health services

The third source of data on patterns of health among men and women reflects use of health care, with data from general practice consultations, in-patient hospital data, discharge data and so on. We have already explored, in chapter 2, some of the factors that affect this kind of data – the ways in which women's and men's use of the health care systems relates to gendered differences in access to services, the way services are funded, appropriateness of care and beliefs about health. Health care use will also reflect factors such as poverty and disadvantage, employment and caring responsibilities. Despite these problems, measures of health care use offer a further illustration of health differences between women and men. What they reveal is a complex pattern which begins with the revelation that, despite having better life expectancy than men, women use health services more often than men, and more than might be expected given the nature of the gap in self-reported health. This is the heart of the gender paradox that we need to explore.

In the UK, women consult general practitioners more often than men for virtually all conditions, and women report slightly more visits to their general practitioner per year than men (McCormick et al., 1995; GHS, 2004). Women also take more prescribed drugs than men, and while some of these relate to reproductive health, particularly contraception (GHS, 2004), there are differences in prescribed drug taking over and above those related to reproductive factors.

In the USA too, women have more primary care consultations than men; women have more visits to out-patient hospital departments; and they take more prescription drugs. Women in the USA are also more likely to receive treatment in hospital, although over the age of 45 men spend more days as in-patients compared with women. Slightly more women than men attend emergency departments for treatment, but this is where the gap between women and men is narrowest, and in some age groups – under 18s and among those aged 65–74, for example – women and men are equally likely to use emergency services (NCHS, 2004).

The use of health care by men and women also varies by ethnic group, albeit in complex ways which reflect a range of factors, including symptoms, perceptions of health, access to health care, and gendered cultural influences on consultation behaviour. As we saw earlier, in England women from minority groups tend to have poorer self-reported health than men. Women from most minority groups in England also make more use of primary care than the female population overall, with high consultation rates in particular among Pakistani women (Erens et al., 1999). In the 1999 Health Survey in England, more men from minority ethnic groups – particularly Bangladeshi men – had seen their GP in the last fortnight compared with the general male population. However, minority women were more likely than men to have used primary care, and these women also made more visits per year. Health consultations increased more with age for some minority groups – Pakistani women over 55, for example, were more than twice as likely to consult a GP than younger Pakistani women, and were also more likely than Pakistani men over 55 to consult. But the highest consulters of all were Bangladeshi men over 55, half of whom had consulted a GP in the previous two weeks, compared with under a third of Bangladeshi women in this age group, and less than 10 per cent of Bangladeshi men aged 16–34. Hospital out-patient treatment (excluding maternity care) is similar for minority groups and the general population, apart from relatively low figures for Chinese men and women, but nearly all minority ethnic groups had less in-patient treatment than the general population. The exception was again Bangladeshi men, who were significantly more likely to be treated in hospital (Erens et al., 1999).

Figures for health care use in the USA show that Asian women and men have fewest health care episodes, including visits to doctors' offices, emergency departments and home visits, while American Indian and Alaska Native Americans have most (NCHS, 2004). However, white women receive more prescriptions than black and African American women or Mexican women (NCHS, 2004).

In Australia and New Zealand, both indigenous men and women are more often admitted to hospital for treatment than the non-indigenous population, and also make more use of out-patient and emergency services (AusStats, 2002).

Health care use in the USA is also related to social class, income and insurance status. Health care use is higher amongst those defined as poor who receive more treatment in doctors' offices, home visits and in emergency departments than the non-poor (NCHS, 2004). More American women than men have health insurance in all age groups up to 55, which means that men have less access to, and are less likely to use, preventive care (HRSA, 2004).

Breaking down figures for health care use into the kind of condition which people consult for, and how serious it is, adds to the emerging picture of the gap between men and women. In Britain women use primary care more than men for both serious and minor conditions, although this varies in relation to the kind of consultation as well as the condition itself. Hunt et al. (1999) report that women consult more than men for serious conditions only in cases relating to mental health, and they suggest that it is perceived rather than actual severity of a complaint that explains patterns of consultation. Data from general practice show that men consult their GPs more than women for serious illness relating to diseases of the circulatory system, respiratory system and digestive system, while more women than men consult for serious musculo-skeletal conditions (ONS, 2005a). Equal numbers of men and women consult for other kinds of serious illness, including infectious diseases, diseases of the blood, injury and poisoning, (ONS, 2005a; GHS, 2004). Similarly, while, overall, women are prescribed more medication, men are more likely to be taking drugs for coronary heart disease, and in older age groups more men take medication for respiratory disease and urinary tract conditions (ONS, 2005a). In figures for out-patient referral, women are more often referred to hospital specialists up to the age of 75, when more men are referred. Women remain the majority of those referred to out-patient psychiatric services throughout their lives, and also the majority of those receiving treatment in primary care for mental health problems (ONS, 2005a).

There are further differences between women and men in their use of hospital care for specific conditions. In England men are the majority of those treated in hospital for cancers of the digestive system, cancer of respiratory organs and cancer of the urinary tract, and more men receive in-patient treatment for cerebrovascular disease, ischaemic heart disease, arterial disease, liver disease, substance-use disorders and psychotic illness (DOH, 2003). Men also receive more hospital treatment than women for accidents and injury, particularly in younger age groups (DOH, 2003). Women, however, are more likely to be treated in hospital for pulmonary heart disease, anaemia, thyroid disease, mood and neurotic disorders, degenerative disease and gall-bladder conditions. Figures for in-patient treatment relating to hypertensive disease, respiratory tract conditions, diabetes mellitus and epilepsy show few differences between women and men (DOH, 2003).

Figures from the USA similarly show more men treated in hospital for some conditions. Men have more in-patient days for coronary heart disease, malignant neoplasms, cerebrovascular disease in all age groups while women have more in-patient days for treatment relating to osteoarthritis and mental illness. Men also have more in-patient treatment as a result of injuries and poisoning up to the age of 75 (NCHS, 2004). In Australia, women have higher rates of treatment for mental health conditions, and women take more prescribed medications, but they also receive more treatment for circulatory conditions and cancer. In contrast, women are less likely than men to receive treatment for accident and injury (AusStats, 2002).

Women and men from different ethnic groups also have different patterns of treatment. In the USA, for example, white women have higher morbidity than other women from Alzheimer's disease, osteoporosis, hip fractures, breast and uterine cancer. Black and African American women, however, have higher rates of morbidity relating to HIV and AIDS, obesity, hypertension, cervical cancer, heart disease, diabetes mellitus and poor health resulting from violence, and are more likely to undergo hysterectomy and myomectomy or the removal of fibroids (Nunez and Robertson, 2003). Latina women also have more ill health than white women due to HIV and AIDS, heart disease, cervical cancer and diabetes mellitus, while Asian women have higher rates of illness than other women for hepatitis and cancer of the stomach and liver (Nunez and Robertson, 2003). These different patterns of illness experienced by specific groups of women reflect the ways in which both biological and gendered risks are mediated by other influences on health.

In addition to figures for health service use, primary research also reveals differences in specific aspects of morbidity. Although these data also often rely on self-report questionnaires, surveys that ask about specific conditions tend to reveal more people with poor health than those which rely on general questions about health status overall. Conditions reported by more women than men include migraine, hypertensive disease, anaemia, gall-bladder disease, irritable bowel syndrome and osteoporosis, while more men report coronary heart disease, emphysema, cirrhosis of the liver, kidney disease, high blood cholesterol, angina and cancer (AIHW, 2004; NCHS, 2004; Bird and Rieker, 1999). Women also report more depression and anxiety compared with men, and are more likely to suffer acute conditions and short-term infectious diseases, including upper respiratory infections and gastroenteritis, for example (Macintyre et al., 1996; Bird and Rieker, 1999).

What these figures for health and morbidity tell us, then, is something quite complex. Country-level indicators of healthy life expectancy suggest that women by and large enjoy a greater proportion of their lives in full health than do men; other data suggest that men are more likely than women to report their own health as excellent or good in many – but not all – countries, and that women and men report similar levels of long-standing illness. However, women use health care services more than men. When we look in more detail at specific conditions, women and men suffer different kinds of poor health, and while both suffer chronic disease, men are more likely to be diagnosed with life-threatening chronic diseases, while women are more likely than men to experience diseases which impact on quality of life.

This suggests that there is no simple pattern in the health status of women and men, and that specific factors explaining the vulnerability of women and men to specific conditions are more useful than generalizations. Sex and gender-linked factors both play a part in these explanations, although the extent and nature of that influence will vary. We now turn to a brief discussion of the potential role played by sex and gender and the ways in which these might intersect with social class and race/ethnicity to produce quite complex effects on health, before our two case studies which explore these various influences for specific conditions.

Sex and health

As we saw in chapter 2, biological factors can be important in explanations of patterns of disease and morbidity. For women, biology often acts to protect them from specific diseases during the reproductive years. Women's lower rates of heart disease during this period, for example, relate to the protective influence of female hormones as well as other differences between women and men. Part of the excess cancer morbidity in men relates to differences in gene expression, which increase men's vulnerability in the presence of factors which may trigger the disease, although with lung cancer genetic vulnerability relates to female not male genes. Most pain conditions show a higher prevalence in women than men, and women also appear to have lower pain thresholds and report more symptoms of pain, and this reflects biological factors – susceptibility relating to female hormones, for example – as well as gendered differences in pain reporting (LeResche, 1999).

Biology also influences the ways in which women and men respond to different therapeutic interventions – for example, antiarrhythmics, antibiotics and antihistamines have a different effect on women's heart rhythms compared with those of men taking these drugs, and these differences increase women's risk of cardiovascular morbidity (Hochman and Tamis-Holland, 2002). The success of pain relief also varies for women and men as a result of biological differences, and some analgesics are less effective for women as a result (Wizeman and Pardue, 2000).

Gender and health

Gender-related factors are also important in understanding different health conditions experienced by women and men. First, gender relates to structural factors and access to resources which might improve health prospects. Morbidity which is associated with disadvantage and deprivation, for example, helps to explain differences between women and men in conditions where vulnerability is increased by lack of resources. Poor-quality housing increases the risk of respiratory disease among those who are at home most – particularly children, women and older people (Rennie et al., 2005). Similarly, a lack of safe water and basic sanitation in many developing countries poses a number of health risks for women through their domestic work, and also because when there are no private toilet facilities, women reduce their food and water intake during the day so as to avoid needing to relieve themselves. This increases their risk of urinary infections, constipation and other conditions, while women are also at greater risk of sexual violence and rape when seeking privacy, often at night, for these basic functions (WHO, 2004e).

Inequalities in access to resources within households are also important in explaining differences between women and men in health, combined with differences in responsibility for unpaid work and care. Lone mothers have particularly poor health in many countries, partly because more of them suffer poverty and deprivation, poor housing and a heavier load of domestic responsibilities. In the UK, lone mothers have high rates of respiratory disease and depression, for example, while lone mothers in the USA and Sweden also have poorer health than partnered mothers (Baker et al., 1999).

Similarly, occupational risk factors vary, and the sexual division of labour in the workplace which means that some jobs are more likely to be held by men or by women affects morbidity arising from hazards at work. Men's increased risk of injury, for example, relates to their work in engineering, construction and manufacturing. Women's occupational risks are associated with other forms of morbidity, particularly repetitive strain injury and upper musculo-skeletal conditions, as well as the impact of low-status, poorly protected and repetitive work on mental health (Messing et al., 2003).

The sexual division of labour found in both high-income and low-income countries and the growing participation of women in the labour market have increased women's exposure to health risks from paid work. In less developed countries, women often occupy jobs with a number of health hazards – in manufacturing work they are frequently exposed to environmental hazards such as smoke, fumes, dangerous chemicals and radiation, repetitive labour, extremes of cold or heat, sexual harassment and violence (Ostlin, 2002). Women also often constitute the majority of the workforce in agricultural work, where the hazards include exposure to chemicals such as pesticides, as well as long hours, physically stressful work and water-borne diseases (Ostlin, 2002). The sexual division of labour in developing countries similarly increases men's risks of specific health hazards, especially in relation to injury as well as exposure to particular chemicals and environmental pollution (Ostlin, 2002). These risks are higher in less developed countries because of a lack of protective policy and legislation. The great majority of workers in low-income countries do not have access to occupational health services, particularly in the Free Trade Zones (FTZs) which have been set up in low-income countries to encourage manufacturing, often by the removal of environmental controls and safety regulations. In such FTZs there is little protection for workers, most of whom are women, and occupational health hazards are a serious problem (Prieto Carron, 2004; McMichael and Beaglehole, 2000).

Paid work can also affect health in a positive way – through opportunities for satisfaction, enhanced self-esteem, social support from co-workers, and through the income earned (Ostlin, 2002; Doyal, 2002). There are further gendered differences in these factors – independent income may be particularly relevant for women when it gives them the opportunity to live outside a household or relationship that is damaging to health, or if it increases their power and their say in household decisions, for example. Social support may be more important in women's well-being, especially that of older women (Doyal, 2002), and research suggests that paid work has a positive impact on women's health, while lack of paid work reduces women's well-being (Lahelma et al., 2002). For men, paid work can also offer opportunities for health enhancement through self-esteem and access to social support, as well as financial benefits, and for both women and men the value of paid work relates to factors such as control and autonomy, occupational status, job satisfaction, and the availability of training, which may increase esteem. The sexual division of labour means that many of these factors are more likely to be present in male paid work – men enjoy higher rates of average pay around the world, for example, and are more often in higher-status jobs within organizations (Messing et al., 2003).

Secondly, while gendered differences in access to resources are an important part of health difference, so are gender differences in health behaviour. Chapter 2 explored differences between women and men in activities which can have a negative impact on health, including diet and weight, alcohol use, smoking and illicit drug use, and these differences in behaviour help to explain men's increased risks of a range of health problems, including cardiovascular disease, cancer, liver disease, and morbidity from accidental and non-accidental injury. The disparity between men's and women's self-reported health may be explained in part by health lifestyle factors which increase the chances of ill health, but are compensated for or discounted when individuals are asked to judge their own health or well-being.

Thirdly, there are gender differences in health service treatment and the use of health care. There are conditions such as irritable bowel syndrome, where women constitute the majority of those consulting for the disease, but survey data from the general population reveal a relatively narrow gap between women and men. This suggests that differences in willingness to consult, and also differences in the way in which clinicians respond to patients, particularly in primary care and referral to specialist treatment, may be important in explaining some of the health gap between women and men revealed by data on the use of medical services.

The intersection between social class, gender and ethnicity

One of the most important issues in health is the way in which social class, gender and ethnicity interact, not only in terms of material effects, but also in the cumulative effect of disadvantage on psycho-social well-being. When we look at self-reported health and at health care, this intersection between specific aspects of inequality is particularly important. In terms of material health effects, those who occupy lower social class positions are likely to have poorer resources, live in poorer-quality neighbourhoods, and have poorer health lifestyles. In addition, where health care is funded in such a way that access depends on financial resources, social class interacts with use of care at all levels. People from minority ethnic groups are more likely to be poor, and so are women. But the health impact of their social position goes beyond lack of material resources: discrimination and membership of subordinate or disparaged groups affects well-being and stress, while those who inhabit privileged positions enjoy privileged health profiles. In the context of self-reported health, the idea of embodied inequality, where the body incorporates social experiences, including not only economic disadvantage but also social relations, may help to explain differences between different groups (Krieger, 2001). It was observed earlier that there is a close correlation between mortality and self-reported poor health, particularly for men, but also for minority ethnic groups. This has been explained by the way in which individuals draw on a range of knowledge in making a judgement about their health, including their experiences of illness and their knowledge of family longevity. However, self-reported health may also reflect their embodied experiences of inequality and social relations.

It may be unsurprising, then, that inequalities in health do not easily fit the gender paradox. Figures for healthy life expectancy, drawn up at national level, show that women spend a greater proportion of their lives in good health compared with men. Another set of data suggests that men have slightly better health, but this varies between countries and also by age. Yet a third set of data suggests that women are more likely to consult doctors; but if we look at specific conditions, sometimes men consult more. In addition, poor health is more common for both women and men who are disadvantaged, from low socio-economic groups, and from minority ethnic groups. Sex alone cannot explain these variations, but sex-linked factors are important in vulnerability to some conditions, in the experience of pain, and in the success of some treatments. Gender plays a part in terms of exposure to risk and also in how health and illness are experienced, but the way in which gender interacts with biology is also connected with other inequalities – particularly those of class and ethnicity. The final part of this chapter explores in more detail two non-fatal chronic conditions which illustrate these influences.

Sex, gender and irritable bowel syndrome

Irritable bowel syndrome is a chronic condition suffered by up to 40 per cent of the population. It is a disorder for which there is as yet no cure, and no 'gold standard' of treatment. People with IBS suffer from a number of symptoms, including alternating diarrhoea and constipation, and gastric pain, and their quality of life is often seriously reduced. Although both men and women suffer from this condition, it is between two and four times more common among women, and women often suffer more severe forms of the illness (Chang and Heitkemper, 2002; Mayer et al., 1999). Despite considerable research into this condition, the underlying causes of IBS remain unclear. The literature suggests that a number of causes may be relevant in each case, and these include both sex-linked factors, or biology, and gender relations.

The main ways in which biology is associated with IBS is through the relationship between hormones and gastric activity. Some women with IBS report changes in the symptoms and pain experienced across the menstrual cycle, and this is thought to relate to the effects of changes in oestrogen levels on sensitivity to pain, as well as the effects of hormones on smooth muscle activity and on gastric emptying. Men, on the other hand, appear to be protected against IBS by testosterone, and men with IBS often have relatively low levels of testosterone (Houghton et al., 2000). There are also differences between women and men in the production of bile, and in bowel transit time, which may be associated with women's greater vulnerability to IBS and the kinds of IBS symptoms experienced by women and men (Legato, 1997). Biological factors are also implicated in research which shows differences between women and men in the efficacy of different therapies and different kinds of pain relief (Chang and Heitkemper, 2002).

However, the differences between women and men in their risks of IBS, and in how it manifests itself, are not constant. For example, while more than three times as many women as men are treated for IBS in specialist gastroenterology clinics, there are only twice as many women as men in primary care, and the number of men and women with IBS symptoms in community surveys is nearly the same (Chang and Heitkemper, 2002). These differences suggest that factors other than biology are involved in explanations of this condition.

Gender-linked factors which also play a part in the epidemiology of IBS include in particular the strong association between stress, mental health difficulties and IBS. A disproportionate number of those diagnosed with IBS suffer from poor mental health, particularly stress-related disorders and depression (Mayer et al., 1999). The higher risk of depression and anxiety among women in the general population therefore forms part of the explanation of IBS among women. In addition, women's experiences of minor psychiatric conditions have been associated with factors which increase stress – poverty, low-status paid work, discrimination, caring responsibilities, and limited opportunities for enhancing self-esteem, for example – and these are factors which have also been associated with IBS (Toner and Akman, 2000).

The second potential explanation for variations in IBS between women and men is the association between this condition and sexual abuse. A high proportion of both women and men with IBS report experiences of childhood sexual abuse or abuse as adults, or both. In one study in France, for example, more than a third of female IBS patients and a fifth of male patients had been sexually abused, including a quarter who had been raped (Delvaux et al., 1997). Another found that nearly half of women with IBS and a quarter of men with this condition had suffered such abuse (LeRoi et al., 1995). A number of different factors might explain this association. One explanation relates to somatic memory, in which the body is described as remembering the abuse through the experience of IBS. Studies which have explored pain sensitivity among IBS patients have found greater reported pain among those with histories of abuse, and suggest that this is because of a greater awareness of physical sensation and increased attention to bodily changes (LeRoi et al., 1995). People who have experienced sexual abuse as children are also more likely to seek health care, and the over-representation of women among figures for treated IBS, particularly in specialist care, may reflect this increased consultation behaviour following experiences of abuse.

However, the greater use that women make of health care in general might also explain IBS figures, reflecting a greater awareness of bodily changes among women. There may also be gendered differences in the impact of IBS on daily life and on quality of life. There is a much greater emphasis in feminine discourse on physical appearance and cleanliness, for example, which women are particularly exposed to through menstruation discourse which stresses the need to avoid leaks and smells which threaten to make public the woman's menstrual status. Thus symptoms of IBS may be more difficult for women to tolerate in the context of the importance attached to freshness and the secrecy of bodily functions.

Finally, IBS illustrates interactions between gender and biology. In recent years research has identified physical changes which result from chronic stress arousal, and suggests that the extreme stress caused by childhood sexual abuse may result in long-term changes in physical functioning, particularly in the hypothalamic-pituitary-adrenal axis, which in turn affect the experience of pain. Gender relations and the sexual abuse experienced by girls in childhood might thus increase their vulnerability to particularly complex chronic conditions such as IBS.

Sex, gender and arthritis

The second case study is again a chronic condition which seriously impacts on quality of life. 'Arthritis' is a broad term which includes a number of different conditions which have different causes and which are experienced differently by women and men. The most common of these is osteoarthritis, a condition which is an increasingly important cause of disability worldwide (Murray and Lopez, 1997). It is around five times as common among women as men, and is a major factor in the health and disability of older women in particular (Dieppe, 1999). In addition to differences in prevalence, osteoarthritis is also experienced differently by women and men – women report more pain than men, for example, and experience more increases in pain during the day (Dieppe, 1999; Keefe et al., 2004).

This is a condition with complex causes, and research suggests that the factors initiating the onset of the disease differ from those which are associated with increasing progression of the disease and its severity (Dieppe, 1999). Thus, differences between women and men in the risk of developing osteoarthritis may not be explained in the same way as differences in their experiences of the condition. However, both biology and gender play a part.

Some of the gap between women and men relates to variations in pain response and women's greater sensitivity to pain. Women with osteoarthritis report more severe pain, more frequent pain, and more disabling pain than men (Affleck et al., 1999). Although the relative contributions of sex and gender to pain are difficult to assess, biological factors and the influence of female hormones on pain receptors affect women's experiences of arthritis (Fillingim, 1999). Non-steroidal anti-inflammatory drugs (NSAIDs) also appear to be less effective in treating pain in women than men (Walker and Carmody, 1998). Physical factors associated with osteoarthritis include changes in, and damage to, cartilage and bone and also to bone turnover (Legato, 1997). Some of these can be connected to biological factors which alter during the life course – bone turnover, for example – but the risk of cartilage and bone damage is also gendered and relates to occupation, physical activity, physical stress factors and poor nutrition (WHO, 2003b). Gender-related factors are also implicated in the association between isolation and depression and higher levels of reported pain and disability among women with osteoarthritis (Dieppe, 1999).

Fibromyalgia syndrome is the second leading arthritic disease after osteoarthritis. It is particularly difficult to diagnose, but is characterized by tenderness in a number of specific points across the body combined with muscular pain. It can cause severe pain in muscles, ligaments and tendons, and other problems including stiffness, fatigue, disturbed sleep, problems in concentration, numbness and intolerance to cold. As with all of these conditions, the severity of symptoms varies, and again there are differences between women and men in their prevalence. Women are approximately four times more likely to develop fibromyalgia than men, although, as with irritable bowel syndrome, the gap between women and men is narrower in community studies than in primary and specialist care, which suggests that women are more likely than men to seek help for this condition (Bradley and Alarcon, 1999; Yunus, 2002; Yunus et al., 2000). Factors which may cause fibromyalgia include other illness, stress and emotional trauma. In particular, there are associations with other conditions where there is also an excess of women, including irritable bowel syndrome, migraine headache and chronic fatigue syndrome, which suggest shared causes, including biological risk factors (Yunus, 2002). However, the gap between women and men in the risk of experiencing this condition is also associated with gender, particularly women's risks of chronic stress and trauma – such as childhood and adult sexual abuse – which increase sensitivity to pain.

Rheumatoid arthritis is less common than osteoarthritis, but also affects more women than men. Women and men have different patterns of onset of the disease, with women experiencing an earlier onset than men. However, although rheumatoid arthritis is more common in women, men are more likely to die of complications from the disease (Lahita, 2000; daSilva and Hall, 1992). There are well-documented biological influences affecting the distribution of rheumatoid arthritis, relating to the influence of oestrogen on the immune system (Lahita, 2000; Jansson and Holmdahl, 1998). In pregnancy, women's rheumatoid arthritis often reduces in severity or goes into remission, for example (Lahita, 2000).

There are also gender differences in the experience of pain and in the impact of pain on quality of life. Women with rheumatoid arthritis are largely younger than men with the same condition, and have different responsibilities as a result of the sexual division of labour. Women's caring work is particularly affected by arthritis, and women are more likely to report difficulties in looking after children or other dependants and in domestic work (Barlow et al., 1999).

Ankylosing spondylitis, which mainly affects the spine, is another condition which falls under the broad heading of arthritic diseases. However, it is more common among men than women, with between two and three times as many male sufferers (Calin et al., 1999). While genetic factors help explain predisposition to the condition, the causes which trigger the illness in an individual are not yet known.

Explanations for differences between women and men in arthritic disease draw on sex and gender as combined influences on pain. There are important differences between women and men in how pain is experienced which relate to biophysical mechanisms and sex differences – including hormonal influences on pain sensitivity and pain receptors (Affleck et al., 1999; Fillingim, 1999). But there are also gender differences in the experience of pain. Social constructions of masculinity and femininity allow women to report pain more readily than men, and encourage different coping mechanisms which affect the experience of pain (Affleck et al., 1999). Keefe et al. (2000) suggest that women are more likely to engage in what they describe as 'pain catastrophizing' – defined as the 'individual's tendency to focus on and exaggerate the threat value of painful stimuli and negatively evaluate one's ability to deal with pain' (p. 326). Pain catastrophizing influences the transmission of pain signals, so that women's greater experience of pain due to osteoarthritis or fibromyalgia, for example, is seen as the consequence of emotional and psychological differences in individual behaviour, rather than hormonal influences on pain sensitivity. This might be read as a fairly critical judgement of women with osteoarthritis or fibromyalgia, and indeed might be seen as victim blaming. But if placed in the context of a feminine discourse in which women do not expect themselves to deny pain, compared with discursive constructions of strong, silent masculinity, for example, 'pain catastrophizing' might be seen as reflecting more complex differences in the performance of gender.

Conclusion

Both irritable bowel syndrome and arthritis illustrate the complexities of health experience and of what we mean when we discuss inequalities in health relating to sex and gender. Overall, women and men do have different patterns of health, but there are also similarities between them, while what we are measuring when we explore health and of illness is based on a range of ways in which these terms might be conceptualized, and gender plays a part in this too. All we can say with certainty is that for both women and men their experience of health and illness is affected by their biological sex, by their experience of gender relations, and by the way in which they perform gender; and these influences are further associated with differences in age, income, sexuality, ethnicity and culture or location. While with mortality data we can say that men are more likely than women to die at every age, with data on health we cannot do this: neither women nor men are necessarily 'sicker' than each other – it depends on how we ask the question.

4 Women, Men and Mental Health

Introduction

Mental health problems are now a major and increasing cause of disability worldwide. Poor mental health accounts for a significant burden of reduced healthy life expectancy and can create serious difficulties both for individuals and for others, including family and friends, employers and the providers of health care. The risk of experiencing mental illness is similar for women and men, but there are important differences between women and men in the prevalence of specific psychiatric problems as well as in their vulnerability to mental health problems across the life course, and in their experience of psychiatric treatment (WHO, 2001; Busfield, 2002). The term 'mental illness' covers a number of diverse conditions, and although there is an over-representation of women for some of these, there are also illnesses where men predominate. Prevalence for specific illnesses also varies by ethnicity and social class. The differences between women and men in their experiences of mental illness are largely consistent from one country to the next, but there are some variations, particularly when we use data which come from treatment for mental illness, which reflect additional gender differences in diagnosis, the location and availability of psychiatric treatment, and other service-related factors.

Explanations of women's and men's mental health draw on both sex and gender. While for some kinds of psychiatric illness biological factors, including hormones, play a part, other influences are also significant. Gender-linked factors which contribute to explanations of mental illness among women and men include constructions of masculinity and femininity in a specific socio-cultural environment and gendered differences in socio-economic conditions, and in access to and the delivery of both primary care and specialist services.

This chapter explores data about mental health of women and men, in the context of other forms of diversity, and explanations of these findings, taking three aspects of mental health – eating disorders, depression and suicide – as case studies to illustrate the issues in more depth. First, however, we need to explore some of the methodological problems involved in measuring mental health, and how these might affect the reporting of differences between women and men in figures for mental illness.

Defining and measuring mental health

It is interesting that both national and international organizations tend to talk of mental *health*, while data and research focuses on mental *illness*. Both are difficult to define, and both are difficult to measure. With measures of mortality, at times we want to question the ways in which causes of death are attributed (this is discussed later in chapter 6), but the fact of death is on the whole seen as indisputable. Other forms of ill health – chronic conditions such as asthma, osteoporosis or diabetes, for example – can to a greater or lesser extent be defined in relation to key symptoms, and the prevalence of the condition can be measured. With all health conditions there is a need to consider what is sometimes termed the 'iceberg' effect – that is, that a proportion of the population suffering a particular condition will not see a medical practitioner, for various reasons, and so remain 'hidden' and not counted in statistics based on treatment. This will be more likely with minor illnesses, in circumstances where there is stigma attaching to the condition, and where services are scarce or difficult to access. The demographics of this hidden population may also vary – if services are less accessible to people without insurance or the means to pay for treatment, for example, or where it is more acceptable for either men or women to use services – and data on treated health problems can underestimate the prevalence of a condition among specific groups.

One way of addressing this problem is through population or community surveys, which use some form of clinical test or instrument (a questionnaire which elicits information about key symptoms, for example) to assess the number of people with a condition. In such surveys, clinical evidence affects which symptoms are included as indicative of a particular condition. There are issues regarding the reliability and accuracy of such measures of general health or specific physical conditions, but measurements of psychiatric disorders are yet more problematic. What is seen by the medical profession as mental illness will reflect current understanding about causes and symptoms of specific conditions; but it can also reflect bias, while the presence of a mental illness cannot be assessed by external diagnostic tools such as a blood or urine sample, or an X-ray. Mental health problems can also be experienced differently: some conditions, particularly depression, recur over periods of time, while others, including psychotic illnesses, are frequently continuous. This can affect comparisons which rely on 'snapshots' of prevalence at a given moment in time, rather than lifelong risks of experiencing mental illness, and differences between women and men in the risk of repeated mental health problems will affect prevalence data (Hankin et al., 1998; Kessing, 1998).

Mental illness data drawn from treatment figures and clinical research include a diverse range of conditions, which are broken down into distinct diagnoses according to criteria defined by the psychiatric profession. The current International Classification of Diseases (ICD), for example, is used worldwide to record treated mental illness, and is also referred to in assessments of mental illness in population surveys. After more than 100 years of existence, the ICD in current use is the tenth revision (WHO, 2004e). It is a highly detailed document which classifies each group or 'chapter' of illnesses by a number of sub-types, which are carefully described. Chapter 5, on 'Mental and Behavioural Disorders', for example, takes up more than 50 pages of the US version of the ICD-10 handbook (NCHS, 2003).

Types of mental illness in this framework include depression, anxiety neurosis, behavioural disorders, psychotic illnesses such as schizophrenia, and substance misuse. These categories have changed over time, with new ones added and some deleted, and the descriptions which accompany each type have also changed, including some alterations to the diagnostic specifications for a condition. However, the existence of chapter 5 of the ICD assumes that it is possible to differentiate between mental health and mental ill health, and between different kinds of mental illness. The fact that the boundaries of the sub-types used have shifted over time, while the use of diagnoses may vary in practice, suggests that these categories are not impermeable. Instead, mental illness categories can be seen as continuously discursively constructed by practitioners, patients, researchers, the media, political circumstances and the availability of treatment, in the context of other cultural and social discourses. Homosexuality, for example, was defined as a form of mental illness for the greater part of the ICD's history, and was not removed until the publication of the tenth revision in 1992 (Smith et al., 2004). Gender plays a part in this mental health discourse, most obviously through the historical and contemporary association between some diagnoses and women's reproductive difference, but also through experiences in practice which lead some categories to be seen as inherently male or female – substance-use disorders, for example. While we explore variations between women and men in their experience of mental illness below, we also need, therefore, to remain conscious of the range of illnesses subsumed under this label and the subjectivity of diagnostic categories.

Women's mental health, men's mental health – what are the differences?

Men and women both experience mental distress which seriously affects their well-being and quality of life, and which affects others around them (Busfield, 2002). A considerable number of people suffer poor mental health – estimates of the burden of mental illness suggest that around a quarter of the population will suffer such illness during their lives, and that at any one time about 450 million people around the world suffer from mental and neurological disorders or problems with substance abuse (WHO, 2001).

There are differences between women and men in the kinds of mental illness they are most likely to experience. Globally, the overall prevalence of mental ill health is similar for men and women: in 2002, for example, neuropsychiatric disorders accounted for around 12 per cent of the total burden of disease among men and 14 per cent of the burden among women (WHO, 2004e). Differences between men and women in mental health relate not to their overall risk of suffering some form of difficulty, but to specific conditions. Women and men are equally at risk for the most severe mental disorders, including psychotic illnesses, although men are more likely than women to experience some conditions, particularly schizophrenia, in early adulthood (WHO, 2004e; Lehman, 2003).

With psychotic illnesses there are other differences between women and men. Men, for example, have a poorer prognosis than women after being diagnosed; they have more in-patient admissions, and are less likely to form lasting relationships. Women with psychotic illnesses often have better social relationships, but they are also more likely to experience hallucinations (MIND, 2002; Astbury, 1999).

Minor psychiatric illnesses are much more common, but figures for differences between women and men in the experience of such illnesses are less consistent. Worldwide, women outnumber men in figures for treated and untreated mood disorders, including depression (WHO, 2001, 2004e; Biji et al., 1998). Post-traumatic stress disorders are also higher among women. Men are more frequently diagnosed with substance-related disorders, although the number of women with these conditions has increased in recent years (Keene, 2002; Biji et al., 1998; WHO, 2001). In 2002, for example, alcohol-use disorders accounted for around five times more disability among men than with women, and drug-use disorders were three times as common in men (WHO, 2004e). Finally, suicide is higher among men, but non-fatal self-injury is higher among women (WHO, 2001, 2004e), and cutting behaviour and self-mutilation are also more prevalent among women (Shaw, 2002; McAllister, 2003).

Differences between men and women within countries only partially reflect these global figures. For example, similar proportions of women and men in England report symptoms of poor mental health – around 22 per cent of women and 25 per cent of men – although men are more likely to report symptoms indicative of co-morbidity, or more than one condition at once (Singleton et al., 2001). Levels of psychotic illness, such as schizophrenia, are similar for men and women. More women suffer from mixed anxiety and depressive disorders, and more women suffer phobias, but there are few differences between women and men in symptoms for depression and anxiety in England, compared with worldwide data, where women predominate (Singleton et al., 2001). However, more men than women suffer symptoms of personality disorders; men are more likely to engage in 'hazardous drinking'; and more men than women are dependent on alcohol and illicit drugs.

Survey data for serious psychological distress among adults in the USA reveal a slightly different picture: overall, more women than men have symptoms of mental health problems (Schiller and Bernadel, 2004). In *Women's Health USA*, for example, more than 10 per cent of women reported a serious mental illness, compared with 6 per cent of men, with particularly high risk of illness among women in early adulthood, up to the age of 25 (HRSA, 2004). Studies in the USA suggest that up to 40 per cent of women and 25 per cent of men suffer from depression, and though relatively small proportions of those with symptoms have been diagnosed clinically, women are also more likely than men to receive treatment (Collins et al., 1999; Sandman et al., 2000). Figures from Australia similarly show more women with anxiety and depression, while more men report hazardous drinking and substance misuse (AusStats, 2002; AIHW, 2004).

Community and population surveys also show that mental health difficulties vary across the life course for women and men. Women in young adulthood and in mid-life report more symptoms of depression and anxiety than men, and the risk of depression among women is greatest during reproductive years (Byles et al., 1999; Piccinelli and Wilkinson, 2000; Collins et al., 1999). For men, mental health problems are more common in early life – boys in early adolescence are more at risk of depression than girls of the same age – and again in later life (Hankin et al., 1998). Substance-use disorders relating to both alcohol and illicit drug use are higher for men than for women, and peak in earlier age groups, decreasing over the life course (Thom, 2003).

Overall, the findings of surveys looking at symptoms in the general population suggest that women experience depression and other 'minor' mental health problems more than men. Data on health care from psychiatric services and from primary care also reveal differences. Prescriptions for psychotropic medicine are higher for women in most countries, with the widest gap between women and men in Spain and France (WHO, 2001). Figures for prescription drugs show that adult women take twice as many antidepressants as men in nearly every age group in the USA (NCHS, 2004).

Figures for general practice in England and Wales also show that more women receive care for anxiety, particularly in older age groups, while younger women are more than twice as likely as men to be treated for depression and to be prescribed antidepressants, SSRIs and hypnotics (ONS, 2005a). In many countries, more women receive hospital psychiatric treatment. In England and Wales, more women than men are admitted to hospital for psychiatric care overall (S. Payne, 1998). In the USA, more than 27 million people received psychiatric treatment in 2002, and of these, two-thirds were women (HRSA, 2004). Similar numbers of men and women are admitted for psychiatric in-patient care in the USA, although men make more use of hospital treatment in relation to substance abuse, and if this was added to figures for general psychiatric in-patient treatment, men would outnumber women by a large margin. However, more than twice as many women receive outpatient treatment. Similarly in Australia, women are the majority of patients treated for psychiatric problems (AIHW, 2004).

Figures for treated mental health problems in developing countries are less often broken down separately for women and men, and models of some illnesses – particularly depression – used in developed countries do not readily fit patterns of mental health difficulties experienced in other parts of the world (Patel et al., 2001). These data also reflect availability of treatment, not true prevalence, and gender differences in who is covered by insurance and who is able to fund care or take time out of work or domestic responsibilities for treatment also affect what we are measuring. In Pakistan, for example, more men than women are diagnosed with schizophrenia and substance-use problems, but more women are diagnosed with depression and manic depression (Karim et al., 2004). In Chile, men's greater insurance coverage is reflected in the fact that more men than women receive hospital treatment for schizophrenia and substance abuse, and men also outnumber women in hospital treatment for depression, manic depression, dementia and emotional disorders, although more women are treated in primary care for these conditions (Stewart, 2004).

Treatment for mental illness also varies for women and men across the life course. In England, for example, psychiatric hospital admission rates overall are the same for men and women, but among those up to the age of 44 and over the age of 85, men are more often admitted, while more women than men are treated as in-patients during mid-life and early old age (DOH, 2004). Men's greater hospitalization in younger age groups applies not only to severe mental disorders, but also to depression, and women with depressive illness are more likely than men to remain in the community (DOH, 2004). In the USA, antidepressants are more commonly prescribed for older groups – although the ratio of women to men taking these drugs remains fairly constant at around two to one (NCHS, 2004). In-patient psychiatric treatment is more common in the USA for younger age groups, and decreases over the age of 65, but as in England, the ratio of women to men admitted changes over the life course. Under the age of 64, more women are admitted, particularly among those aged 45–64, while over the age of 75 slightly more men than women are treated as in-patients (NCHS, 2004). But again, if we were to add in-patient treatment for drug- and alcohol-related problems to these figures, men would dominate hospital figures for those under the age of 44.

In England some patients are, at present, detained in hospital under provisions of the 1983 Mental Health Act, a process often known as 'sectioning', in reference to the relevant Sections of the legislation. This Act is currently under review, but longitudinal surveys and annual data returns from the Department of Health reveal an excess of male patients detained in this way from the mid-1990s onwards, following earlier periods when more women were treated involuntarily (Audini and Lelliott, 2002).

Differences in the risk of poor mental health in relation to ethnicity, socio-economic class and sexuality are also important. In the UK, population-based surveys reveal poorer mental health among women in almost all minority ethnic groups compared with white women (Erens et al., 1999; Sproston et al., 2002). Women's higher risk of mental health problems compared with men is particularly marked for Indian and Pakistani populations. However, among the Bangladeshi population, men have more symptoms of poor mental health than women (Erens et al., 1999; Sproston et al., 2002). Both men and women from all minority ethnic groups are also at greater risk of involuntary detention in psychiatric hospitals in England and Wales under the provisions of the 1983 Mental Health Act, but some men, particularly black British, black African, African Caribbean and Asian men, are much more likely than white men to be sectioned under the Act (Audini and Lelliott, 2002; MIND, 2002). Both women and men from minority groups are also more likely to receive high-dose medication, and are less likely to be offered psychotherapy and counselling by the National Health Service (Wilson, 2001; Audini and Lelliott, 2002; MIND, 2002).

In the USA, treated mental illness and self-reported psychological distress are both greater among black and minority ethnic groups. American Indian and Alaskan Native men and women, in particular, report the highest levels of serious psychological distress, and are more than twice as likely as the white population to have symptoms of poor mental health (NCHS, 2004).

There is also an over-representation of people from lower social class groups in figures for both treated and untreated mental illness, in all countries. Both depression and schizophrenia are associated with low socio-economic status (Muntaner et al., 2004; Lorant et al., 2003). Research exploring the relationship between social class and mental health difficulties has suggested that socio-economic status may to some extent be affected by poor mental health through poorer education and work opportunities, for example, but social class also affects mental well-being, through the stresses caused by material deprivation, social exclusion and discrimination. In the USA, people who are poor have higher levels of psychological distress than non-poor populations (NCHS, 2004), and surveys report higher levels of depression among lower socio-economic groups (Lorant et al., 2003). In the UK, women and men with symptoms of psychotic illness or depression are also more likely to come from the lowest two social classes (Singleton et al., 2001; Weich and Lewis, 1998).

In addition, sexuality is associated with differences in mental health. Both gay men and lesbians have a greater lifetime risk than the heterosexual population of experiencing poor mental health, including, in particular, depression and substance-use problems (Sandfort et al., 2001; King et al., 2003; Moran, 1996).

Overall, then, differences between women and men in mental health are not always straightforward. On the whole, disorders related to substance misuse are more common among men; severe illnesses, including psychotic disorders, are relatively equally distributed between women and men, while figures for depression and anxiety suggest that women are more likely to report and to be treated for such conditions, although there are differences across the life cycle and in how such illness is treated. Recent trends suggest that more men are now receiving care for depression than in the past, possibly reflecting changing perceptions of the nature of depression and increased recognition of men's depressive illness.

Within this overall picture of risk for men and women, there are important variations – men and women from most minority groups are more at risk of being diagnosed with mental health problems than white populations in the USA, Australia and the UK, for example, although the gender gap is not consistent within minority groups. Higher levels of distress are experienced by men and women in lower social classes and poorer populations, and gay men and lesbians are similarly more likely to report symptoms of poor mental health, and to be treated for mental illness, particularly depression and substance abuse.

How well do sex and gender factors explain these patterns of mental health? The following sections explore the ways in which biological factors and gender relations might increase vulnerability of women or men to specific mental health problems, while in the final part of the chapter we use three case studies – eating disorders, depression and suicidal behaviour – to draw out these interrelationships in more depth.

Biology and the mental health of women and men

Biological factors, particularly those associated with reproductive differences, have long been seen as important in the mental health of women in particular. Historically, psychiatry defined women's reproductive nature as rendering them more susceptible to insanity than men (Smith-Rosenberg, 1974; Showalter, 1987). Women are still seen as vulnerable to poor mental health as a result of their female bodies, particularly in relation to pregnancy and childbirth and the menopause, and in recent years pre-menstrual syndromes have been added to the list of illnesses which affect women of reproductive years (Ussher, 2003).

However, evidence for biology as a factor in the mental health of either women or men is relatively lacking. For men, lower levels of male hormones have been associated with poorer mental health and increased risk for some conditions, including psychotic illness and depression (Seidman and Walsh, 1999; Orengo et al., 2004). Although some antipsychotic medications affect hormone levels, studies on medication-free men have suggested that levels of testosterone are higher in men with schizophrenia and bipolar disorders than in the general population (Ozcan and Banoglu, 2003). Depression may be more common among men with low levels of testosterone, particularly in later life (Seidman and Walsh, 1999). Taken overall, research on the association between testosterone and mental health remains inconclusive, however. Testosterone levels vary greatly over the life course, and the impact of such changes on functioning also varies, which means that deterioration in mental health among older men cannot be ascribed simply to biological factors (Sternbach, 1998). Older age is also a time when men's lives are changing in other ways – the loss of paid employment and status, loss of personal relationships, and increased isolation can all affect mental well-being.

Women's increased risk of some conditions, particularly depression, at times of hormonal change, including menstruation, pregnancy, childbirth and the menopause, suggest that sex-linked factors may play a part in mental health (Legato, 1997). Post-natal depression among women, for example, is associated with rapid and marked changes in hormone levels post-partum (Harris et al., 1994). However, other factors, including exhaustion and lack of sleep, and changes in employment, social status and isolation, are also important (Busfield, 2002). Similarly, recent findings that men also experience depression after the birth of a child and that poor mental health in one parent increases the risk of similar difficulties in the other parent reinforce the suggestion that biology alone cannot explain women's risks of mental health problems (Matthey et al., 2001).

Evidence on mental health during the menopause is also mixed. One of the problems in assessing this relationship lies in the difficulty of defining the menopause itself, and also the variability in symptoms experienced and the severity of symptoms. Studies exploring the relationship between hormonal changes associated with the menopause and mental illness have concluded that while biological factors play a part, so too do social factors, including changes in status, sources of support, caring responsibilities and feelings of self-esteem in cultures where youth is particularly valued for women (Winterich, 2003).

As with men, there is evidence that women's risk of psychotic illness is associated with hormone levels – women with schizophrenia appear to have lower levels of estradiol than other women, while men diagnosed with this illness also have lower than expected levels of this female hormone, leaving some question over the possible protective effect of estradiol for both women and men (Huber et al., 2005).

Substance-use problems among both men and women are associated with higher risks of having experienced abuse or violence as a child or an adult (Redgrave et al., 2003). Such risks are gendered – women are more likely than men to have experienced childhood sexual abuse and sexual abuse as adults, for example, but men in some occupational groups have increased risks of post-traumatic stress disorder, and men are also at greater risk of some kinds of violence (Bremner et al., 1996). While gender shapes risk, biological factors are also involved in the effect of abuse and violence on mental health. Chronic stress arousal, for example, including experiences of abuse in childhood, appears to trigger physiological changes – changes in brain function – which are associated with addictive behaviour later in life. Although both men and women are vulnerable to poor mental health following such physiological changes, differences in brain function between men and women also mean that memory is stronger for women, and that emotionally charged events have more long-lasting and powerful effects on women's mental health, particularly with depression and post-traumatic disorders (Legato, 2003).

What this suggests is that biological factors are relevant in the distribution of mental illness, but that they may not fully explain the differences between women and men. For example, the strongest evidence relating to biological factors in mental illness is found in the context of severe disorders where women and men are similarly at risk. Social factors are also significant in poor mental health, including those relating to gender, as well as class and experiences of discrimination related to ethnicity and sexuality in particular.

Gender and the mental health of women and men

There are a number of ways in which gender relations affect the risk of mental health for both women and men. These consist of social and structural factors, including resources, responsibilities and roles, for example; factors relating to the costs of gender relations, including sexual and other forms of violence; factors relating to the construction of gender difference, including masculinity and femininity and emotional expression; and factors relating to service delivery. These interact with each other, while other kinds of difference also play a part.

Social and structural influences on gendered differences in mental health

A number of studies, in both high- and low-income countries, have found an association between poverty, social exclusion and poor mental health (e.g. S. Payne, 2000; Tulle-Winton, 1997; Patel and Kleinman, 2003). Both minor and more severe mental health problems are more common among women and men living in poverty or deprivation, while use of psychiatric services and suicidal behaviour are more frequent in poor and deprived areas (Gunnell et al., 1995).

Although the direction of causality is problematic – does poverty increase the risk of mental health difficulties, or do these difficulties increase the risk of poverty? – the association itself is well established. If we look at the distribution of poverty by gender, this might explain differences between women and men when it comes to mental illness. In any society, some people are more at risk of poverty, because the causes of poverty – lack of paid work and savings, financial responsibility for others, access to other forms of income, and control over household resources, for example – are not evenly distributed. Poverty is concentrated among people in low-income groups, who have less job security, spend longer periods out of paid work and have fewer savings to fall back on. However, in all countries, women are more at risk of poverty due to lower pay, fewer work-related benefits, less job security and less access to the labour market due to their caring responsibilities. All over the world, women raising children alone are poor, and women are poorer in old age as a result of their caring work, fewer years in the labour market and lower earnings (Miranda and Green, 1999; Patel et al., 2001; Patel and Kleinman, 2003). In addition, in societies where women's paid work outside the home is limited by gendered expectations, women are at risk of deprivation within the household, and women often feel unable to use resources for themselves, or go without in order to provide for others, particularly children (Graham, 1984).

Poverty can also limit use of health services for poor mental health, particularly in countries where access to treatment relies on insurance status or the ability to pay, and more women than men are unable to seek care because of financial constraints (Miranda and Green, 1999).

Fewer studies have explored mental health and poverty in developing countries, but those that have reveal higher levels of mental health problems among women compared with men, partly reflecting gender differences in access to resources and the fact that responsibility for managing scarcity often falls to women (Patel and Kleinman, 2003; Patel et al., 2001). In India, for example, post-natal depression is more common among poorer and disadvantaged women (Patel et al., 2001). Similarly, in Zimbabwe, high levels of depression among women are associated with loss, significant life events including infertility and unwanted pregnancy, and also with poverty (Patel et al., 2001). Food insufficiency is more common among women, and is associated with poorer mental health (Siefert et al., 2001). However, job insecurity also increases the risk of poor mental health among men in low-income countries. Not knowing how long employment will last or where alternative employment might be found increases stress and anxiety, for example, which may be particularly acute for men trying to provide for their families: 'when I don't have [any food to feed my family] I borrow, mainly from neighbours and friends. I feel ashamed standing before my children when I have nothing to help feed my family. I'm not well when I'm unemployed. It's terrible' (Patel and Kleinman, 2003: 611).

Work and mental health differences

Poverty and disadvantage are closely related to employment status, and gender differences in the availability of paid work combined with expectations about unpaid work are important in understanding differences in mental health between women and men.

Paid work may contribute to mental well-being, through the income it brings and when it provides opportunities to increase self-esteem, particularly where the work is interesting, where the individual has control over their work, and where there are opportunities for advancement, and support for such progress (Bildt and Michelsen, 2002). Work can also improve mental health through the opportunities it provides for interaction and social support. However, paid work can affect mental health adversely, particularly when work is undervalued, repetitive, unrewarding, insecure, in a stressful environment, where it is carried out in isolation, and where the worker cannot control the speed of work (Ferrie et al., 2005). In both developed and developing countries the sexual division of labour means that women's paid work is more likely to be concentrated in service industries, and in lower-grade work with lower rates of pay, less job security and fewer opportunities for enhancing self-esteem and mental well-being (Doyal, 2002). In addition, in some countries the mental health of women working outside the home is further threatened by sexual violence and harassment in the workplace. There are also specific employment-related risks of post-traumatic stress disorder for some occupations, including fire-fighters, rescue services, police and military personnel, most of whom are men (Krug et al., 2000). Finally, the 'double burden' of paid work and domestic work may pose particular mental health threats for women who combine employment with domestic labour and responsibility for the care of children or other vulnerable people, although women who have paid work outside the home tend to have better mental health than women who do not (Emslie et al., 2002; Patel et al., 2001).

Sexual abuse, sexual violence and mental health

Sexual violence includes forced sexual contact, coercion and trafficking, as well as unwanted sexual advances and harassment (WHO, 2003g). Sexual violence can take place both inside and outside the home, in the workplace, school, health centre or other public arenas; it can be a single act or repeated; and it can be perpetrated by one person or form part of a systematic oppression, as in conflict situations, for example. Sexual violence is associated with a number of adverse mental health outcomes, including post-traumatic stress disorder, depression and anxiety, eating disorders, alcohol and substance misuse, and suicidal behaviour (Palmer et al., 1993; Weiss et al., 1999; Collins et al., 1999; Siriwanarangsan et al., 2004; Ganju et al., 2004a, 2004b). Women and men who experience sexual violence are more at risk of stress, poor self-esteem, and loss of confidence, as well as feelings of stigma, self-blame and 'silencing' (Ali et al., 2000). Sometimes there is additional stress due to the loss of support from others – for example, being unable to remain at home, either because that is the source of sexual violence or because of stigma attached to those who have suffered sexual violence (WHO, 2003g).

Figures for all forms of sexual violence underestimate the number of women and men who experience it. Men may be particularly unlikely to report sexual violence due to embarrassment and shame, or fear of revealing homosexual activities (Ganju et al., 2004b). In addition, the myth that only gay men experience sexual abuse and rape makes it less likely that men will report violence (MIND, 2002). However, women also fail to report violence out of shame and stigma, fear of repeated violence, fear of losing paid work or home, and in some countries fear of further acts of violence by those in authority, including the police (WHO, 2003g). Bearing this in mind, it is estimated that up to 15 per cent of women have experienced sexual violence in their lifetimes, and just under a tenth of all women have experienced sexual violence against them in the past five years (WHO, 2003g). Women are particularly likely to experience sexual violence from an intimate partner – studies in Peru and Mexico, for example, report that over 40 per cent of women have been sexually assaulted by a partner, while in Thailand, a third of women have experienced such violence (WHO, 2003g). Studies also suggest that up to a tenth of male children are sexually abused, and in some countries sexual assault on adult men is high as well. In Peru, for example, a fifth of men report experiencing sexual assault by another man (WHO, 2003g). Although less research has been carried out on the effects on men of sexual assault, such violence impairs men's mental well-being in ways which are similar to the effects on women.

Physical violence

Physical violence in the home and in other settings affects both physical and mental well-being, related to the severity of the attack, the injuries caused, whether it is repeated violence, and who the perpetrator is (Robinson and Keithley, 2000). Regular violence from a close family member or intimate partner generates stress, hopelessness, depression, anxiety and substance misuse, for example. Gender differences in the impact of violence on mental health partly reflect differences in the kinds of violence experienced. More women experience regular and long-term violence in the home, increasing low self-esteem, feelings of worthlessness, depression, anxiety disorders, including panic attacks and phobias, and use of alcohol or illicit drugs (Abbott and Williamson, 1999; Redgrave et al., 2003). Poor mental health also makes it more difficult to leave a situation of violence.

Men are more often the victims of violence outside the home, both in specific occupations and because men are more often subjected to violent crime (Porcerelli et al., 2003; Courtenay, 2000; Robinson and

Keithley, 2000). In Britain and the USA, for example, more men are hurt in violent attacks by strangers (Smith and Allen, 2004; Porcerelli et al., 2003). Street violence can reflect masculinity, particularly for those men whose social position closes off other avenues of expression (Courtenay, 2000). Gendered performances of violence also increase men's risk of experiencing violence and the risk of ensuing mental health problems, while masculinity may also mean that men who have been the victim of violent crime find it difficult to share their mental distress. Women are also at risk of attack outside the home, and although this risk is less than that experienced by men, for many women the fear of such attack restricts their activities at night, and sometimes during the day, and adds to their feelings of anxiety and isolation.

Experiences of sexual and physical violence also affect the mental health of refugees and people subjected to enforced migration. Refugees are more at risk for a number of factors leading to mental health problems, including the stress of their status, the traumas which led to their becoming refugees, experiences of loss, isolation, lack of material resources, language and communication problems, and of course anxiety and uncertainty over the future. But there are further risks, for women in particular and also for children, of sexual abuse, coercion, enforced prostitution and violence, which can increase mental health problems (WHO, 2003g; Hynes, 2004). Domestic and sexual violence in the home can also increase in post-conflict situations, with further costs for women's mental health (Hynes, 2004; Thara and Patel, 2001).

Gender and emotion

Women's and men's vulnerability to mental health difficulties also reflects gender differences in emotional expression. Lupton (1999) suggests that men and women are expected to experience and express emotions in different ways – women have long been seen as naturally 'emotional', able to recognize their feelings and willing to express them, while the cultural stereotype of masculinity means that men's emotions are more likely to remain buried. Hegemonic masculinity requires men to display a strong unemotional exterior, which leaves little space for aspects of the self that belong in the irrational, the subjective and emotional world. This does not mean that men are unemotional, however: men express those emotions which are culturally or socially sanctioned as legitimately male, particularly anger and jealousy (Lupton, 1999; Lee and Owens, 2002). These differences connect with the mental health of both women and men in complex ways – for example, the sanctioning of negative emotions such as grief for women may be helpful in terms of mental well-being, in that women can confide in others and seek support, or it may be detrimental if their emotional expression is treated as problematic and in need of medication. Similarly, where jealousy or anger are sanctioned for men, this may improve their well-being if it prevents the internalization of negative feelings which reduce self-esteem and increase the risk of some forms of illness. But expressing anger can also jeopardize men's well-being – if the expression is inappropriate in degree, time or place, for example – while men's expression of anger or jealousy can adversely affect women's mental and physical health when they are on the receiving end of such emotions.

Gendered and racialized constructions of mental health and illness

Women typically receive more psychiatric treatment in both primary and specialist care in most parts of the world. In the USA, more women are treated as in-patients, and more receive out-patient and private treatment. In the UK, women outnumbered men in figures for admission to psychiatric hospitals for many years, although in younger age groups and among the very old, men now outnumber women (S. Payne, 1998). In primary care, more women are treated for both minor and more severe mental health problems (ONS, 2005a). These differences in treatment reflect gender differences in the use of health care, but also relate to discursive constructions of mental illness which are gendered and relate to psychiatry's 'differential involvement' with the problems of women and men (Busfield, 1983).

Gender differences may affect men's and women's assessments of symptoms, the assessments made by others, and health care-seeking behaviour, as we have seen. However, gender may also be a factor in the availability of help and access to care, including differences in those countries where access to mental health treatment is dependent on either insurance status or ability to pay. In China, for example, men receive more in-patient mental health treatment, and women's stays in hospital are both less frequent and shorter, reflecting perceptions about women's work in the home and domestic responsibilities, as well as their lack of insurance (Pearson, 2005). The ways in which services are designed affects not only how easy they are to use at a pragmatic level, but also how far stigma and negative stereotypes about mental illness are diminished or reinforced. Once an individual seeks help, the ways in which services operate, and in particular the role of the primary care practitioner as a gatekeeper to specialist psychiatric services, may influence who is seen in the community, who is referred for specialist treatment, the diagnosis they acquire, and what form the treatment takes. The rapid reduction in the number of in-patient psychiatric beds in England and Wales from the 1980s onwards increased the importance of 'risk' assessment, in which gender played a part and the decreasing availability of in-patient psychiatric beds was followed by an increase in the proportion of admissions made up by young male patients (S. Payne, 1998).

Similarly, racialized discourse in which gender plays a part affects the construction of mental illness. Psychiatric care and hospital admissions for black women and men are affected by stereotypes of mental health and risk which are both gendered and racialized (S. Payne, 1998). Discursive constructions of black femininity mean that black African and Afro-Caribbean women are often seen as strong, able to cope with stress, less likely to need help, and also as being difficult to treat. These ideas combine to increase the invisibility of black women's mental health difficulties and the likelihood that when black women are treated by the psychiatric services, they will be admitted to hospital and detained involuntarily (Wilson, 2001). Stereotypes about Asian women similarly mean that women from Indian, Bangladeshi and Pakistani communities in the UK are seen as having less need of psychiatric care because of family support, but also as being put under pressure by those same families to conform. Again, their difficulties are less likely to be identified, but when they are recognized, Asian women are pathologized as being part of a problematic culture (Burr and Chapman, 2004).

Mental health services also fail men from minority ethnic groups. Asian men receive poorer-quality services from the British NHS, partly because they are seen as a group with a low risk of mental illness. Their distress is less likely to be recognized, for reasons similar to those experienced by Asian women, and also because they are less likely to discuss emotional and mental health difficulties with their GPs because they don't want to 'moan', and because they are ambivalent about seeing mental health problems as an illness compared with physical problems (Burr and Chapman, 2004). However, they are also invisible in the absence of culturally sensitive and appropriate services with a clear understanding of symptoms of distress in this community (Bhui et al., 2002).

Other black minority men are also stereotyped. Young black British men, for example, are seen as lazy and irresponsible, or as aggressive, risky and in need of hospitalization (Bhui et al., 2002; S. Payne, 1998). The construction of this group as problematic is reinforced by the number of studies which are carried out on psychotic illness among Afro-Caribbean and black British men – studies which are reported regularly in medical journals – despite the fact that psychotic illness is rare in this population compared with other less dramatic health conditions such as depression and anxiety (Sproston et al., 2002).

Overall, then, figures suggest that women and men are both vulnerable to mental health problems, but that there are differences in the kinds of illness experienced, the treatment offered, and the part played by sex and gender. To some extent these differences are associated with the ways in which symptoms are interpreted by individuals, by those around them, and by the health care system, how psychiatric treatment is funded, and the sanctioning of particular kinds of behaviour or emotional expression. But there are also important gender differences in the exposure to various risks which impact on mental well-being. These various influences are explored now in more detail in three case studies of mental health: eating disorders, depression and suicidal behaviour.

Sex, gender and eating disorders

Eating disorders, particularly anorexia nervosa, have a relatively long medical history, although it is only in the latter decades of the twentieth century that they became widely recognized and discussed, primarily as conditions affecting women. Sayers (2002) suggests that, historically, fasting has been met with both approval and disapproval, being seen as signifying alternately holiness or heresy. The terms 'anorexia nervosa' is itself gendered, originating in a description of female mental disorder in the nineteenth century (Sayers, 2002). In clinical terms, anorexia is defined as a Body Mass Index of less than 17.5 combined with an intense fear of gaining weight or of being fat and, for women, loss of menstrual periods. Bulimia nervosa is described as binge eating, purging, including self-induced vomiting and the use of laxatives, and also as a preoccupation with shape and with weight. However, anorexia is increasingly used as a term which encompasses a range of conditions which have problematic eating behaviour at their core. Anorexia, bulimia and other eating disorders are also often experienced together with other health conditions – in particular, substance abuse and mood and anxiety disorders.

Anorexia is a well-known concept in the West – most teenage girls, for example, could tell you what it means – but it is also rare, with an estimated lifetime prevalence of around 1 per cent in developed countries. It is more common in some groups of men and women, particularly those involved in sport, modelling and dance (Klein and Walsh, 2003). Bulimia is estimated to affect around 2 per cent of the population, while a category known as 'Not otherwise specified eating disorders' is estimated to affect between 3 and 30 per cent of the population of the developed countries where it has been used (McNulty, 2001). Given the higher levels of body dissatisfaction among women, it is not surprising that both anorexia and bulimia are more common among women than men – there are somewhere between 10 and 20 times as many women with anorexia, for example (Klein and Walsh, 2003; McNulty, 2001). However, men suffering from anorexia and other eating disorders are similar to women with such disorders in terms of their levels of body dissatisfaction, age of onset, and their risk of co-morbidity particularly with mental health problems – although fewer men seek treatment than women (Lee and Owens, 2002). Eating disorders are also more common among gay men than heterosexual men, and this relates to higher levels of body dissatisfaction as well as the role of appearance in gay culture (Lee and Owens, 2002; Siever, 1994). Rates of eating disorders are lower among lesbians compared with heterosexual women, however (Siever, 1994).

Eating disorders also vary for ethnic minority women and men. Anorexia is less common among African American women, while over-eating and compulsive eating disorders are higher (Beauboeuf-Lafontant, 2003). Eating disorders are also higher among women from South Asian groups, particularly Pakistani women, in comparison with white women (Furnham and Adam-Saib, 2001). There are fewer data on eating disorders among women or men in low-income countries in comparison with the literature from developed regions; but where research has been carried out, it suggests that cultural differences in the perceived value of particular body shapes mean that women and men are protected from such conditions (Khandelwal et al., 1995; Furnham and Adam-Saib, 2001).

How can we explain the risk of eating disorders? Both sex and gender have been identified as potential explanations in the aetiology of anorexia and bulimia. Evidence relating to biology is mixed, but new developments in molecular biology and the influence of genes on women's compulsive behaviour, including eating and fasting, are currently being explored.

Gender-related factors have tended to dominate explanations of eating disorders, partly reflecting the disproportionate number of women who experience these conditions. Both men and women with anorexia, bulimia and other eating disorders report higher levels of body dissatisfaction, negative self-image and low self-esteem, and these are also more common in women in general (Lakkis et al., 1999; Malson and Ussher, 1997). Eating disorders are also more common among men and women who have been sexually abused as children, partly because abuse affects feelings of self-worth, body image and levels of body satisfaction, and partly because eating disorders may offer a sense of control in the face of traumatic experiences (Logio, 2003). Other health conditions associated with experiences of sexual abuse, such as self-harm and alcohol problems, are also associated with eating disorders, particularly for women (Shaw, 2002; Redgrave et al., 2003).

Beyond these precipitating factors, writers have explored the gendered meaning of eating disorders. Anorexia, for example, has been viewed as a form of control, and gender differences in opportunities to exercise power are relevant. Women with anorexia are described as using food restriction as a means of exerting control over the body and as a way of coping with areas of life which are out of control. Disordered eating among younger people can also be seen as a part of an adolescent struggle for identity which particularly affects women: for young women the body is the realm where they can exercise power, while young men are able to exercise power elsewhere (Logio, 2003).

Both anorexia and bulimia nervosa have also been contextualized as part of the increasing celebration of thinness as a desirable attribute, evidenced by media portrayals of the ideal female body, and by the thinness of celebrity musicians, models and actors. The growing emphasis on the thin ideal in the late twentieth century has been seen as part of a backlash against women's political, economic and social advances. Thus thinness restates the primacy of women's physical appearance – being rather than doing – while taking control of one's body is also a means through which women are offered the promise of freedom and self-control (Lovejoy, 2001). 'Doing' anorexia might then meet several different needs – to be thin is to be successful economically, it is to be desirable as a woman, but it also allows control and denial of mature femininity.

Feminist analyses of gender differences in anorexia and bulimia have further highlighted the part played by the sexual division of labour in the home and the responsibility that women carry for feeding the family, for shopping and cooking. In carrying out these jobs, women are expected to suppress their own needs – both physical and emotional – in order to provide for others. Anorexia and bulimia can be read as strategies to exert autonomy within the feminine realm, strategies which are culturally sanctioned for women.

Others have related anorexia to prevailing and interconnected discourses in high-income countries in which the separation of the body and the mind sets them at war with each other. Within this construction, the emphasis on control and discipline, particularly among higher-class groups, inside discourses of power and gender relations, creates the body as the site of struggle in which women's attempts to exercise power lead to anorexic and bulimic behaviour. For Bordo (1993), for example, weight control strategies reflect contradictions of feminine discourse in that such strategies simultaneously reproduce women's oppression and offer freedom.

However, men's eating disorders need to be open to such gendered constructions, if these ideas are to make sense. Are men who are anorexic or bulimic doing femininity, suffering from low body dissatisfaction because shifts in masculine discourses render some men at risk, or are these men also exercising power and control over their bodies? The large proportion of men with eating disorders who have also experienced sexual abuse suggests similar pathways, particularly issues around body dissatisfaction, self-worth and control, although these issues may be more pronounced in the context of discourses of masculinity, which mean losing control over one's body is particularly problematic (Courtenay, 2000).

Overall, then, eating disorders are highly gendered, and although there have been increases in men's risk of both anorexia and bulimia in recent years, women remain more likely to be diagnosed with these conditions. A range of factors is involved in eating disorders, but in particular, aspects of gendered discourse and gender identity are important. Although relatively rare, these conditions are very difficult to treat, and are often chronic, enduring health difficulties which carry a significant mortality risk, as well as implications for physical health.

Sex, gender and depression

Depression is now a major cause of disability around the world – it is likely to be the second largest cause of global disease after ischaemic disease in the next few years, while among younger age groups depression accounts for more disability worldwide than any other cause (WHO, 2001; Thara and Patel, 2001). Both the prevalence of the disorder and the relative importance of depression as a cause of disability vary greatly from one country to another. Community studies suggest high rates of depression in Chile, where nearly one-third of the population in one study reported symptoms of depression, compared with 17 per cent in the UK and the Netherlands, and under 3 per cent in Japan (WHO, 2001). These variations in depression reflect differences not only in symptoms, but also in diagnosis, availability of treatment, how depression is perceived, and differences in the stigma attaching to mental illness. The role of depression in a country's health profile also relates to the relative contribution to total morbidity from other conditions – depression accounts for a greater proportion of morbidity in high-income and more developed countries than in low-income and developing countries, where communicable diseases and other conditions related to poverty are more widespread.

More women than men are treated for depression in general practice and specialist care, and population surveys suggest that more women experience depression (Piccinelli and Wilkinson, 2000; Busfield, 2002; Singleton et al., 2001). The gender gap in depression varies with age. In early adolescence slightly more boys suffer from depression, while depression increases dramatically among girls in later adolescence. This high risk of depression early in life in turn increases figures for lifelong prevalence among women, as they are more likely than men to suffer recurrent forms of the illness (Hankin et al., 1998; Piccinelli and Wilkinson, 2000).

Depression is multi-factorial; that is, it has a number of causes, and in recent years research exploring depression has emphasized the complexity of the condition. Different factors play more or less of a role in the illness, and while these factors may vary from one individual to the next, they also change over time in the same individual. However, differences between women and men reflect a wide range of gendered social processes which exacerbate or interact with biological factors (Bird and Rieker, 1999).

Sex and depression

Evidence relating to the role of biology in depression is mixed, but on the whole – and perhaps surprisingly – suggests that sex-linked factors are relatively minor aspects of the explanation of the increased risk of depression among women. Studies have suggested that genetic factors may explain some susceptibility to depression, but socially constructed factors remain significant (Khan et al., 2002). Female hormones are implicated in women's excess of depression during reproductive years particularly, with higher risks associated with changes in oestrogen levels especially pre-menstrually, after childbirth and in the years leading up to the menopause (J. Payne, 2003).

Among older men, depression is associated with falling levels of testosterone, although this is not universal (Seidman and Walsh, 1999). Men present with different symptoms – men are more likely to talk about apathy, insomnia, appetite changes and fatigue, and these symptoms may mirror other, physical, illnesses – and this may reflect both biological and social factors (Orengo et al., 2004). The evidence relating to women's risk of depression in later life following hormone changes – particularly the menopause – is also inconclusive (Hunter, 1996). Biological factors appear to be less important in the gap between women and men in depression compared with gendered factors, and although there is evidence of a physical explanation for some depressive illness, this does not explain the differences between women and men.

Gender and depression

For both men and women the risk of depression appears to be associated with a number of gendered factors. The risk of depression is increased in response to adverse life events and stresses, role-related factors, the experience of childhood sexual abuse, relationship issues, the presence of other illness, substance dependence, coping strategies and emotional behaviour. Each of these might explain differences between women and men in the risk of depression, although not all explain the greater risk experienced by women, and some would suggest that men suffer higher risks.

As we have seen, there are gendered differences in the experience of poverty (Harris, 2003), but while poverty increases the risk of poor mental health and depression for both men and women, poor women suffer symptoms of depression more often than poor men (S. Payne, 2000). Women suffer from increased levels of depression during the years when they are most likely to be responsible for children, partly as a result of the stress associated with caring for children, but also because parenting often reduces their opportunities for paid work, particularly when children are young, and increases their risk of deprivation and isolation (Piccinelli and Wilkinson, 2000; Harris, 2003).

Paid work outside the home also offers opportunities for enhanced self-esteem and a sense of self-worth, which may reduce the risk of depression.

This suggests that a number of factors are involved. In the USA, for example, a detailed study of women's status across different states concluded that women were less likely to suffer from depression in states where there was greater gender equality – where women had more access to employment and more autonomy. In states where women's economic position was poor and where women were disadvantaged in other ways in relation to men – including West Virginia, Kentucky and Alabama, for example – depression among women was greater (Chen et al., 2005).

Some risk factors, including life events and adverse circumstances, also have a greater impact on women. Stresses such as housing difficulties, problems with children or reproductive health, and lack of social support may create greater mental health risks for women, partly because of gendered differences in responses – women more frequently internalize anger, for example – but also because women have more involvement and more emotional investment in family and private worlds than men (Harris, 2003), and women carry more of the responsibility and stress associated with domestic work, child care and the care of other dependants.

Harris (2003) also suggests that women are more vulnerable to depression than men in the face of life events, because they are more at risk of what she describes as 'humiliation' – from a partner's infidelity, for example – and because women have fewer opportunities for validation from other social and public roles. Women may feel more trapped in humiliating relationships because gender roles make it more difficult to extricate themselves (Harris, 2003). Similarly, depression may be more common among female adolescents, because a greater focus on interpersonal relationships in their development leaves them with poorer instrumental skills and greater difficulty coping with stressors outside interpersonal relationships (Cyranowski et al., 2000). That is, young women are better at negotiating personal relationships, but may be less able to deal with other kinds of crisis or difficulty. Men, on the other hand, are increasingly constructed in relation to fatherhood and the family, not simply as breadwinners but also in terms of their emotional engagement, which in some discourses is anticipated as being similar to that of women, even if the nature of that engagement is distinctly gendered. In many countries masculinity means being a father, both biologically and socially, and the loss or diminution of this role may impact on men's mental health. In addition, marital status is related to mental health: married men and women are less at risk of depression than single, divorced and separated men and women, possibly because marriage and cohabitation offer opportunities for emotional support, although other factors, including income and social status, may also have an effect (Simon, 2002).

Depression is also a response to violence, both physical and sexual, and to insecurity. Depressed women are more likely to have experienced physical, sexual and emotional abuse from intimate partners than non-depressed women, for example (Hegarty et al., 2004), and women's increased risk of violence and abuse, economic need, displacement, and the stresses associated with rapid change following globalization may be a key factor in women's depression worldwide (Thara and Patel, 2001).

For both men and women the experience of sexual abuse as a child or adult is also associated with depression in adulthood (Hegarty et al., 2004; Weiss et al., 1999). Although most of the research looking at this association focuses on women, the incidence of depression is also higher among men who have been abused, compared with men in general (Weiss et al., 1999).

Depression is also more common among men and women who are suffering from life-threatening and chronic illness, at all ages, and this also helps to explain the relative risks of depression among men and women. For example, there are high levels of depression among people with HIV and AIDs and also among people with painful conditions such as arthritis. Depression is also common after cardiac events, but more women with heart disease suffer from depression than men with this condition (Chang and Heitkemper, 2002). People with other mental health problems, particularly substance dependence and abuse, are also more at risk of depression, and while substance-related conditions are more common among men than women, the association between depression and substance misuse is stronger for women than men (Redgrave et al., 2003). However, the underlying factors related to substance-related disorders are similar to the factors implicated in depression – stress, adverse life events and sexual abuse, for example – and it is possible that the more marked association between these for women simply reflects their greater exposure to such experiences.

In all of these explanations, masculinity, femininity and social constructions of gender play an added part. Depression is an illness associated with loss of self-esteem, feelings of low self-worth, loss of face or confidence, and feelings of guilt, but experiences of negative feelings and expression of emotional difficulties relate to gendered discourse. Similarly, adverse life events may be more or less likely due to gender differences in responsibilities and resources, but the impact varies in relation to gender as well. In the association between unemployment and depression, the meaning of unemployment will be associated with the job that has been lost, the impact on income, and the potential for new employment, but also with the role of paid work in the construction of the self. For men, unemployment may have a particular effect due to the status of the job itself, the meaning and importance of being a provider, or the loss of a place where masculinity is enacted on a daily basis, while women who lose paid work may have other ways in which they can 'do' gender. However, masculinity may mean that negative feelings – sadness or grief – associated with unemployment prompt different kinds of responses, including suicide, substance use, violence and failures in intimacy (MIND, 2002). Masculinity may also reduce the likelihood that men's depression is diagnosed and treated (MIND, 2002), both because men are less able to recognize that they are ill and seek treatment, and because men more often present with symptoms of fatigue, sleep problems and appetite changes than 'the blues', and doctors are less likely to consider depression as a possible explanation. In an effort to challenge stereotypes about this illness, a recent campaign in the USA, by the National Institute of Mental Health in America, included these personal stories of men who had suffered from depression:

> 'Here I am in the Air Force and I'm one of the senior leaders in the enlisted ranks. And that would be a sign that well maybe I'm not a leader. And then my career's derailed or maybe I'll lose my security clearance. I can't let anybody know, I've got to gut it out, I've got to fake my way through it . . . You don't know where to turn for help. You don't want to be perceived as weak, you finally get to a point where you say, let all that be damned, you don't care how you're perceived, because you are barely breathing, you're barely getting up.'
>
> 'It depended who I was speaking to about how much I can admit to how I was feeling. You know your head is screwed up, that somebody is going to look at you like you're crazy, that you're weak for admitting that you're having a problem. Especially in the fire service. Fire service, police service; it's an entirely macho atmosphere. So it's just natural that you'll be looked upon as weak if you admit that you're having some kind of problem dealing with something.'
> (<http://menanddepression.nimh.nih.gov/>)

Suicide and suicidal behaviour

While depression is a significant cause of disability, which affects more women than men, suicide is an important cause of mortality, particularly premature mortality, which is more common among men. Estimates by the World Health Organisation suggest that around a million people worldwide commit suicide every year, with a further 10–20 million people attempting it (WHO, 2001). More people die each year as a result of suicide than in armed conflict, and the number of suicides is also increasing, particularly among younger people (McKenzie et al., 2003). There are wide variations between countries in terms of suicide mortality, with very low rates in some South and Central American countries, compared with high rates in northern Europe, and although variations in the way suicide is recorded affect these comparisons, particularly in countries where suicide goes against religious beliefs, such variations do not fully explain differences between countries (McKenzie et al., 2003; Gunnell, 2000).

More men commit suicide every year in every country in the world apart from one, China (Cheng and Lee, 2000; Phillips et al., 2002). Suicide ranks among the top causes of male mortality worldwide, and the male excess in suicide mortality is particularly marked in younger age groups, with the exception of China, where suicide is greater among young women (Hawton, 2000; Cheng and Lee, 2000; Phillips et al., 2002; WHO, 2004d). Male suicide mortality rates have also increased in recent years in comparison with female rates, although not in all countries (WHO, 2001). In the USA, Japan and China, for example, suicide has fallen in the past decade, while Mexico, India, Brazil and the Russian Federation have all experienced dramatic increases in suicide death (WHO, 2001).

The ratio of male to female suicides also varies. Lithuania currently has the highest male suicide rate in the world – 80 per 100,000 population, compared with a global suicide mortality rate of 15 (WHO, 2004d). Suicide is also high among men in the Russian Federation and Belarus. Female rates are lower than those of men, and the countries with the highest rates are different: in China, the female mortality rate was 26 per 100,000 population over the period 1995–99, while Sri Lanka had a female suicide mortality rate of 17 per 100,000 population in 2002, and in Japan the rate was 13 (Phillips et al., 2002; WHO, 2004d). Thus the gap between women and men in suicide deaths also varies – the widest gap is found in Belarus, Poland, the Russian Federation, Ukraine and Romania, while the narrowest gap is in Sweden, Kuwait and the Netherlands (WHO, 2004d).

In the USA men are more than four times as likely as women to commit suicide (CDC, 2004). In Europe, the widest gap between men and women for suicide mortality is found in Greece (a ratio of seven males for every female death) and Ireland (five male deaths for every female death) (Stone et al., 2002). In England and Wales, men are around three times as likely to commit suicide as women (ONS, 2003).

The risk of suicide, and the gap between women and men, varies further over the life course. In Australia, for example, the widest gap between men and women in suicide deaths is found in young adults and among those aged 70 and over (AIHW, 2004). In the USA, the vast majority of suicides among those aged 15–24 or over 65 were men (CDC, 2004). In New Zealand, men are more than three times as likely to commit suicide, but in younger age groups this increases to a four-fold risk (NZMOH, 2004).

There are additional differences between women and men in how they commit suicide, which reflect the availability of different methods. More men use violent methods, including hanging, jumping and guns, while women are more likely to use poisoning, including paracetemol, prescription medication, including antidepressants and sleeping tablets, and liquids such as pesticides and cleaning agents (Gunnell, 2000). In Australia, for example, nearly half of all male suicides are by hanging, while a further tenth of male suicides are from gunshot wounds (Hassan, 1996; NZMOH, 2004). Among women in Australia, hanging is also the most common method, accounting for just over a third of female deaths, but another third of women use self-poisoning with liquids and solids. Similar numbers of women and men use motor-vehicle exhaust gas as a method of suicide (AIHW, 2004). In comparison, in the USA, over half of male and female suicide deaths were gunshot-related, including 60 per cent of male deaths, compared with a fifth of suicide deaths in France and New Zealand, and less than 3 per cent in England and Wales (CDC, 2004; Hemenway et al., 2002).

In China, the majority of suicides and suicide attempts come from the ingestion of pesticides, particularly in rural areas of the country. This choice of method, and the scarcity of treatment facilities, is associated with increases in female suicide rates in recent years, particularly for impulsive suicide (Phillips et al., 2002).

Methods used in suicide also vary with age, which again reflects differential access to methods, especially guns – particularly in the USA – and cars. Three-quarters of the suicides over 65 in the USA, for example, use a gun, compared with just over half of those in the 15–24 age group (CDC, 2004).

In many countries, people from minority ethnic groups have lower rates of suicide than white populations, but this is not the case throughout the world, and suicide mortality is increasing among minority ethnic groups at different rates for men and women (O'Donnell et al., 2004). In Australia, for example, suicide is higher among Aboriginal and Torres Straits Islanders than the white population, for both women and men (McKenzie et al., 2003; Hassan, 1996). Figures for New Zealand also reveal differences in the risk of suicide – with high rates of suicide among Maori people, particularly Maori males (NZHIS, 2005). In younger age groups Maori men are nearly twice as likely to commit suicide as white men, and while suicide rates for young women are lower than those for young men, young Maori women are also more at risk than their white counterparts (NZHIS, 2005). In the USA, suicide has risen faster among young black men than among white men or black women, mainly associated with increasing rates of suicide in which guns are used (CDC, 2004). In 2001 white men were four times as likely to commit suicide as white women, whereas black African and American men were more than five times at risk than black African and American women (NCHS, 2004). Over the past 50 years, suicide among white men in the USA has decreased, while rates for black men have increased, and the fact that suicide rates are still higher in the white population overall reflects the wide gap between white and black Americans in older age groups where suicide is more common (McKenzie et al., 2003). However, among younger age groups, American Indian and Native Alaskan males, rather than white males, are most at risk of suicide (NCHS, 2004).

In the UK, data on suicide by ethnic group are more difficult to track, because death certificates in the UK do not include information on ethnicity (McKenzie et al., 2003). Research suggests that there are higher suicide rates for men in Irish and Scottish groups, and suicide rates have also increased among young black males (McKenzie et al., 2003). Among women there is a marked risk of suicide among young Asian women. This risk is low in comparison with young men of all ethnic backgrounds, but is much greater than that of white women in the same age group and has increased in recent years (Raleigh, 1996; Bhardwaj, 2001; McKenzie et al., 2003; Fikree and Pasha, 2004). Asian women up to the age of 35 are three times more likely to commit suicide than non-Asian women in this age group, and are particularly at risk from self-poisoning (Bhardwaj, 2001; Thompson and Bhugra, 2000).

However, we need to be cautious here. Suicide research has tended to highlight these differences, and in a sense has pathologized both Asian women and Asian culture by attributing blame for female suicide to family pressure and the refusal to allow young Asian women to adopt Western lifestyles (Bhardwaj, 2001). Experiences of racism and discrimination and health services which are insensitive to gender and culture contribute to the pressures facing young Asian women, and are obscured in a discourse constructed solely around familial and cultural factors.

Similarly, the higher rates of suicide among indigenous populations in Australia and New Zealand have been subjected to a discourse of pathological lifestyles, particularly substance use, among Aboriginal and Maori populations, rather than the acknowledgement of issues relating to discrimination, structural factors and service delivery.

Suicidal behaviour is also greater among gay and bisexual men than heterosexual men, and again this reflects both stress and adverse life events, higher use of substances associated with increases in suicide risk, and services which are, or are felt to be, homophobic and insensitive to the needs of gay men and women (MIND, 2002).

While, worldwide, more men commit suicide, more women than men make suicide attempts (CDC, 2002; NZMOH, 2004). In the USA, for example, about three times as many women attempt suicide in comparison with men (CDC, 2004). The Eurosave project in Europe also estimated that women are about three times more likely than men to attempt suicide (Stone et al., 2002). In Britain, however, suicide attempts have increased in recent years, particularly in younger age groups, and the ratio of women to men in deliberate self-harm has also narrowed considerably, with more men making suicide attempts than previously (Hawton, 2000).

Explaining gender differences in suicide

The primary explanations for differences between men and women in suicide mortality and parasuicide relate to gendered differences in exposure to events and factors which might precipitate suicidal behaviour, and to the ways in which masculinity and femininity may operate to increase or reduce risks.

Masculine discourse around pain, aggression and violence increases the likelihood of selecting methods of suicide which are both violent and the most lethal, and which make it more likely that the act will end in death. Women, on the other hand, are more likely to choose less violent methods, which increases their chances of survival. The risk of suicide is also increased by access to some methods of suicide. The higher rate of substance use among men increases their access to a relatively lethal means of suicide, for example (Hawton, 2000; Higgitt, 2000). The choice of method also relates to whether the act is planned or impulsive, as some of the more lethal methods are associated with a greater degree of impulsiveness (CDC, 2004). In China, India and Sri Lanka, the availability of toxic pesticides in rural areas, for example, is connected with impulsive suicide particularly among women, while growing rates of suicide among young black males in the USA are also connected with the availability of the most common method used by this group, guns (WHO, 2001; CDC, 2004). Women's relatively high suicide mortality in Asia and their choice of method also reflect women's circumscribed lives in Asian cultures, and their lack of voice (Pearson and Meng, 2002).

Impulsive suicide is also connected with alcohol and substance use, and higher levels of substance use and dependence among men further explain their excess suicide mortality. High rates of suicide and the growth in suicide mortality in the Baltic states and the Russian Federation, for example, are associated with heavy levels of alcohol consumption among men in these countries, as well as economic stress (WHO, 2001).

One of the most important 'explanatory' factors is the close correlation between suicide and poor mental health. Depression, substance misuse and discharge from psychiatric in-patient treatment are key risk factors for suicide (WHO, 2001; Blair-West et al., 1999). Both women and men who have ongoing mental health problems are at greater risk of suicide, but men more often lose contact with specialist psychiatric services and with general practitioner care, particularly in age groups where suicide rates are highest (Booth and Owens, 2000). Although women are more at risk of suicide immediately after being discharged from in-patient psychiatric treatment, after a few weeks men's suicide risks overtake those of women (Goldacre et al., 1993).

Masculinity – being strong, coping with difficulties, and not showing emotions, for example – also makes it unlikely that men will seek help from others when faced with emotional crises or problems. Surveys suggest that both women and men view completed suicide as a reflection of strength, and attempted suicide as a sign of weakness (Stillion, 1995); and suicide may be more acceptable for men than women. Media reports more commonly depict male suicide, particularly among famous celebrities, and help to construct a gendered discourse in which male suicide is seen as a legitimate response to stress (Canetto and Sakinofsky, 1998).

There are also gendered barriers to mental health services involving cost, the appropriateness or acceptability of services, and perceptions of stigma attaching to mental health services, and these differentially affect the suicide risk of men and women around the world (WHO, 2001).

In addition, socio-economic factors have been implicated in suicide risk. Research suggests that poverty, deprivation and social exclusion may all substantially increase the risk of suicide, but that the effect may be greater for men than for women (Hawton, 2000; Gunnell et al., 1995). In Scotland, for example, young men in deprived areas are six times more at risk of suicide than young men in the least deprived areas (Boyle et al., 2005). The very high rates of suicide among men in former Soviet states have also been attributed to high levels of psychosocial stress associated with increases in deprivation, combined with poor health care and men's alcohol and substance abuse (Puras et al., 2004). Stone et al. (2002), in a review of suicide mortality in Europe, found that unemployment was a key risk factor for men in a number of countries. Other research suggests that unemployed men are at increased risk of suicide (Crawford and Prince, 1999). In the USA, unemployment is also associated with increased risks of suicide for both women and men (Kposowa, 2001). Figures revealing lower suicide mortality rates in the USA among black single mothers despite poverty and deprivation suggest that there are complex mediating factors, but that responsibility for children, while increasing the risk of both mental health difficulties and poverty, may act to protect women from suicidal behaviour. Similarly, research in Denmark found that having a child under 2 protected women – but not men – from suicide (Fernquist, 2004).

Domestic violence is an important risk factor in suicidal behaviour for women. Women who experience physical violence from an intimate partner are more likely to have thought of committing suicide than women who have never experienced such violence (Abbott and Williamson, 1999; WHO, 2001). Women's suicide in India is associated with poor marital relationships and violence, and with factors which increase the risk of violence, including young age at marriage and bearing girl children (Thara and Patel, 2001). Sexual violence and enforced prostitution are also significant aspects of suicidal behaviour among women in China (Yip et al., 2000).

Gender plays a further part in explanations of trends in suicide, although a number of factors are involved. Hawton (2000) suggests that changing gender or social roles for women and men have enhanced women's independence and decreased their risk of the kinds of adverse events which trigger suicide. For example, if women are able to leave relationships which are not working, or which are abusive, because they have more economic independence than in the past, this may add to women's protection against suicidal behaviour, whereas marital breakdown or relationship loss increase the risk of suicide among men. Women's 'social embeddedness' in parenting and in social roles compared with that of men also helps to protect women from suicide (Chaudron and Caine, 2004).

Conclusion

Overall patterns of mental health for women and men are complex. As with other kinds of morbidity, risks associated with sex and gender are also mediated by other aspects of diversity, including ethnicity and sexuality, and risks change over the life course. Differences around the world and comparisons between countries are made more difficult by variations in what is defined as mental illness, what is measured, and how figures are constructed; but there are important similarities in the patterns revealed for men and women.

Key factors in mental health problems – poverty, disadvantage, adverse events, experiences of trauma and abuse, for example – play a part in explaining why women are more at risk of some common mental disorders and why men have greater risks of suicide, but in order to explain variations in the kinds of mental health problems faced, other aspects of gender, and in particular differences in expression of emotion, are also important. In addition, service-related factors which affect the diagnosis and treatment offered, and gendered constructions of mental distress, are significant in understanding the distribution of mental illness.

There are also gaps in our understanding. Data are lacking on differences between women and men in mental health in developing countries, partly because of a failure to recognize gender as a significant variable. For example, a recent series of papers reviewing mental health profiles of developing countries included little discussion of differences between men and women and very little about gendered factors in mental health or gender sensitivity in mental health services (Jenkins et al., 2004; Parameshvara Deva, 2004; Puras et al., 2004).

One of the most significant gaps in the literature relates to men's mental health. When men's mental health or risk of illness is discussed – in on-line resources about men's health, for example – the focus of such discussions is largely suicide. A search on 'Medline' for literature relating to men's mental health produces papers which focus on the mental health of gay men rather than all men or heterosexual men. What is interesting about this lack of discussion is that the difficulties created by constructions of masculinity which mean that men are less able to recognize depression or to talk to about emotions are reflected in the invisibility of men's mental illness even in websites devoted to the topic and in clinical research.

5 Gender, Sex and Sexual and Reproductive Health

Introduction

The most obvious health differences between women and men are those relating to the reproductive system – so obvious that variations between women and men relating to mortality and morbidity which stem from, or appear to relate to, women's different reproductive capacity are highly researched and form part of common-sense notions of what explains overall health experience. Differences relating to reproductive health also reveal some of the most marked gaps in health experience between women, particularly in terms of the dangers associated with reproductive events for women in less developed countries compared with those living in more developed parts of the world. Following the International Conference on Population and Development in 1994 and the Cairo Declaration, there has been an increasing recognition of the importance of reproductive rights for women's well-being (Locke, 2002). Since then, however, despite the promotion of women's reproductive rights by the United Nations, the World Health Organisation and others, women around the world still do not have full access to the services they need; nor do they always have the power to determine their sexuality and reproductive choices (Locke, 2002).

In comparison, men's sexual health and reproductive health are rarely discussed in policy or in research, and while in many ways men continue to exercise power over women's sexual and reproductive well-being, this runs alongside a continued failure to attend to men's sexual and reproductive health needs. In this chapter we explore some of the key differences between women and men which relate to reproductive health, focusing on stages in the reproductive life course, and also differences relating to sexual health and sexual behaviour. The two case studies at the end of the chapter highlight the ways in which sex and gender play a part in reproductive and sexual health through a more detailed focus on pregnancy and childbirth, and on HIV and AIDS.

The meaning of reproductive and sexual health

Significant distinctions between the male body and the female body – most obviously in terms of the reproductive organs, but also differences in hormonal constitution – are described as differences in terms of the sex of the individual. Most data on health which are reported by subgroups within total populations refer to these biological sex differences – mortality rates, life expectancy and hospital admission figures, for example, are reported separately for women and men. In the study of differences in reproductive health, this biological perspective is important, as some illnesses are associated with reproductive organs. Women do not suffer from testicular or prostate cancer, and men do not suffer from cervical or ovarian cancer, for example. Conditions associated with pregnancy and with menstruation, including dysmenorrhoea, amenorrhoea and menorrhagia, are biologically female, while specifically male disorders are similarly defined by virtue of their association with male sex. However, 'male' and 'female' disorders can also be seen as being discursively constructed in ways which affect the experience of the illness, screening services and the treatment which is offered.

This is best illustrated by the association between sexual behaviour and sexual morbidity. Cervical cancer – cancer in the neck of the womb – is a female condition which in the past has been attributed to women's sexual behaviour, and in particular 'sexual promiscuity', including early age of first sexual intercourse, the number of sexual partners and the kinds of contraceptive protection women use in sexual intercourse (Foster, 1995). This reading of cervical cancer as a cancer contracted by immoral or promiscuous women stems from both medical research in the 1960s and 1970s and also representations of research findings in the media (Kavanagh and Broom, 1997). This affects women's behaviour in relation to screening – for example, when women see themselves as not being at risk because they are in same-sex relationships, or because they are not 'promiscuous', or when they feel responsible and stigmatized for their own 'risk-taking' behaviour (Hann, 1995). This discourse of blame is reinforced by health professionals: 'the doctor said that normally it was with promiscuity that you got this sort of thing, but then he said you know nuns have had it, little old ladies or whatever' (Kavanagh and Broom, 1997: 1388).

In comparison, promiscuity is also discussed in relation to prostate cancer, but in a different way. A number of risk factors have been identified in the epidemiology of cancer of the prostate men, but, just as nuns 'do not get' cervical cancer, there are similar associations between sexual behaviour and the risks of prostate cancer. For example: 'Eunuchs do not get prostate cancer, castration has a palliative effect on cancer . . . certain aspects of sexual activity also appear to be indicative of a higher prostate cancer risk. These include early age of first intercourse and a history of venereal disease' (Mant and Silagy, 1998: 17–18).

However, although there is a highly visible discourse relating to women's sexual behaviour and cervical cancer risk, which has affected women's (and men's) interpretations of negative cervical smear results, treatment-seeking behaviour and the public health imperative for women to protect themselves by being 'good' (Lupton and Barclay, 1997), there has not been a similar discursive construction of men with prostate cancer as 'bad' boys, or of men needing to protect themselves by saying 'no' and minimizing their sexual partners or their sexual activity. While for women it is 'sexual promiscuity' and 'multiple sexual partners' that put them at risk (Biswas et al., 1997), for men the risks are described as 'a greater number of sexual partners' (Ilic et al., 1996: 1682). Although by the late 1990s the term 'promiscuity' is found in relation to men's risk of prostate cancer, penile cancer and also anal cancer, the term remains more common in the study of sexually transmitted diseases and HIV infection among homosexual men and the transmission of HIV in developing countries. The sexual health of women and men is not framed simply around biological difference, then, but reflects gender as well, both in how different conditions are viewed and in the way in which problems are treated or researched.

Sexual health

Sexual health encompasses a number of different experiences and conditions. At the broadest level, sexual health refers to well-being in the context of sexual relationships, particularly relating to power and control over sexual activity. More narrowly defined, sexual health refers to specific conditions which are sexually transmitted, or which affect sexual performance. This section explores some of the major variations between women and men in these health experiences.

There are important differences between men and women in their risk of contracting sexually transmitted infections (STIs) and in the impact of such disease on their health. HIV and AIDS are discussed in the case study later in this chapter, but first it is useful to explore broader differences in such infections. STIs include chlamydia, gonorrhoea, syphilis, genital and anogenital warts, herpes and a range of other infectious diseases. STIs can affect both morbidity and mortality, reduce fertility, and increase the risk of HIV infection due to the vulnerability of inflamed tissue. Rates of STIs have increased in recent years in many countries, partly as a result of changing levels of sexual activity and safe sex practices (James et al., 2004; Lowndes and Fenton, 2004). In the UK, for example, new diagnoses of syphilis increased eightfold between 1997 and 2002, with the greatest increase in young men (Brown et al., 2004). However, there are other important differences in STI infections: those most at risk, for example, are younger, low-income and poorer populations of men and women (Klausner et al., 2001; Duncan and Hart, 1999).

Sex-linked or biological factors are important in both the impact of STIs and the mechanisms of transmission. One of the main factors affecting cervical cancer is the highly infective human papilloma virus which is transmitted during sexual intercourse and which puts women at risk of developing this disease. Without treatment, cervical cancer is often fatal, and although women in developed countries are screened for cervical cancer, and their mortality from this disease has been greatly reduced, cervical cancer is the most common form of cancer for women in developing countries and a leading cause of death for women in poorer countries (Suba and Raab, 2004).

Chlamydia trachomatis – the most common STI – has increased in recent years, partly because it can remain asymptomatic for a long time, partly due to changing sexual practices, and partly because knowledge about chlamydia in general populations has been limited until relatively recently. Both men and women may be infected with chlamydia, but if the disease is untreated, the impact on women's health is particularly severe, with increased risks of pelvic inflammatory disease, infertility and ectopic pregnancy. Among men, untreated chlamydia can lead to other conditions, including epididymitis which can also result in sterility, although this is relatively rare (Donovan, 2002). Another STI, trichomoniasis, has been associated with increased risks for women of cervical neoplasia, post-operative infections, adverse pregnancy outcomes, pelvic inflammatory disease and infertility, and increased risks for men of urethritis and infertility.

While the ways in which STIs affect health reflect biological differences between women and men, gender relations are also important. Sexually transmitted reproductive tract infections are often under-reported by women, and women often resort to self-medication for symptoms of infection, due to cultural perceptions that these conditions stem from promiscuity and unacceptable sexual behaviour, or the belief that symptoms are a normal part of ageing or an outcome of child bearing and need not be treated (Manderson, 1999).

The spread of STIs reflects sexual risk taking associated with constructions of masculinity and gendered differences in power, in particular. Heterosexual masculinity includes risk-taking behaviour, while the construction of male sexual pleasure as of primary importance in heterosexual relations decreases the likelihood that condoms will be used during intercourse (James et al., 2004). Some constructions of homosexual masculinity similarly construct risky sex, including 'bareback' sex, or unprotected anal intercourse, as more exciting, more pleasurable and more intimate (Crossley, 2004; Bauermeister and Carballo-Dieguez, 2004). Scarce (1999), however, suggests that unprotected anal sex has been used in the media and public health debates as an opportunity to construct gay men as promiscuous, foolhardy and to blame for their own illness (again), and points out that although the attention paid to 'barebacking' has increased dramatically, there is less evidence that the practice itself has increased.

STIs are passed on in sexual encounters particularly where the receptive partner – whether a woman or a gay man – is unable to determine the use of condoms. This includes relationships where women fear violence, encounters between younger women and older men, which are common in many countries, and also both male and female sex-workers who can earn more for sex where a condom is not used.

In addition to the risk of STIs, there are differences between women and men in health risks arising from sexual violence. Many conditions, including mental health problems, irritable bowel syndrome and substance misuse, are associated with sexual abuse as a child or adult (Chang and Heitkemper, 2002). Both men and women experience sexual violence, although it is more common among women (Ganju et al., 2004a, 2004b). However, the silence and stigma which surround homosexual acts in many countries can particularly affect younger men who are victims of sexual coercion by other men and who feel unable to seek medical help or support, who may blame themselves for their infection, and have more risk of subsequent health problems (Ganju et al., 2004b). Male sexual violence, against either women or other men, is located within culturally specific discourses of masculinity as an expression of men's power, but the health of both women and men is jeopardized by such violence (Lee and Owens, 2002).

Sexual health problems also include sexual dysfunction for both women and men. Among men the most common form of sexual difficulty is erectile dysfunction, which is more common among older men. In recent years the drug sildenafil, marketed as Viagra, has increasingly been used to treat male erectile dysfunction. While Viagra has brought benefits to thousands of men and women, there are some risks involved for men who take it, including angina, nausea, dizziness and allergies. In addition to these health risks, Viagra helps to reinforce penetrative sexuality as a gold standard of sexual relationships, while bringing particular stresses for female partners, who feel pressurized to agree to sexual intercourse once the tablet has been taken (Marshall and Katz, 2002). Viagra has been inscribed with a range of meanings, which together construct sexuality as penetrative, as a coupled phenomenon, and as a practice in which male pleasure is paramount (Mamo and Fishman, 2001). More recently, pharmaceutical companies have begun to target female sexual dysfunction. Estimates have been produced by such companies which suggest that up to half of the female population may suffer from sexual dysfunction, including lack of sexual desire and inability to orgasm, and both Viagra for women and testosterone patches have been promoted as treatments to 'restore' women's libido and sexual pleasure, despite a lack of evidence to date that these treatments are safe or effective for women (R. Moynihan, 2005).

Some groups are less often addressed by sexual health services – particularly younger men (Yamey, 1999). Where young men are visible in the literature – in leaflets directed at both male and female adolescents, for example – they tend to be addressed within the bounds of traditional hegemonic masculinity, portrayed as the initiators of sexual intercourse, while women are seen as taking responsibility for enforcing safe sex and protection, and as having better information about sexual health (Jewitt, 1997). While men's embarrassment and their lack of familiarity with their bodies prevents them from seeking help for STIs (Manderson, 1999), discursive constructions, in public health promotion and more generally, of young women as responsible and knowledgeable does little to challenge this notion.

Reproductive health

Reproductive health includes a wide range of conditions which affect both men and women. These can be further divided into reproductive health conditions over the life course – relating to puberty, menstruation, the menopause and the concept of the male menopause, or andopause – and conditions which relate to reproductive events – the health effects of contraception, abortion, fertility treatment and infertility, and pregnancy and childbirth.

The health of men and women changes during the life course in response to variations in hormone levels reflecting reproductive and biological factors. A number of those conditions which affect women's health during adolescence and adulthood relate to menstruation – the loss or absence of periods, periods which are heavy, too frequent or which last too long, and periods which are painful. However, while menstrual health problems are clearly associated with biological difference, they are also socially structured.

Menorrhagia, for example, refers to the experience of heavy periods, where the blood loss is above a certain level – usually 80 ml measured over three consecutive menstrual periods (Bonnar and Sheppard, 1996). Measurement of heavy loss, however, is difficult, but the method used, involving chemical treatment of sanitary protection to assess blood loss, allows menorrhagia to be clinically defined, associated factors to be assessed and different treatments to be evaluated. For research purposes, a woman either does or does not suffer from menorrhagia according to the outcome of such a test, while her own perception of what is normal or abnormal blood loss is seen as unreliable. Of course, in practice, women define what they mean by heavy blood loss through their actions – most obviously in deciding whether or not to seek help, but also in other ways: in conversations with others, for example, and in the way blood loss affects daily life by interrupting employment, child care, or social activities and so on. Clinicians discuss with women the extent of their 'heavy' loss, referring to the number of pads used, for example, but this is not a scientific judgement. Women who consult for this condition, then, are women for whom the bleeding and the problems this causes within the context of their lives are severe enough to warrant anxiety (over their state of health and potentially threatening underlying causes, for example) or a desire to explore solutions (when the difficulties of managing the blood loss are too great). Other factors also intervene. South Asian women with severe menorrhagia are less likely than other women to seek help, in part because of a preference for female doctors who may not be available (Chapple et al., 1998). However, cultural differences relating to beliefs about the meaning of menstrual loss and the role of diet are also significant – some South Asian women value a heavy flow, because blood is thought to be 'dirty' and 'impure', and because a scanty period is thought to result in abdominal weight gain and pain. When menstrual blood loss is thought to be 'excessive', women will often avoid 'hot' foods such as meat, fish and eggs rather than seek medical help (Chapple et al., 1998).

Thus, what is scientifically a biologically female disorder, and is to some extent measurable, is also socially or discursively constructed, through both the individual herself and her context. Statistics on the incidence of menorrhagia reflect women's attitudes towards seeking help and social attitudes towards menstruating women, as much as they reflect the distribution of a female health problem.

This is true for other specifically female disorders – figures for dysmenorrhoea, or pain during menstruation, for example, are affected by the ways in which the experience of painful periods is discussed by women and the medical profession, and whether and how treatment is sought for this condition.

One aspect of menstruation and women's health which has been discussed extensively in both medical literature and public arenas is the association between monthly hormonal changes and a collection of symptoms known as pre-menstrual tension (PMT) or pre-menstrual syndrome (PMS). A further condition relating to pre-menstrual mental health – pre-menstrual dysphonic disorder (PMDD), described as being more severe than PMT or PMS – was introduced in the American classification of diseases, the DSM-IV, in 1994. Despite estimates that a significant number of women suffer from PMT, PMS or PMDD, and despite treatment interventions which focus on hormonal imbalance, evidence suggests that these conditions are not simply biological phenomena, but relate also to psychosocial factors and to gender. In particular, pre-menstrual conditions can be seen within a social construction of women's hormones as generally problematic (Davis, 1996). Pre-menstrual conditions have been used to deny the reality of some women's complaints or experiences, including domestic or partner violence and abuse, as well as unhappiness and stress, while the potential for positive changes in the pre-menstrual phase – increased levels of energy, creativity or sensitivity, for example – are obscured in medicalized definitions which see PMS as something to be cured (Laws et al., 1985).

The female menopause is similarly a period of hormonal change which is at the same time both a biological reality and a social construction. The menopause is not easily defined. In medical terms, it is known only after the event – when 12 months or more have passed since the last menstrual period. Menopause discourse in developed countries reveals not only a largely biological focus on the experiences of women during this phase of the life course – the physical and mental changes going on in oestrogen-starved bodies – but also a largely negative rendering of this period in which the menopause is the end of reproductive life, while medical intervention through hormone replacement therapy is the solution (Davis, 1996). This discourse is widespread, and both women themselves and their doctors see the menopause in medical and biological terms, and as the start of physical decline (Morris and Symonds, 2004). Menopausal discourse in the West has shifted more recently, and women currently experiencing the menopause are more likely to see the menopause as a normal, if problematic, stage in the life course (Morris and Symonds, 2004). The menopause is also culturally specific, and cross-cultural comparisons reveal differences in which symptoms are experienced and in the severity of such symptoms – in Japan, for example 'hot flushes' are rarely identified, while in the USA or the UK, these are one of the main indicators that a woman is menopausal (Winterich, 2003; Lock, 1998).

Hormonal changes through the life course may also affect sexual health in other ways. Sexual desire for both women and men during later life may be reduced, but Winterich (2003) suggests that the impact will be felt differently by men and women. If men's libido decreases, their female partners often have to do without sex, whereas a woman's decreasing libido may not mean that she can refuse sex to a male partner. During and after the menopause, physiological changes experienced by some women, including thinning of the vaginal walls and dryness, can mean that sexual intercourse is painful, accompanied by bleeding and discomfort; but the construction of heterosexual intercourse as penetrative increases problems for a woman, particularly if she cannot discuss these difficulties with her partner or if he does not pay attention to her needs.

The alternative discourse of the male menopause, or andopause, also needs to be considered. Despite considerable research, partly funded by a pharmaceutical industry which stands to gain if the existence of the andopause can be demonstrated, there is no evidence that men experience the equivalent of the menopause. Testosterone levels do decrease, for both women and men, and decreasing male hormones may be associated with depression, anxiety and loss of libido, but there are wide variations between men in the changes experienced (Sternbach, 1998; Seidman and Walsh, 1999).

Other aspects of the reproductive life course which affect health include contraception, abortion, fertility and conception. Male contraception methods are limited to condom use, vasectomy and withdrawal.

Withdrawal increases the risk of STIs for both men and women, as well as pregnancy. Condoms have minimal risks for men, although there is a slightly greater risk of pregnancy compared with other forms of contraception. Vasectomy is a largely non-reversible surgical intervention which may carry some risks for men's health associated with the operation itself, and with suggestions that men may be more likely to develop prostate cancer following a vasectomy, although evidence remains inconclusive regarding this risk (Giovannucci et al., 1993).

The case study below explores in more detail aspects of fertility relating to pregnancy and childbirth. However, infertility is also an important aspect of reproductive health that affects both women and men, with around a third of all infertility caused by male-factor problems (Brugh and Lipshultz, 2004). Infertility may be related to a range of biological and gendered factors. STIs, as we have seen, can increase the risk of infertility in both women and men, although many STIs have a more marked effect on women's fertility. Lifestyle factors also affect fertility – for example, smoking decreases the fertility of both men and women (LSC, 2003). Gender differences are also important in the way in which infertility is treated in women and men, and in the past male-factor infertility was obscured in treatment which focused on women as the source of the problem and the focus of treatment interventions (Corea et al., 1987). Infertility also has different meanings for women and men in terms of medical intervention, the chances of success, and the impact on the sense of self. Although the particular stress for women of being unable to have a child has been widely discussed in medical literature and popular media, the impact on men of both their own infertility and that of a partner has only recently been recognized as a source of stress and difficulty (Gannon et al., 2004). However, while for both men and women there are important emotional consequences of infertility treatment, particularly when it is extended over a long time and when it is unsuccessful, there are further physical and mental health costs for women from hormonal treatments and various surgical interventions (Bergart, 2000).

Pregnancy and childbirth

While pregnancy and childbirth are clearly events which happen to women, there is increasing interest in the impact of a partner's experiences on men's health. However, we start with the question of women's health and the role of reproductive events in women's well-being. First, pregnancy and childbirth carry risks of both ill health and premature death, but these risks vary greatly around the world.

Maternal mortality is defined as death during pregnancy or death within 42 days of the end of pregnancy from causes which are associated with the pregnancy or conditions which are aggravated by the pregnancy (WHO, 2004e). Maternal mortality data include, therefore, deaths which result from complications in childbirth and complications after labour or after the termination of a pregnancy, including both miscarriage and induced termination. The data also include figures for women who die as a result of deteriorations in their health or in pre-existing conditions which are caused by a pregnancy, but the data do not include deaths during pregnancy relating to accidents or other incidental causes.

Although maternal mortality figures are often incomplete, due to difficulties collecting data (AbouZahr and Wardlaw, 2001), global estimates of maternal morbidity and mortality reveal a large number of women who suffer from health problems related to pregnancy and childbirth. Around the world, 8 million women experience pregnancy-related health complications each year, and over half a million women die (WHO, 2004b). The risks of maternal mortality vary globally, and are highest in poorer and developing countries (WHO, 2004b). In 2000, for example, the maternal mortality rate was 2,000 per 100,000 live births in Sierra Leone, 1,900 in Afghanistan, 1,800 in Malawi and 1,700 in Angola (WHO, 2004b). To put these mortality figures in perspective, maternal mortality in Ireland in the same year was five per 100,000, and women in Sierra Leone were 400 times more likely to die from pregnancy and childbirth than women in Ireland and many other Western and developed countries (WHO, 2004b). Maternal mortality is particularly high in countries in West, East and South Africa, with rates of 1,000 or more per 100,000 live births in Chad, Burundi, Central African Republic, Kenya, Niger, Mozambique and Somalia (WHO, 2004b).

The World Health Organisation lists five causes of maternal mortality which together explain nearly three-quarters of all deaths resulting from pregnancy. The most common cause of death in childbirth, explaining around a quarter of maternal deaths, is post-partum haemorrhage. This is a condition which requires rapid treatment if it is not to become fatal, treatment which is unavailable to women in the poorest countries, women who give birth some distance from health facilities, and women who cannot access the financial resources necessary to pay for such health care (WHO, 2004b). Infection, eclampsia and obstructed labour also all require medical intervention, and these pregnancy outcomes together account for nearly half of all maternal deaths. In addition, unsafe abortion with unclean instruments or by untrained personnel is responsible for a further 13 per cent of deaths among pregnant women around the world (WHO, 2004b). The proportion of maternal deaths which are accounted for by unsafe abortion is greatest in countries where there are good prospects for pregnancy and childbirth combined with legal restrictions on abortion – in Argentina, for example, although the maternal mortality rate is relatively low, a third of these deaths are the result of unsafe abortion (Gogna et al., 2002).

It is estimated that, globally, up to half of all pregnancies are unplanned, and a quarter of all pregnancies are unwanted (Costello et al., 2004). While data on abortion are particularly likely to be underreported (Hanson, 1999), estimates suggest that of the 46 million abortions carried out each year, more than 40 per cent are performed in countries where it is illegal, with the attendant risks of untrained providers and unhygienic conditions (WHO, 2004b). Women who have had an illegal abortion are often afraid to seek treatment if there are complications, both because of legal redress and also when they have kept their actions secret from their families, and this further increases the risk of death. Even in countries where abortion is legal, the attitudes and beliefs of health care workers and policy planners may mean that safe abortion is hard to access (Koster-Oyekan, 1998; Harrison et al., 2000). Despite these difficulties, women will choose to risk abortion as one way of retaining control over their bodies when they do not have contraceptive rights, and without access to safe abortion, women will continue to die.

A further fifth of maternal deaths are the result of complications to a woman's health which arise from the pregnancy, defined as indirect maternal deaths (WHO, 2004b). These are also 'avoidable' deaths, which could be prevented given improved access to appropriate antenatal, natal and post-natal health care. However, it is not only a question of health care: other factors increase the risk of death in pregnancy and childbirth, including both age and parity (the number of previous viable pregnancies or births). Deaths in pregnancy and childbirth are more common among younger women, and youth is an additional risk factor particularly in the absence of good services and when nutritional status is poor (Craft, 1997; WHO, 2004b). Globally, women under 20, for example, have twice the risk of dying in childbirth as women over 20, while girls under the age of 15 have five times the risk of dying, (WHO, 2004b; Save the Children, 2004). And if they do survive, both mother and child have a high risk of poor health in later life. An estimated 70,000 such young women die each year around the world, with the highest risks experienced by young women in the Niger, Liberia and Mali, while the lowest risks for younger women are found in Sweden, Denmark and Finland (Save the Children, 2004).

Older women also have a greater risk of complications from pregnancy and poor outcomes – for many of these women their risk is increased as a result of the number of pregnancies and deliveries they have already experienced (Craft, 1997). In all cases, and in all countries, it is women in the most disadvantaged income groups, and women without access to money in their own right, who are most at risk of maternal death due to their poorer nutritional status, reduced access to contraceptives, their greater risk of unplanned pregnancies, the lack of information about safe abortion, and poorer health care (Sundari Ravindran, 2000; Schwarcz and Fescina, 2000; Costello et al., 2004).

Further risks in pregnancy arise when the woman is suffering from other health conditions, including HIV and AIDS, malaria, hepatitis and leprosy, all of which are more common among pregnant women in low-income countries, particularly in Africa (Sundari Ravindran, 2000; Hanson, 1999). Malaria, for example, increases the risk of illness and mortality among pregnant women, while the risk of contracting malaria increases in pregnancy because of women's reduced immunity (WHO, 2004b). Women with HIV and AIDS suffer higher risks in pregnancy and childbirth – for example, in parts of Uganda the maternal mortality rate among HIV-positive women is more than five times the rate for HIV-negative women (WHO, 2004e). There is also an additional risk of malaria and TB among HIV-positive pregnant women, which again increases the hazards of pregnancy and childbirth for such women (WHO, 2003d).

An additional factor affecting maternal health for many women is the practice of female genital mutilation (FGM), most commonly found in African countries, including those with high maternal mortality rates. FGM practices vary, but infibulation, which includes the removal of the clitoris and all or part of the labia minor, followed by the cutting and sewing up of the labia majora, can lead to increased risks in childbirth resulting from extensive internal and external scar tissue, particularly where adequate obstetric care is not available (Black and Debelle, 1995). Many women require operative labour or Caesarean sections after FGM, but this is less available in poorer countries and carries an increased risk of maternal mortality (AbouZahr and Wardlaw, 2001).

If we look at high-income countries, the concerns of most pregnant women are very different. While there are risks of maternal mortality in more developed regions, these risks are slight, with maternal mortality rates of less than 10 per 100,000 live births (WHO, 2004b).

Maternal deaths in more developed countries relate largely to complications in pregnancy and labour, only some of which can be classed as avoidable. In the UK, for example, indirect causes of maternal mortality, such as the aggravation of pre-existing disease due to pregnancy, outnumber direct causes, such as complications in labour (Lewis et al., 2001). Among direct causes, the most common were thrombosis, which accounted for just over a third of direct maternal deaths, and hypertensive disease, which accounted for a sixth of direct deaths. The most important indirect cause relates to cardiac disease, although deaths from suicide are also increasing (Lewis et al., 2001). A high proportion (over 60 per cent) of direct deaths are classified as being due to substandard care by health professionals, while nearly a fifth of deaths relating to indirect causes are also the result of substandard care by the relevant professionals.

The risk of maternal death is not spread evenly across all women in developed countries. In the UK, women from disadvantaged backgrounds are 20 times as likely as non-disadvantaged women to die in pregnancy and childbirth (Lewis et al., 2001). In addition, women from minority ethnic groups in the UK are more likely to die, particularly when women rely on interpreters, often from their own family, to communicate with health providers. Such a reliance on interpreters in pregnancy and labour is likely to increase difficulties where women are unable to communicate easily with a health care provider, and when women feel unable to share important information through an interpreter. Women from the travelling community in the UK also have higher risks of maternal death, related to inadequate standards of care (Lewis et al., 2001). Women who are HIV-positive in developed countries and who have access to health care resources are at greater risk than HIV-negative women, but their chances are good in comparison with women in poorer countries.

As in developing countries, women with a high number of previous pregnancies are more at risk of maternal death, and being very young also carries greater risks of maternal mortality in the developed world. The UK Confidential Enquiry into Maternal Deaths in 2001 reported a specific concern over deaths from indirect causes among young women which were attributable to substandard care. However, the report also highlighted the complexity of factors leading to maternal death – the younger women who died also suffered high levels of disadvantage, domestic violence and sexual abuse (Lewis et al., 2001).

In the USA, the picture also shows higher maternal mortality in disadvantaged populations. Although the risk of dying in childbirth has decreased substantially over time, black and African American women are more than four times as likely to die following complications of pregnancy and childbirth and post-natally compared with white women, and the risk increases substantially for black women over the age of 39 (NCHS, 2004). For white women, being unmarried – and more at risk of poverty – is a risk factor, whereas for black and African American women, the risks are higher for those who are married. The leading causes of death for all women are embolism, haemorrhage and hypertension, although more black women die as a result of anaesthetic complications. Other research has shown that black mothers in the USA are more at risk of having low birthweight and premature babies, regardless of their socio-economic position – something that may be explained by their experiences of racism and violence, rather than exposure to poverty alone (Rich-Edwards et al., 2001).

The concerns of pregnant women overall in more developed countries have in recent years tended to focus on the delivery itself, rather than on questions of safety – in particular, where and how women will deliver, and the issue of power and control. The women's health movement and the natural childbirth movement have campaigned to allow all women to choose how and where they will give birth, and to reduce the medicalization of birth and the disempowerment of women in labour (Lee and Jackson, 2002). Women in more developed countries are also unhappy with the extension of the medical gaze over pregnancy and childbirth – for example, the role of ante-natal care in regulating women, and the use of foetal tests to monitor the unborn child and detect 'abnormalities', and the construction of the pregnant body as pathological, both in the labour ward and beforehand. In most countries where abortion is legal, for example, the grounds for abortion rest on the threat posed by the foetus to the health of the woman (Lee and Jackson, 2002).

Men's involvement in pregnancy and childbirth has been more widely discussed in recent years, and in many high-income countries men's participation in childbirth has increased substantially. The role of men in childbirth is largely seen – by women, by professionals and by men themselves – as that of supporter, whose task is to enable women's labour (Early, 2001), and this is often associated with the idea that a woman may thereby retain more control within the medical setting, by calling on her partner to support her choice over how to labour and how to deliver. It is also possible to see this increased involvement of men in childbirth as related to decreasing funding and reductions in formal health care resources, particularly in the number of staff available. More recently, men's presence at the birth has also been seen as necessary to enable the new baby to bond with the father (Early, 2001).

However, this expectation that men will be involved in childbirth is culturally specific, and the involved father discourse in which men are seen as necessary and valuable to labour is situated within Western practice, while in other cultures the father remains absent (Lupton and Barclay, 1997). As this discourse has grown, the role of the father has extended from supportive helper and bonding father, and in discussions about the psychological consequences of childbirth he is now also referred to, in his own right, as the traumatized father following a difficult birth (Early, 2001).

Biologically, men's health is unaffected by pregnancy, although men may have experienced various health consequences prior to conception if they have gone through infertility treatment. Gender does impact on men's health, however, when their partner is pregnant, and gendered expectations of what men can and should do may carry implications for their physical and mental health. Studies of associations between cancer and parity, for example, have found increased risks of some cancers among women which relate to parity. These findings have been interpreted as indicative of a biological risk factor. More recent studies which have explored men's cancer and associations with parity, however, have found similar relationships between men and the number of children they have, suggesting that more complex social factors associated with parenting are significant (Kravdal, 1995).

What, then, are the solutions to inequalities in pregnancy and childbirth, particularly the gap between women in the developed world and those in less developed countries? Policies to improve outcomes of pregnancy and childbirth and to reduce maternal mortality primarily focus on the availability of good health care and removing barriers to access, especially in an emergency (Berer and Sundari Ravindran, 1999). The majority of maternal deaths occur because of a combination of poor-quality, expensive or inaccessible obstetric services, women's lack of control over resources, particularly the economic resources often needed to access care, women's lack of access to contraception, and women's lack of sexual and reproductive rights.

The World Health Organisation (2004b) estimates that over 80 per cent of maternal deaths are avoidable, and could be prevented with better care or through avoiding action – that is, of the half million deaths annually around the world, the lives of 400,000 women might be saved.

The WHO in 2004 suggested, in the opening pages of a review of maternal deaths, that 'maternal mortality offers a litmus test of women's status, their access to health care and the adequacy of a health care system in responding to their needs' (WHO, 2004b: p. vii). Reproductive rights, including the right to a safe pregnancy, were a part of the 1994 Cairo agreement arising from the United Nations International Conference on Population and Development and have since been reaffirmed at the 1995 Beijing conference and by the inclusion of a target on maternal mortality in the Millennium Development Goals. Recent reports indicate, however, that the goal of reducing the maternal mortality ratio by three-quarters is not being met, with very high levels of maternal deaths continuing in large parts of Africa and Asia (United Nations, 2003).

Skilled health workers and birth attendants are seen as among the central solutions to high maternal mortality (Hussein et al., 2004), but difficulties in making such skilled attendants available wherever necessary include not only the lack of personnel and difficulties in ensuring access, but also income factors and the relatively high cost of obstetric services for low-income families. There are indications of improvements in North Africa, Latin America and Asia in the proportion of births which are attended by skilled health workers, but not in sub-Saharan Africa (AbouZahr and Wardlaw, 2001). The high cost of obstetric care and the unpredictable nature of the total amount which may become necessary – including sometimes 'under-the-table' payments – deter women with complications in pregnancy and childbirth from seeking help when it is needed (Afsana, 2004). In addition, too great an emphasis on clinical solutions should not come at the cost of traditional birth attendants whose skills may be more widely available and more acceptable and appropriate for a majority of deliveries.

In order to reduce maternal mortality, the disadvantage which impairs nutritional status and overall health of women, and affects their strength and resistance during childbirth and labour, must also be addressed. A third strategy focuses on changing the status of young women so that they may be able to delay pregnancy and childbirth until they are older and the risks of maternal injury and death have decreased (Save the Children, 2004). Education both reflects and reinforces improvements in women's status, and also has a positive effect on young women's maternal health and reproductive rights. In addition, strategies to tackle female genital mutilation are needed to reduce the increased risks of maternal morbidity and mortality for women in countries where FGM is practised.

A further related problem is the high risk of adverse health consequences, including unplanned and unwanted pregnancy, resulting from coerced sex and sexual abuse (Ganju et al., 2004a). Younger women are more at risk of maternal injury and death, as we have seen, but for many the cost is compounded by the coercion and abuse which led to the pregnancy in the first place (WHO, 2004b).

Through pregnancy and childbirth, biology has major implications for one aspect of women's health experience. It is women who get pregnant, women whose pregnancies end either in natural or induced abortion or in labour, and therefore it is women's reproductive bodies that carry specific risks for their survival and their health. However, gender is a key factor mediating this risk – gendered divisions of power, for example, limit women's access to financial resources or decision-making processes within the household which might enable them to take advantage of health care to minimize the risk of giving birth. Gender is also implicated in the practice of female genital mutilation, which leads to increased risks in childbirth for women. Gender affects women's health in pregnancy and childbirth in both low-income and high-income countries, although the precise pattern and the weight of impact will vary. However, while gender is important, there is also the wider context in which pregnancy and childbirth take place, and in particular the costs and risks associated with both local global inequalities in income and resources – gender alone does not provide the full explanation for differences in the risks experienced by pregnant women in different parts of the world.

HIV, AIDS and the health of men and women

The second case study we use to explore the influences of sex and gender on the reproductive and sexual health of women and men is HIV and AIDS. As with other conditions, the risks of contracting HIV/AIDs, and of dying from it, are greatest in the poorest parts of the world. Africa, for example, has just over a tenth of the world's population and over two-thirds of the HIV/AIDs population (WHO, 2004e). These inequalities in the risks of HIV- and AIDs-related deaths are a reflection of health status and factors such as nutrition and poverty, of difficulties in accessing treatment in developing countries, of the stage of the epidemic in these regions, and of factors reflecting women's status in particular.

In 2004 the World Health Organisation suggested that 20 million people worldwide have died from AIDS, that between 34 and 46 million more people were living with the virus, and that 6 million people in developing countries would die 'in the near future' without treatment (WHO, 2004e). Data on the prevalence of HIV and AIDS are problematic, for a number of reasons, including lack of disclosure, unknown infection, and difficulties collecting baseline population figures to calculate rates. However, estimates of HIV prevalence among the most affected adult population, those aged 15–49, range from less than 0.1 per cent in many countries around the world, including, for example, Afghanistan, the Czech Republic, Finland and Norway, to a quarter of the population in Zimbabwe, just under a third in Lesotho, and more than a third of the population in Botswana (WHO, 2004e). HIV and AIDS rates are increasing in some countries, but not others, reflecting a range of factors. HIV/AIDS is most widespread in sub-Saharan Africa, with around three-quarters of the world's AIDS deaths in 2003 taking place in these countries (UNAIDS/WHO, 2003; WHO, 2004e). In Asia there were more than 7 million people with HIV/AIDS in 2003, with national prevalence rates averaging around 1 per cent. These rates disguise, however, extremely high prevalence in some groups within countries – up to 80 per cent of drug-users and sex-workers in parts of Vietnam, for example (UNAIDS/WHO, 2003).

Figures showing prevalence rates separately for women and men are subject to the same difficulties, but overall estimates suggest that nearly 50 per cent of the world's HIV- and AIDS-infected population are female (UNAIDS, 2004; WHO, 2004e). The ratio of men to women varies between countries. In the USA, for example, around three-quarters of people living with HIV or AIDS are male (CDC, 2003). In Australia, more than four-fifths of the population with HIV or AIDS are male (National Centre in HIV Epidemiology and Clinical Research, 2004). In other countries – particularly those where the epidemic is greatest – women outnumber men. For example, in Africa, 57 per cent of those infected are female, while among the youngest age groups the proportion of female cases rises to 75 per cent; and female infections have been rising more than male infections around the world (UNAIDS, 2004).

The main health consequences of HIV/AIDS are mortality and high levels of morbidity associated with the greater risk of opportunistic infections. Some of the specific conditions associated with HIV/AIDS, including tuberculosis, malaria and various forms of cancer, occur most often in poorer parts of the world, creating an additional burden of disease for the most vulnerable (Crampin et al., 2004; Bates et al., 2004). While both women and men suffer from such complications, women are further at risk from sex-specific health conditions, including recurrent yeast infections, severe pelvic inflammatory disease, and increased risks of cervical abnormalities and cervical cancer. Women also suffer more from other associated diseases, including STIs, herpes simplex and bacterial pneumonia, which seriously limit their health and make treatment more difficult (NIAID, 2004). In contrast, men with HIV and AIDS are much more likely than women to suffer the form of skin cancer known as Karposi's sarcoma, which may lead to painful swelling, fever and weight loss (NIAID, 2004).

While HIV/AIDS reduces fertility for both women and men, there are implications for pregnancy for women with HIV/AIDS – partly in terms of the treatment needed to reduce the risk of transmission of the virus to the foetus or child, and partly because of the implications of HIV/AIDs status for the woman's health during pregnancy. For example, women with HIV/AIDS are more likely to experience complications of pregnancy, including puerperal fever and anaemia, and infant mortality is also higher (WHO, 2003a; Ross et al., 2004).

Thus there are differences between women and men in the implications of HIV/AIDs for health. How is HIV transmitted? Worldwide, HIV is transmitted primarily through unprotected sexual intercourse between men and women, although unprotected sexual intercourse between men, injecting drug use, unsafe blood transfusions and other injections also account for a proportion of new infections (NIAID, 2004; WHO, 2004e). In addition, there are increasing rates of transmission between pregnant women who are HIV-positive and their children. The risk of this vertical transmission is greatest in low-income and less developed countries, where the maternal viral load is greater, where there is less access to the treatment interventions which might reduce the risk of transmission, and where breast-feeding, which increases opportunities for transmission, continues for longer periods (Bates et al., 2004). For example, one estimate suggests that fewer than 1 per cent of pregnant women in areas with high levels of HIV infection are able to access services and treatment to minimize the risk of transmission to their child (UNAIDS/WHO 2003).

Who is most at risk? Patterns of HIV and AIDS are uneven, both among certain sub-populations and also regionally or geographically.

In Europe, for example, the highest rates of HIV/AIDS are found in Eastern countries with high levels of poverty and deprivation, particularly the Russian Federation, where around 1 million people, mostly men, have HIV/AIDS (UNAIDS/WHO, 2003).

Rates of HIV and AIDS also vary between different ethnic groups. In the USA, half of all HIV and AIDS cases diagnosed in 2003 were black Americans (CDC, 2003), and estimated prevalence rates for HIV and AIDS ranged from 58 per 100,000 population among the black population, 20 per 100,000 in the Hispanic population, 8 per 100,000 among the American Indian and Alaskan Native population, and 6 per 100,000 in the white population (CDC, 2003). Two-thirds of the US population living with AIDS in the USA in 2003 were from black, Hispanic or minority groups. In addition, survival after diagnosis is poorest among black Americans (CDC, 2003).

Most striking are the disproportionate numbers of minority women with HIV and AIDS: three-quarters of the female AIDS population in the USA are African American and Hispanic, although women in these groups make up only a quarter of the population as a whole (NIAID, 2004).

Similarly, in England, Wales and Northern Ireland in 2003, minority ethnic groups made up less than 15 per cent of the population, but just under half of all HIV patients were from minority ethnic groups (HPA, 2003). In Australia, HIV and AIDS rates are similar for indigenous and non-indigenous populations, although in 2002–3 there was a higher rate of HIV diagnosis among the indigenous population compared with the non-indigenous population (National Centre in HIV Epidemiology and Clinical Research, 2004).

One of the features of the disease is that the distribution between men and women changes over time, reflecting different patterns of risk for women and men at different stages of the epidemic. Figures for HIV infections from the Russian Federation illustrate this – in the earliest years of the epidemic, extremely high rates of HIV/AIDS were found in younger people, predominantly among injecting drug-users and predominantly among young men. However, more recently, the number of women being infected has increased dramatically – mostly through heterosexual transmission – and this in turn has led to an increase in vertical or mother–child transmission and growing numbers of children with HIV/AIDS (UNAIDS/WHO, 2003). Similarly, in the UK, infections among heterosexual populations have increased in recent years, while in the first years of the disease the majority of those infected were gay men (HPA, 2003).

Differences between women and men in their risk of infection relate to both sex and gender influences on health. The most common route of transmission worldwide is heterosexual intercourse, and the most significant sex-related factor in such transmission is that women appear to be more vulnerable to infection than men in unprotected heterosexual intercourse (NIAID, 2004; WHO, 2003a). Women's vulnerability to this disease may be greater due to a number of interrelated factors, but in particular because in unprotected vaginal intercourse a large surface area of mucous membrane – the wall of the vagina – is exposed to infectious fluid and because this fluid – semen – carries higher levels of the virus than other bodily fluids (WHO, 2003a). Younger women may be particularly at risk of infection due to immaturity of the vaginal walls and tissue (UNAIDS/WHO, 2003; <www.Aids.net.au>, 2004). Unprotected anal sexual intercourse, between men and men or between men and women, also carries high risks for the receptive partner, due to exposure to seminal fluid and because there is a danger of tearing (WHO, 2003a). It is not yet clear whether women are consistently at greater risk, or if other factors are also involved, and more research on transmission during vaginal and anal intercourse is needed, particularly in relation to men's risks of HIV in heterosexual relationships. Studies of infection in Uganda, for example, have suggested that women and men have similar risks in vaginal intercourse, possibly because more men in Uganda than other African countries are uncircumcised, and this may increase men's risk of infection (NIAID, 2004). Another explanation relates to differences in viral load. Women appear to have lower viral loads than men in the early stage of infection, due to hormonal differences, though this does not appear to affect the progression of the disease in women (Cohn and Clark, 2003; NIAID, 2004). Men's higher viral load, particularly early on, might explain women's greater risk during heterosexual intercourse (WHO, 2003a). Other STIs, which are often asymptomatic and thus go untreated among women, also increase their risks of HIV/AIDS infection (Bates et al., 2004). Pregnant women suffer additional risks of infection through unsafe transfusions and other blood products after complications such as haemorrhage in childbirth, in countries where blood is not screened for the virus (WHO, 2003a).

However, these biological factors interact with gender factors to increase women's risks of HIV/AIDS, and while the nature of this interaction and its impact may differ from one country to the next, the underlying issues often remain the same – for example, cultural pressures for early marriage for women in many countries increase their risk of infection (Fikree and Pasha, 2004). The major gendered factor is that of sexual rights and the extent to which women are able to exercise choice over their sexual freedom. Women's negotiating power in heterosexual encounters – their ability to insist on protected intercourse or to refuse penetrative sex – is shaped by gender. In many countries women are less able to exercise power over their sexual rights in a relationship, while both women and men engaged in sex work may be unable to insist on condom use or may be paid more for sex without the use of a condom (WHO, 2003a). Women may also be forced into sex for economic survival, and this reduces their ability to negotiate safe sex practices, while the cultural ideal of motherhood also reduces women's power to resist unprotected intercourse (WHO, 2003c). Women may be reluctant to take steps to increase their protection for fear of being seen as sex-workers, or as promiscuous, or may be unable to refuse sex because of fear of economic reprisal. Women who are refugees, for example, are often coerced into exchanging sex for travel or protection, and are at increased risk of sexual violence (Kerimova et al., 2003). Sexual abuse and sexual violence impact on women's health in a range of ways, but the risk of HIV infection is a particular threat, not only because women are not protected in intercourse but also because the risk of tearing is greater, and this increases the chance of transmission (Garcia-Moreno and Watts, 2000).

Women with AIDS also have a greater chance of premature death compared with men (WHO, 2004e), which reflects their younger age when infected rather than differences in survival, though variations in survival are difficult to measure when the point of infection is not known. Women's age at infection is affected by the tradition in many developing countries for younger women to marry older men, combined with different perceptions of the acceptability of numerous sexual partners for men and women and the reluctance of men to practise safe sex.

Information about HIV and AIDS and means of protection from the virus is also poorer among women compared with men in low-income countries and among those most at risk – again, particularly younger women (WHO, 2004e). For example, women in Rwanda are twice as likely as men not to know where to go to get a condom, despite the fact that a high proportion of both women and men know that condom use is a key means of preventing HIV infection (DHS, 2000). Similarly, in Zimbabwe, twice as many women as men do not know how to avoid HIV infection (DHS, 1999).

In addition, there are differences in the effects of treatment and in access to treatment (WHO, 2003c). Although in the past it was thought that treatment was less effective for women with HIV/AIDS than for men, it is becoming clear that this is associated with access to interventions and age at onset, as well as with the value of different kinds of intervention for men and women. Higher mortality rates among women with HIV/AIDS may reflect delays in obtaining care, combined with different age profiles. Let us look at these different factors affecting survival separately.

At present, treatment for HIV and AIDS acts to prolong life and maintain health, and there is no cure for the disease. There are also interventions which may reduce the risk of a pregnant or breast-feeding woman transmitting the disease to her child. The main treatments in use are antiretroviral therapy, sometimes described as ARV or ART, including highly active antiretroviral therapy, or HAART. These treatments have side-effects and are accompanied by problems with resistance, but are presently being advocated by WHO and others as the main hope for millions. However, use is not widespread: among the 6 million people in developing countries described as in urgent need of ART, some 93 per cent are not being treated (WHO, 2003f).

The efficacy and side-effects of different treatments vary for women and men. Side-effects of the treatment include muscle wasting, heart failure, nerve damage, degeneration of the liver, and inflammation of the pancreas, as well as nausea and vomiting – and these side-effects may make it difficult for people with HIV and AIDS to continue therapy (NIAID, 2004). Recent research suggests that women may be more responsive to anti-HIV therapy (WHO, 2003c). However, body weight and body fat are important influences on the way in which treatment works: on average women weigh less than men and have higher levels of body fat, which can alter the way in which drugs work in the body, reduce the efficacy of the treatment, and alter the risk of side-effects for men and women (NIAID, 2004). Some studies have also suggested that women's bodies are more able to fight the progression of the disease, although research in this area is still limited (WHO, 2003c).

While treatment is less available in poorer parts of the world and in rural areas, barriers to treatment affect women and men differently. Financial barriers are very important throughout the world, particularly where state-funded care is minimal or non-existent. Women are less able to access treatment due to financial constraints because of the ways in which decisions are taken in households or because women are poorer in their own right. In the USA, for example, women find it harder to access treatment as a result of high costs, lack of insurance and their caring responsibilities (NIAID, 2004). Research also suggests that treatment is more inaccessible for women suffering domestic violence, women who lack support and homeless women (NIAID, 2004).

Gender also affects both women's and men's ability to follow treatment regimes. One of the difficulties affecting HIV/AIDS treatment is the complexity of the regime which must be followed. The medication, particularly those therapies still in use in poorer countries, means that a number of different drugs need to be taken, sometimes after fasting, and the intervals between doses are very precise. For both men and women this can present problems in situations where revealing HIV status may result in discrimination, stigma and loss of employment or family support. These problems are often greater for women, who suffer blame and prejudice due to cultural gendered beliefs about responsibility for the disease, cultural differences in standards of sexual behaviour for women and men, and because women are more often financially dependent on men within the household (WHO, 2003c). Some of the therapies are also not suitable for pregnant women, and women who are unable to disclose their HIV status may find it difficult to resist pressures to become pregnant in countries where a high social value is placed on motherhood, which in turn could put both their own and any child's health further at risk (Manderson, 1999). Even where women are able to tell partners about their status, their fears over becoming mothers are profound. A study of women with HIV in the USA describes their sadness over decisions to limit their fertility for fear of passing on the virus:

> 'We know what this virus does. There is no need playing with that. I just don't feel that you should put a child through that.'
>
> 'You may have a baby to love and to remember and cherish. But when you see that child waste away under your eyes, and you know that you could have avoided that pain.' (Ingram and Hutchinson, 2000: 123)

In treatment strategies for HIV and AIDs identified by the World Health Organisation and other organizations, gender equity in the promotion of information about treatment and access to services is critical. Attempts to halt the spread of the disease particularly among women will falter unless these identify barriers to women's or men's participation in treatment. There is a need for gender-sensitive treatment protocols, and also for better understanding of the side-effects and allied health conditions experienced by women or by men – for example, gynaecological complications of HIV/AIDS need to be monitored more carefully.

A further dimension in HIV and AIDS is the role of socio-economic status, poverty and disadvantage. Low socio-economic status is associated with greater exposure to HIV risk and to HIV infections (Sanders-Phillips, 2002). The rapid rise in the level of infections among African American women in the USA, for example, reflects complex influences, including both social and cultural factors. Among social factors, environmental stress and economic inequality are significant variables. Zierler and Krieger (1997), for example, write of how the dramatic increase in poverty in the USA following economic recession and social and economic policies during the Reagan era pushed millions of women – particularly African American and Hispanic women – into poverty. Such poverty, combined with experiences of racism and gender discrimination, affects health and the risk of HIV infection, both through decreased resistance to infection, as women's power in negotiating sexual relationships is reduced, and as women turn to drugs and sexual intimacy to escape their poverty.

Some of the greater risk experienced by black women may reflect differences in exposure to sexual trauma. Both women and men with a history of sexual trauma, including childhood sexual abuse and rape, are more at risk of HIV than those without such a history, because of an association between sexual trauma and subsequent risk-taking behaviour and because increased alcohol use also contributes to HIV-related risks (Wyatt et al., 2002; McNair and Prather, 2004). A study of HIV-positive and negative American women, for example, found that HIV-positive women had higher rates of sexual trauma, but rates were greatest among African American HIV-positive women, suggesting that this may be an important contributory factor to the disproportionate number of minority women with HIV/AIDS in the USA (Wyatt et al., 2002).

Women from minority backgrounds also describe using alcohol and drugs – particularly crack cocaine – to 'numb the pain' following such abuse, as well as the pain of experiences of racism and prejudice: 'That's my easy way out, get high, it was easy. That's my way out of bein' hurt, angry, in pain' (cited in Ehrmin, 2002: 780). Such substance use increases their risk of a number of health problems, but also HIV infection both if injecting and also when prostitution is the means of funding substance use. In addition to the pain of sexual trauma, racism and prejudice, women in such impoverished circumstances must also deal with other forms of loss – from neighbourhood violence or the deaths of others with HIV/AIDS and other diseases, for example (Zierler and Krieger, 1997). Similarly, in a study in London of African women living with AIDS, one of the most common problems was loss, both of their identity as mothers – many had children left behind in Africa, while others were afraid of becoming mothers – and of their children who had died of AIDS (Doyal and Anderson, 2005). For black and minority women, whether in the USA or elsewhere, the risk of HIV infection follows the intersection of race/ethnicity, gender and socio-economic class – the factors affecting their increased vulnerability reflect material resources, poverty, neighbourhood deprivation, access to health care, but also different aspects of discrimination, power, exposure to specific risks such as violence and abuse, and responses to pain, including substance use and sexual risk taking.

One development which may reduce the transmission of HIV and which may empower both women and men is the role of microbicides in the prevention of HIV and other STIs. Microbicides are products which may be self-administered vaginally or anally, and clinical trials suggest that there may be few side-effects. As such, these interventions offer women and men the opportunity to protect themselves against infection. This is particularly valuable for those who have little control over their sexual rights, including those at risk of sexual violence who cannot insist on safe sex practices, and sex-workers. As yet, microbicides offer more hope than help, however, as they are still on trial, and are not yet freely available (NIAID, 2004).

Gendered dimensions of power are also significant in understanding the transmission of the virus in sexual practices between men and men. Homosexual acts continue to be stigmatized and denied in many parts of the world, creating an environment in which information on safe sex for gay men is minimal, as is information about the spread of the disease and the risks involved. Factors influencing the risk of transmission through unsafe heterosexual sex and through unsafe homosexual sex include gender and constructions of masculinity around penetrative sex, unprotected intercourse and coercive sex, which carries greater risks of infection for the victim. Masculinity also creates an environment in which homosexuality remains hidden, and while coercive sex between men increases risks, it may be less frequently reported in some areas due to the shame and the stigma which surround homosexual practices (Ganju et al., 2004b).

Conclusion

This chapter has focused on reproductive and sexual health. These are perhaps areas where the part played by biological factors in the health of men and women, and in explanations of health differences between men and women, might be expected to be most significant. And of course there are important variations in this aspect of health which reflect sex and biology – women do experience specific risks of poor health and mortality as a result of pregnancy, childbirth, menstrual and menopausal conditions, for example, while men experience other biologically specific conditions. However, gendered factors remain important in explanations of exposure to risk and what happens once a disease is contracted. The most important gender-related factors in explaining the differences between women's and men's health worldwide are differences in access to resources, differences in power – particularly over sexual and reproductive rights – and the ways in which masculinity and femininity shape behaviour and the delivery of health care.

6 Death, Dying, Sex and Gender

Introduction

Earlier chapters have explored the relationships between health, sex and gender, looking at patterns of ill health and morbidity, mental health, and reproductive and sexual health. This chapter looks at the ways in which the risk of death and the causes of death vary for men and women across the life course. To what extent are our chances of a long life related to our biological sex, and what part is played by gender in longevity? Data on life expectancy, age at death and causes of death for men and women are central to this exploration of differences between men and women in relation to sex or gender.

Death, is of course, a fairly limited way of measuring health – increases in life expectancy in both developed and developing countries have rendered the use of mortality data alone to measure health more and more inappropriate. However, mortality remains helpful when exploring differences in the health experience of men and women, because the gap between them in expected life span persists, alongside other inequalities in death – between those who live in the more developed world and those in developing countries, for example, between those who live in affluent circumstances and those who are poor, between different social classes, and between people from different ethnic groups. As in earlier chapters, the intersection between gender, social class and race/ethnicity is also important in explaining differences in the risk of mortality.

A major part of this chapter is taken up with discussion of such inequalities in death, but first we need to consider the extent to which death is socially constructed and 'gendered' – are there differences in the experience of death, and in the way death is recorded and measured which reflect gender relations?

The meaning of death

There are many studies which use mortality data to identify who dies, from what, and at what age. This research draws on a range of sources, but in particular aggregate data compiled from documentation at the level of the individual about the causes of death and about the person who has died. When a death occurs, it must be catalogued and explained. In the USA, for example, death certificates are completed by funeral directors, attending physicians, medical examiners and coroners' courts, and they include information on sex, age at death, causes of death, parents' names, address, race and ethnicity, level of education, occupation, and whether the deceased was ever in the armed forces. In the UK, death certificates collect information on sex, age at death, residence, occupation and marital status, together with medical data on the causes of death, given by an attending physician. Explanations are sought for what is seen as 'premature death', 'undue mortality' and 'avoidable' death, terms which divide death into two categories of mortality: that which is expected, understood and inevitable, and that which is unexpected, unacceptable, and which could have been prevented.

When the data collected are aggregated, this reduces the individual death to a quantifiable event, the risk of which can be predicted in advance, given precise and sufficient information about characteristics which affect risk, including age, sex, ethnic group, area or location, behaviour and individual history. Such predictions are not wholly accurate – there are individuals who adopt risky behaviour but who die of old age, rather than prematurely, just as there are those who confound prediction by dying young despite a healthy lifestyle. However, in the act of calculating mortality risk, these deaths become exceptions, and therefore statistically explicable 'outliers' which help to define the normal. In contrast to medical and epidemiological approaches to death, in which the moment and cause of death are seen as knowable, social science research has opened up the idea of death as a social or discursive construction in which spiritual and religious beliefs and cultural and lay understandings also play a part in defining its meaning.

Death and discourse: 'survival as a social construct'

In modern and late-modern societies in the developed world, our understandings of death and of survival are culturally and socially constructed. The causes of death – the information contained on the death certificate, for example, and the way this information is aggregated – reflect social as well as medical factors. Prior's (1989) research on the social organization of death in Belfast suggests that many of the apparently taken-for-granted aspects of death are less clear-cut than might be thought. Prior (1989) looks at the ways in which death is categorized into specific causes of death reflecting social discourse, about 'good' and 'bad' death, and natural and avoidable death, as well as medical discourse. The doctor certifying the death, for example, may offer a number of explanations of death on the death certificate, yet the person who abstracts this data from the certificate has to decide on the most significant of these causes. Age, gender and socio-economic status all affect the allocation of causes of death and whether death is viewed as 'natural'. Prior (1989) found that the deaths of men, particularly employed men, were more frequently referred to the coroner compared with those of women (Prior, 1989: 59). Similarly Phillimore (1989) found that middle-class men in the North of England were more likely to have several causes of death listed on the death certificate than men from lower socio-economic groups. Classification of death as unnatural in the Western world relates to two things: the availability of a medical interpretation, even where the actual cause remains unclear, and the involvement of human agency. Sudden infant death syndrome (SIDS), for example, is classified as a 'natural death', because it fits within medical discourse of conditions affecting young children, despite the medical profession's incomplete understanding of the syndrome. More adult male deaths are 'unnatural' than those of women, because more men than women die as a result of human agency through suicide, homicide and accidental death (WHO, 2004e); but men's 'natural' deaths are not always obviously natural – Prior's research in Belfast, for example, found that deaths resulting from the use of plastic bullets among men in the 1980s were classified as 'natural' despite the involvement of human agency.

Even the event of death itself is seen in different ways. Medical perspectives focus on determining the moment of bodily death, just as debates over termination of pregnancy focus on the moment at which life begins. Social science literature, however, has explored death as a social process, shaped both by individual history and by the culture in which death takes place. In non-Western cultures people may be understood by the community to be both physically alive yet socially dead, particularly those who are nearing the end of life (Prior, 1989). In many countries the practice of moving the dying out of a main public ward to a side ward in the hospital can be seen as part of the transition to death which offers the family privacy at an intensely emotional moment, but which also avoids confronting the survivors with the fact of dying and their own mortality. There are also differences in location of death: studies in the USA suggest that some people – those who are unmarried (especially men), non-white and from low socio-economic groups in particular – are more likely to die in an institution than white, high socio-economic and married people (Grundy et al., 2004). But in this transition discourse, few questions have been asked about gender, or whether men and women 'do' death differently.

In theory, at least, mortality data have fewer flaws than data on health or morbidity, precisely because death is seen as unarguable, and the sections that follow present statistics on deaths of men and women, and other groups, as though this is true. But there are gaps in mortality data, particularly for deaths in developing countries and, where mortality is calculated as a ratio based on the living, then inaccuracies in population data are also important. We need to remain aware of these gaps, and also of potential gendered differences in how data on death are collected, in the figures we are about to explore.

Death, sex and gender

Statistics for death can be explored over the life course – life expectancy from birth and death rates at different ages, for example – and also for different causes, some of which will be more common at certain ages. Such data reveal some key differences between women and men in the risk of death and the cause of death which relate to both sex and gender, while also being mediated by factors such as ethnic group, income and social class.

The most obvious difference between men and women in both developed and developing countries is that men suffer an increased risk of death in comparison with women at every age. Crude death rates and figures for life expectancy, for example, largely show an excess of male mortality, and greater life expectancy for women, throughout the world (WHO, 2004e). However, the advantage that women have over men in terms of longevity has not remained static over time, and the gap between women and men is not constant throughout the life course. For example, in 1978 global figures for life expectancy at birth suggested that men had on average three years less life expectancy than women; by 1998 the gap was four years (WHO, 1999). The size of the gap between women and men is also not consistent for all countries.

Table 6.1 Male and female life expectancy at birth, 2002, and sex ratio in life expectancy – ten countries with highest and lowest life expectancy for both sexes, 2002

Countries with highest and lowest life expectancy at birth, 2002	Female life expectancy at birth	Male life expectancy at birth	Female life expectancy as percentage of male
Japan	85.3	78.4	108.8
Monaco	84.5	77.8	108.6
Switzerland	83.3	77.7	107.2
San Marino	84.0	77.2	108.8
Sweden	82.6	78.0	105.9
Australia	83.0	77.9	106.5
Andorra	83.7	76.8	109.0
Iceland	81.8	78.4	104.3
France	83.6	76.0	110.0
Canada	82.3	77.2	106.6
Burkino Faso	42.6	40.6	104.9
Burundi	43.0	38.7	111.1
Botswana	40.6	40.2	101.0
Malawi	40.6	39.8	102.0
Angola	42.0	37.9	110.8
Zambia	40.2	39.1	102.8
Swaziland	40.4	36.9	109.5
Zimbabwe	38.0	37.7	100.8
Lesotho	38.2	32.9	116.1
Sierra Leone	35.7	32.4	110.2

Source: WHO, 2004e, Annex Table 1

Table 6.1 illustrates some of the differences in the ratio of female to male life expectancy for countries with the best overall life expectancy and those with poorest overall life expectancy in 2002. In both those countries with the best overall life expectancy at birth and those with the poorest life expectancy, women can expect to live longer than men. The advantage, in terms of additional years of life anticipated, is generally better for women in the high life expectancy countries, but this is not always the case.

Table 6.2 shows those countries which have the widest gap between male and female life expectancy and those with the narrowest gap between women and men. In the Maldives, for example, female life expectancy at birth is lower than that for males, but life expectancy overall is in the middle range. Male life expectancy in Qatar is slightly

Table 6.2 The gap between male and female life expectancy, 2002 – countries with 10 or more years' difference, and countries with 1 year or less

Country	Male life expectancy at birth	Female life expectancy at birth	Gap in years between female and male life expectancy at birth
Russian Federation	58.3	71.8	13.5
Estonia	65.1	77.1	12.0
Belarus	62.6	74.3	11.7
Lithuania	66.2	77.6	11.4
Latvia	64.6	75.8	11.2
Ukraine	61.7	72.9	11.2
Seychelles	67.0	77.2	10.2
Kazakhstan	58.7	68.9	10.2
Malawi	39.8	40.6	0.8
Pakistan	61.1	61.6	0.5
Botswana	40.2	40.6	0.4
Nepal	59.9	60.2	0.3
Zimbabwe	37.7	38.0	0.3
Niger	42.6	42.7	0.1
Bangladesh	62.6	62.6	0.0
Maldives	66.5	65.6	−0.9
Qatar	74.8	73.8	−1.0

Source: WHO, 2004e, Annex Table 1

higher than that for females, but life expectancy in general is relatively high there. However, in other countries where the gap between women and men is narrow, life expectancy generally is poor. There are factors which affect the mortality risk of both women and men in some of these countries – including, in particular, high rates of HIV and AIDS – but these factors are not high contributors to mortality in all those countries where the gap between women and men is narrow.

The top half of table 6.2 shows those countries where women's chances of a longer life are considerably greater than those of men – over 13 years more in the case of the Russian Federation. It is striking that seven out of eight of these countries are clustered together both geographically and in terms of recent history. These are 'new' countries from the former state socialist bloc, and they are countries with high levels of poverty and deprivation (Mosley and Kalyuzhnova, 2000). In these locations life expectancy for men has fallen dramatically in recent years. Explanations of why this should be the case for men rather than women converge around health behaviour, particularly higher levels of smoking, substance and alcohol misuse among men, together with high levels of suicide and violent death among men in these countries, and increasing HIV infection rates (Marmot and Bobak, 2000). It is also possible that men's health reacts more quickly to deteriorations in material circumstances, although as Sally Macintyre (2001) points out, there is little research on the ways in which men and women are affected by such changes in the physical and social environment.

What these tables suggest is that there is no 'natural' mortality gap between men and women – the differences in the ratio of female to male life expectancy seen in table 6.2 reflect a variety of factors, including both biology and gender relations, which vary culturally, economically and socially. In countries where women's life expectancy advantage over men is low, the question we need to ask is what has prevented women from moving to a position of advantage similar to that found among women in other countries. In countries where the gap between women and men is widest, the question is instead what has prevented men from keeping up with women, particularly where overall life expectancy is increasing at different rates for women and men.

The data on the differences in life expectancy between men and women highlight the extent to which explanations need to explore both social differences between men and women as gendered subjects and biological differences between males and females. We can illustrate this through two examples.

A number of studies have explored life expectancy and mortality for nuns and monks, particularly those living in very similar circumstances. Such studies have found that while nuns retain some of the female advantage in life expectancy, the gap narrows to around one year (Luy, 2003). There are particular differences which affect these findings – the figures begin in adulthood, and therefore do not include mortality in early life due to biological risk factors, and also the absence of reproduction among nuns affects their biological health risks. However, the narrowing of the gap between women and men in such cloistered populations does begin to suggest the importance of gender-related factors.

The second illustration of the influence of sex and gender comes from the relative risks of premature death for girl and boy children. Around the world, female children have better chances of survival in the womb, at birth and in the early years of life (Craft, 1997). However, in some countries this is turned on its head: in India and China, for example, the male to female ratio is unusually high at birth, boys are more likely survive their early years than in comparable countries, and life expectancy at birth for female children is reduced (Allahbadia, 2002; Murphy, 2003). The major threat affecting female foetuses and children in these countries is social, rather than physiological, in origin – the selective termination of a pregnancy on the basis of sex, infanticide affecting female but not male children, and neglect of the girl child (Pearson, 2005).

The ratio of male to female deaths also changes across the life course. In the Russian Federation, for example, the ratio of male to female deaths varies from slightly more male deaths than female deaths up to the age of 4 and also over the age of 75, with a much wider gap in the years in between, particularly in young adulthood, when men are around four times as likely to die as women. Similarly, in Japan the ratio of male deaths to female deaths is fairly narrow during infancy and early childhood, but between the ages of 15 and 75, the male death rate is at least twice that of females (WHOSIS, 2005). In the UK, the risk of mortality is slightly higher for younger boys than for girls, but the differences are much greater over the age of 15, with particularly high mortality among 15–24-year-old men. Data on mortality by age and sex are harder to find for the countries with the poorest life expectancy, particularly those countries in the lower half of table 6.1, although infant mortality figures are often available. In the UK, for example, the male infant mortality rate is 6.5 per 1,000 live births, compared with the female rate of 5.5, and in the USA, male infant mortality is 7.2 compared with a female infant mortality rate of 5.8 per 1,000 live births. However, in the Russian Federation the male infant mortality is over 17, compared with a female rate of 13, while in Côte d'Ivoire, male infant mortality is 114 per 1,000 births, and the female rate is 80 (WHOSIS, 2005; <cia.gov, 2005>).

If we look at the probability of dying prematurely, table 6.3 shows that in countries where life expectancy is highest overall, there is a wider gap between women and men in later life than earlier on, while in countries where life expectancy overall is low, there is less difference in the gap between males and females in different age groups. This can be interpreted in a variety of ways, and a number of factors play a part, including the effect on mortality of conflict, violence, poverty and specific infectious conditions, including HIV. However, these gaps also indicate the extent to which biology and gender play different roles in shaping the health of women and men in various circumstances. In particular, in more affluent countries the much greater risk of mortality suffered by adult men is related to gendered differences in health lifestyles, including smoking, substance and

Table 6.3 Probability of dying per 1,000 population, ages 0–5 and 15–60, in countries with highest and lowest overall life expectancy

Country	Probability of dying under 5*		M : F ratio	Probability of dying between 15 and 60*		M : F ratio
	M	F		M	F	
Japan	4	4	1: 1.0	95	46	1: 2.1
Monaco	5	3	1: 1.7	109	47	1: 2.3
Switzerland	6	5	1: 1.2	92	51	1: 1.8
San Marino	5	3	1: 1.7	85	31	1: 2.7
Sweden	4	3	1: 1.3	83	53	1: 1.6
Australia	6	5	1: 1.2	91	52	1: 1.7
Andorra	5	4	1: 1.2	113	43	1: 2.6
Iceland	4	3	1: 1.3	85	55	1: 1.5
France	6	4	1: 1.5	135	60	1: 2.2
Canada	6	5	1: 1.2	95	58	1: 1.6
Burkino Faso	232	217	1: 1.1	597	522	1: 1.1
Burundi	189	177	1: 1.1	692	563	1: 1.2
Botswana	104	102	1: 1.0	786	745	1: 1.0
Malawi	197	190	1: 1.0	657	610	1: 1.1
Angola	279	247	1: 1.1	594	481	1: 1.2
Zambia	191	176	1: 1.1	700	654	1: 1.1
Swaziland	150	142	1: 1.0	818	707	1: 1.1
Zimbabwe	115	107	1: 1.1	821	789	1: 1.0
Lesotho	166	160	1: 1.0	902	742	1: 1.2
Sierra Leone	322	303	1: 1.1	682	569	1: 1.2

Source: WHO, 2004e, Annex Table 1
*Original data also include uncertainty level figures which have been omitted here.

alcohol use, the way men use health care, and risk-taking behaviours resulting in accidental and non-accidental injury. In poorer countries, where levels of health care and standards of living and nutrition are poor, young girls and women do not enjoy the same advantage in life expectancy over men, and this reflects access to resources in particular. Hart (1987), for example, suggested that improvements in female life expectancy following growth in national income reflect the 'biological superiority' of women, which becomes evident when women, even in unfair societies, have access to more resources, particularly better standards of nutrition. In comparison, men's health is impaired by the same growth in resources, due to their increased participation in unhealthy behaviour, especially smoking and alcohol consumption.

Table 6.4 Deaths by major cause, sex and mortality, 2002, in WHO member states

Cause of death	All '000	Males '000	Percent of all male deaths	Females '000	Percent of all female deaths
Cardiovascular diseases	16,733	8,120	27.2	8,613	31.7
Infectious and parasitic diseases	10,904	5,795	19.4	5,109	18.8
Malignant neoplasms	7,121	3,974	13.3	3,147	11.6
Respiratory infections	3,963	1,989	6.7	1,974	7.3
Respiratory diseases	3,702	1,912	6.4	1,790	6.6
Unintentional injuries	3,551	2,307	7.7	1,244	4.6
Intentional injuries	1,618	1,157	3.9	461	1.7
Digestive diseases	1,968	1,094	3.7	874	3.2
All causes	57,029	29,891	100.0	27,138	100.0

Source: WHO, 2004e, Annex 2

Causes of death

Just as there are differences between women and men in data on health which relate to specific kinds of illness, so there are further differences in relation to some of the major causes of death in both developed and less developed countries around the world.

In 2002 there were more than 57 million deaths worldwide, including 30 million male deaths and 27 million female deaths (WHO, 2004e). Table 6.4 shows the number and percentage of male and female deaths in each of the major categories, which together accounted for nearly 90 per cent of all mortality in 2002. As the table reveals, there are only small differences between women and men in mortality when we break it down by cause: cardiovascular disease, for example, accounted for a slightly greater proportion of deaths among women, while similar proportions of women's and men's mortality resulted from infectious disease, cancer and respiratory conditions. It is only with injury-related mortality that we see a greater proportion of deaths among men.

More than half of all deaths worldwide are from non-communicable diseases (NCDs) largely associated with environmental and lifestyle factors, including tobacco use, alcohol, diet, occupation and pollution. A slightly higher proportion of female deaths are due to NCDs compared with those of men. Communicable diseases include HIV/AIDs, respiratory infections and tuberculosis, and in total account for just under a third of all deaths, with slightly more male than female deaths.

Injury-related deaths, including homicide, suicide, accidents and deaths from conflict situations, account for a further eighth of all deaths worldwide, including twice as many deaths among men as women (WHO, 2004e).

However, the contribution to total mortality made by different causes of death varies in different countries. A greater proportion of mortality in poorer regions results from deaths from HIV/AIDS and other infectious conditions, and fewer deaths are the result of cardiovascular disease and neoplasms. In contrast, a higher proportion of mortality in developed countries comes from non-communicable diseases, particularly heart disease and cancer. In the poorest parts of Africa, for example, three-quarters of all mortality is due to communicable disease, with 20 per cent resulting from NCDs and 7 per cent from injury. In those parts of North and South America which have the greatest life expectancy, mortality from communicable disease is 6 per cent, while NCD mortality accounts for nearly 90 per cent of deaths (WHO, 2004e).

The risk of death from different causes of mortality also varies across the life course in both high- and low-income countries: accidental death, for example, is a more significant cause of death among younger age groups, whereas deaths from cardiovascular disease increase in later life.

Looking in detail at mortality figures for women and men, cardiovascular disease is the most common cause of death for both, accounting for nearly 17 million deaths, over a quarter of all male deaths and a third of female deaths (WHO, 2004e). Ischaemic heart disease alone accounted for more than 7 million deaths worldwide in 2002, and while the mortality rate for this disease is stabilizing in developed countries, the number of such deaths in less developed countries is increasing rapidly. Ischaemic heart disease mortality is higher among men – for example, in northern Europe male mortality rates are around twice those for women (WHO, 2004e). However, there are slightly more female deaths than male deaths from cerebrovascular disease and stroke, which together accounted for more than 5.5 million deaths worldwide (WHO, 2004e).

While overall, women and men have very similar risks of dying from heart disease, there are marked differences in the risk of cardiovascular mortality in relation to age. With cerebrovascular disease and stroke, for example, once mortality is adjusted for age, the mortality rate for men is higher than that for women (EUROSTAT, 2003). Men are more at risk of premature death from heart conditions, while cardiovascular disease fatalities among women are more common in later life (Weidner, 2000; Shaw et al., 2000). In England and Wales in 2002, ischaemic heart disease deaths for men of working age are more than four times greater than such deaths among women of the same age, and in total nearly five times as many years of life are lost as a result of premature mortality among men than women (ONS, 2003).

What accounts for the differences between women and men in their risk of fatal heart disease? Explanations of the different risks of cardiovascular mortality experienced by women and men over the life course are complex, and draw on both biological factors and gender-linked ones. Differences between women and men in patterns of heart disease which relate to biological causes are particularly associated with hormonal factors. Being male is a risk for early heart disease due to the protective influence of oestrogen for women (Pollard, 1999), while women in later life, particularly after the menopause, are more at risk than either younger women or men of the same age. However, although heart disease is more common among older than younger women, the risk increases most over the age of 70 – that is, a number of years after the menopause has ended. This suggests that other factors may also be involved in women's risk over and above the changes associated with declining levels of oestrogen (Wenger, 1997).

Gendered explanations of differences in heart disease relate to lifestyle factors which increase men's risks, in particular the fact that in many cultures men smoke more than women, drink more alcohol, are more likely to be overweight (but not obese), and more often have diets which are high in fat and low in fruit and vegetables.

There are also gender differences in diagnosis and treatment, reflecting the stereotype of heart disease as something experienced by men, which increase women's risks of mortality. For example, women are more likely than men to suffer what is described as 'silent' myocardial infarction, where symptoms are not obvious, and to experience atypical symptoms, which may mean that treatment is delayed. More women die following a heart attack than men, partly because of these differences in symptoms, but also because women's heart disease is less well understood due to the fact that it is still relatively under-researched (Pollard, 1999; Gijsbers Van Wijk et al., 1996). Differences between women and men in the way in which heart disease manifests itself and in associated mortality also reflect interactions between sex and gender. Smoking, for example, is a gendered behaviour which affects cardiovascular health of both men and women, but it is a behaviour which appears to raise women's risk of heart disease more than it does for men as a result of biological factors, including the impact of smoking on reductions in oestrogen (Judelson, 1994; Prescott et al., 1998; Pollard, 1999).

Infectious and parasitic diseases are the second most significant cause of death worldwide. These diseases contributed just under one-fifth of both male and female mortality around the world in 2002 (WHO, 2004e). Within this category the most significant causes of death were diarrhoea, childhood diseases such as measles and whooping cough, HIV/AIDS, tuberculosis (TB) and malaria. Most of these accounted for similar proportions of male and female deaths, although there were slightly more male than female deaths due to TB. These conditions are a more significant cause of mortality in developing parts of the world than in more developed countries. In 2002 nearly 80 per cent of the total deaths from infectious and parasitic conditions took place in Africa and South-East Asia, for example, with a particularly high proportion of TB deaths in South-East Asia, and high levels of HIV/AIDS and malaria deaths in Africa (WHO, 2004e).

Most malaria deaths are among children under 5, with very similar numbers of deaths for boys and girls (WHO, 2004e; Bates et al., 2004). Malaria mortality among adults is also fairly evenly distributed among men and women, although women are particularly vulnerable to infection during pregnancy, and malaria deaths are an important part of maternal mortality in some countries (Bates et al., 2004; Tolhurst and Nyonator, 2002). While women's biology increases their susceptibility to tropical diseases in comparison with men, gender-linked factors also affect vulnerability. For example, gender divisions of paid and unpaid labour in many parts of the world mean that women are responsible for water collection and harvesting, both activities which increase exposure to infection (Bates et al., 2004; United Nations, 2003). Women's roles in agriculture in a number of countries have increased in recent years, while men's work in this sphere has decreased, and this is likely to add to women's risks of malaria, as well as increased risks of other infectious diseases, including schistosomiasis (Amazigo, 1998; Vlassoff and Bonilla, 1994). Women are also less able to access malaria treatment where there are out-of-pocket expenses, cultural restrictions on travel to clinics for treatment, and where seeking treatment for malaria by women is seen as constituting weakness (Tolhurst and Nyonator, 2002; Jones and Williams, 2004).

Cancer deaths are the third largest group, representing more than 12 per cent of all mortality worldwide, with similar proportions of male and female deaths (WHO, 2004e). Lung and associated cancers are the most common cause of cancer mortality, and despite the fact that increasing numbers of women smoke, male deaths continue to outnumber those for women by three to one. There is a similarly high male to female mortality ratio for deaths from liver, stomach and bladder cancer. Cancer of the female reproductive organs in 2002 accounted for more than 900,000 deaths among women, nearly a third of all cancer deaths among women, while male prostate cancer was responsible for less than 7 per cent of male cancer deaths (WHO, 2004e).

Although the total numbers of cancer-related deaths among women and men are very similar, gender and biology play different parts in their overall risk of cancer mortality. For men the major disease, lung cancer, is primarily associated with lifestyle and behaviour. For women, however, the major causes of cancer-related deaths are associated with female biology and reproductive factors. Other gendered factors which are also significant in explaining cancer mortality for men and women include differences in diet, obesity, alcohol use, environmental pollution, and work-related exposure to carcinogens (Waldron, 1991). There is increasing evidence that a diet rich in fruit and vegetables may reduce cancer risk, for example, and while in many parts of the world men and women have diets lacking in fruit and vegetables, more women than men consume fruit and vegetables at levels which may offer them protection against some forms of cancer (Cummings and Bingham, 1998). Alcohol use has been associated with increased cancer of the oral cavity and pharynx, oesophagus and larynx, and also liver cancer (Bagnardi et al., 2001), and men's greater consumption of alcohol in comparison with women puts them more at risk of these cancers. Although some women work in jobs which expose them to carcinogens, more men overall have employment which places them at higher risk of occupational-related cancers (Wunsch et al., 1998). Women, on the other hand, suffer higher risks of exposure to pollution at home, particularly in parts of the world where coal-based fires are used for heating and cooking (Luo et al., 1996; Keohavong et al., 2003). However, differences in cancer survival also affect mortality rates: women seem to survive longer than men after cancer is diagnosed. For example, in one study in the USA, two-thirds of white women diagnosed with Non-Hodgkin's Lymphoma survived five years or more, compared with just over half of white men. While black and African American men and women had poorer survival rates than the white population, over half the women survived five years or more, compared with two-fifths of the men (NCHS, 2004). Among both white and non-white populations, women are more likely to survive the first five years after diagnosis with lung cancer (although generally survival for lung cancer is particularly poor), pancreatic cancer, cancer of the rectum and colorectal cancer (Petrek et al., 1985; Keller et al., 2002).

These differences in survival relate to both biology and gender, including differences between women and men in treatment-seeking behaviour, the use of screening services, and the availability of screening. For example, screening programmes for breast and cervical cancer in developed countries help to identify cases early enough to influence outcome, while screening for prostate and testicular cancer is less widely available, and screening for lung cancer is also rarely used (Wisnivesky et al., 2003). Screening may not be offered where tests pick up too many 'false positives' leading to unnecessary interventions and stress. Lung cancer screening, for example, produces a number of false positives, as well as identifying pre-cancerous lesions. A relatively small proportion of prostate cancer is fatal if untreated, and in many cases the medical decision is not to treat, as the treatment itself is highly invasive and carries health costs (Siddall, 1993; Rumm and Johnson, 2002). In contrast, cervical cancer screening and early treatment have significantly reduced mortality in developed countries, and while cervical cancer remains a major cause of cancer-related mortality among women in less developed countries, this is because screening is not widely available, and women with this cancer are not diagnosed in time (WHO, 2003b; Sankaranarayanan et al., 2001).

The fourth group of mortality causes in terms of contribution to global mortality relate to the infections of the respiratory system, which accounted for nearly 4 million deaths in 2002. Most of these were deaths of children – slightly more boys than girls – and most were caused by acute lower respiratory infections (ALRIs), including pneumonia (WHO, 2004e).

Mortality from non-communicable respiratory diseases, rather than respiratory infection, accounted for around 6 per cent of deaths worldwide in 2002. This figure included similar numbers of male and female deaths from chronic obstructive pulmonary disease (COPD), which is associated largely with smoking and environmental pollution. Again, different factors are involved which reflect gender – differences in smoking, work-based and home-based pollution, in particular.

A further 5 million deaths resulted from accidental and non-accidental injuries in 2002, including nearly twice as many male as female deaths (WHO, 2004e). Deaths from both injuries and violence are particularly marked in low- and middle-income countries, and account for a high proportion of premature mortality among younger men in these countries as well as more widely (Krug et al., 2000). The case study at the end of this chapter explores these differences in more detail.

Sex, gender and mortality

These, then, are the major causes of death and the ways in which they vary worldwide for women and men. Overall, the picture shows many similarities. Variations do exist for some causes of death, and also in the risk of death from specific causes at different ages. However, for some causes of death, particularly infectious diseases, the most important health variations relate to part of the world, income inequalities, and stage of development, rather than sex or gender.

Overall, biological factors reduce women's risks of premature death through the protective effects of female hormones, and men have a correspondingly greater risk of death in middle life because they do not have this protection, particularly in association with heart disease. Biology also affects the risk of cancer mortality, not only in relation to specific reproductive cancers but also more generally. Both smoking and non-smoking women have a greater risk than men of lung cancer at the same level of exposure, for example, as a result of sex-linked differences in gene expression, while men have a greater risk of other cancers (Wizeman and Pardue, 2000). The gap between women and men in mortality is also affected by differences in cancer survival, which are partly associated with biological factors.

Gender-linked factors also affect the mortality of women and men. First, health behaviour and lifestyle increase men's risks of death in adolescence and early adulthood, and also in later life. Gendered differences in the use of tobacco and alcohol, in substance misuse, diet, aggressive behaviour and risk taking, and in their use of health care all act to reduce men's life expectancy by increasing their risk of cardiovascular disease, some cancers and violent death. Women's reduced mortality risk reflects the fact that they smoke less – or have in the past – and are less likely to drink hazardous amounts of alcohol or to use illegal substances, while their diets are often healthier, particularly in the developed world. Women's and men's mortality also reflects socio-economic factors, including differences in exposure to work-based stress, risks and pollution, and differences in access to economic and social resources that may increase or decrease opportunities for health. Domestic factors, including the sexual division of labour in the home and in unpaid caring work, and the risk of sexual and physical violence, also affect women and men differently. Although in many countries women's access to health care is restricted by social, economic or cultural constraints, where women can make use of the services which are available, there are further differences relating to the way in which health care is gendered, and this too contributes to differences in mortality.

To sum up, then, patterns of difference between women and men in terms of mortality at different points in the life course are complex. The risk of death for women and men reflects both sex and gender, as well as interactions between these, and is further mediated by other forms of difference, including economic and material factors and ethnicity. The following section explores the part played by these factors in more detail, looking at deaths resulting from accidental and non-accidental injury.

Violent death, sex and gender

Although overall figures for violent death are relatively low, compared with other causes of mortality, there are important differences between men and women in the risk of injury-related death. Throughout the world men are more likely to die as a result of both non-intentional violence, or accidental death, and intentional violence, including homicide and suicide, although women are also at risk of accidental and non-accidental injury, particularly resulting from domestic and intimate partner violence. While the extent of men's over-representation in figures for violent death varies from country to country, and within countries in relation to age, ethnicity and socio-economic status, an excess of male mortality remains.

Accidental death, sex and gender

Most unintentional injury-related deaths occur as a result of road traffic accidents, although poisoning, falls, fires and drowning are also important causes of accidental death. In 2002 there were more than 3.5 million unintentional deaths in WHO member states, and more than two-thirds of those who died as a result of accidents were men (WHO, 2004c). Men were three times as likely as women to die in road traffic accidents, twice as likely to die by drowning or from poisoning, and nearly twice as likely to suffer fatal falls. In comparison, more women than men died as a result of fires (WHO, 2004e).

In England and Wales, accidental deaths have been decreasing in recent years, mainly as a result of a reduction in road traffic fatalities, but there continue to be more accidental deaths among men than women. In 2001, two-thirds of those who died as a result of all accidents were men (ONS, 2003). Around three times as many men died from road traffic accidents and drowning, and more men died from accidental poisoning, while similar numbers of women and men died from accidental falls.

In the USA, there are similar differences between women and men in the risk of accidental death. More men died in 2002 from accidental injury, including more than twice as many men in road traffic and other vehicle accidents, and more than four times as many men from drowning. More men died from smoke and fire, and due to accidental poisoning, but the number of deaths from falls for American men and women was similar (CDC, 2004).

Around the world, men are also more likely than women to die as pedestrians from injuries caused by vehicle accidents, partly after drinking alcohol and partly due to greater risk-taking behaviour – jumping on and off moving buses, for example – which increases the risk of fatal injury (WHO, 2002a; CDC, 2004).

The risk of accidental death varies with age for both men and women, with both experiencing a greater risk of accidental death in early adulthood and again in older age, and the ratio of male to female accidental deaths also varies across the life course. In England and Wales, for example, young adult men are more than four times as likely to have a fatal accident as women of the same age, but over the age of 75 there are more accidents among women. The risks are particularly marked for the most common cause of fatal injury: in 2001 more than four times as many young men as women died as a result of vehicle accidents in England and Wales, for example (ONS, 2003).

Although accidental death rates are different for men and women, there are also differences in relation to ethnicity, reflecting a range of factors affecting risk. In Australia, indigenous populations are three times more likely to die from external causes compared with the white population, and external causes of death are particularly striking for men (<http://www.aihw.gov.au>). In 1999–2001 both men and women from indigenous groups were more likely to die following transport accidents than the white or European population (<http:// www.aihw.gov.au>). Ethnic minority groups in the USA also have different risks of accidental death, particularly for motor-vehicle injuries. American Indian and Alaskan men and women are twice as likely to die as a result of motor-vehicle injuries. Although in all groups more men die as a result of road traffic accidents, the ratio of male to female mortality ranges from nearly three to one for black and African Americans, to two to one among Asian and Pacific Islanders (NCHS, 2004).

Accidental deaths from work-related hazards are also higher among minority groups and immigrant populations in developed countries such as the USA, the result of working in lower-status jobs, which are more hazardous and where employers do not follow safety precautions, and in some cases due to language difficulties (Herbert and Landrigan, 2000; Frumkin, 1999).

Non-accidental death, sex and gender

Non-accidental death includes a number of different causes, which have distinct patterns of risk for men and women. Worldwide, deaths from homicide and suicide in 2002 accounted for more than 1.5 million deaths, including 1 million male deaths and 0.5 million female deaths (WHO, 2004e). Of these, more than 700,000 deaths were due to violence inflicted by others, including conflict-related deaths, and over 80 per cent of those who died in this way were male. Deaths related to violence, including homicide and suicide, are much more common in low- and middle-income countries – the mortality rate for violence-related deaths in high-income countries in 2000, for example, was less than half the mortality rate for poorer countries (WHO, 2003g). Violent death also varies across the life course: young adults are most at risk of homicide, and the relative risk for men compared with women is also greatest during these years. In 2000, on a global basis, men aged between 15 and 44 were more than five times as likely as women the same age to die as a result of homicide (WHO, 2003g).

Not surprisingly, these findings hold true at country level. In the UK, more men than women die as a result of intentional injury inflicted by others. In 2001, more than twice as many men as women died as a result of assault, and young adult men were three times more likely to die from violence from others than women of the same age (ONS, 2003). Among the very old, more women than men died as a result of homicide or intentional harm, mainly from those they knew, rather than stranger violence.

In the USA, the male homicide mortality rate is more than three times the female homicide mortality rate. Again, there are differences between women and men in age at death, and also in whether the person who kills them is known to them. Among males, for example, most homicide deaths take place between the ages of 15 and 25, though rates are also high for boys under the age of 1. For females, the highest risk is in early life, under the age of 1, and though girls and women also have an increased risk of being killed between the ages of 15 and 44 compared with later in life, their risk remains much less than that of men of the same age. In adolescence and early adulthood, men in the USA have a particularly high risk of being killed by gunshot – they are seven times more likely than women of this age to be killed in this way (CDC, 2004). However, more women are shot and killed by partners and intimate acquaintances, while men are more at risk than women of gun-related homicide from people outside their immediate family (Hemenway et al., 2002).

There are further important variations in non-accidental death for different ethnic groups. In the USA, for example, unintentional injury and homicide are among the top ten major causes of death for minority groups (NCHS, 2004). Homicide mortality is lower among Asian and Pacific Islanders than the white population, but black and African American men have much higher risks of homicide than other groups – in 2002, the homicide mortality rate among black and African American men was 36 per 100,000 population, more than seven times the mortality rate of white men and five times the homicide mortality rate of black and African American women (NCHS, 2004).

Black and African American males are particularly at risk from death from firearm-related injuries, including not only homicide but also suicide and accidental death. Men in this group are more than twice as likely to die from gunshot wounds than white males, and six times as likely to die as Asian and Pacific Islander men (NCHS, 2004). Deaths from firearms are much lower for all women, but differences relating to ethnicity remain. Black and African American women are eight times less likely to suffer firearm mortality than their male counterparts, for example, but are more likely than white or other women to die in this way (NCHS, 2004).

There are also differences between women and men in the risk of mortality in conflict situations. In 2002, there were more than 170,000 deaths worldwide due to war, and nine-tenths of these were among men (WHO, 2004e). While war, conflict and their aftermath carry major health costs for both women and men, the risk of dying from violence in such situations is higher for men around the world – reflecting the fact that men continue to make up the great majority of military and paramilitary organizations, and the masculinization of warfare and conflict: 'Norms of masculinity contribute to men's exclusive status as warriors, and preparation for war is frequently a central component of masculinity' (Goldstein, 2001: 12). However, among civilian populations women and children suffer greater risks of mortality from increased levels of infectious disease, as well as homicide and accidental death arising from the conflict (Hynes, 2004).

Explaining the risk of violent death

Compared with other causes of death, then, the gap between women and men in the risk of violent death is marked. While such deaths represent a minority of all deaths, the much greater risk experienced by men is of importance in their premature mortality, and explanations for this increased risk, particularly those related to gender, help to illustrate the complexities of men's and women's risks of mortality more generally.

Sex and violent death

Sex-linked or biological factors have only a limited a role in shaping differences between men and women in death as a result of external agencies. The major biological difference between men and women which has been explored in research is that of testosterone and how this might influence male behaviour, including the relationship between testosterone and both homicide and suicide. Research has largely been inconclusive about the likely effect of this male hormone, however, particularly because individual testosterone levels change in association with a number of factors, including social and environmental influences (Zitzman and Nieschlag, 2001). If there is a link, testosterone might be better as an explanation of men as perpetrators of violence, rather than of their experience of violence, although it might be relevant in understanding suicidal acts, and in particular the more violent methods of suicide chosen by men. Men who die as a result of the violence of others might be seen as 'victims' of their own testosterone, if this relates to an increased risk of fighting, for example; but gender factors are also important in their influence on men's and women's use of public space, whether violence is endorsed or sanctioned, while discourses of masculinity in which being a man is associated with aggression, winning and not backing down in the face of argument, add to the risk.

There is also some evidence that there are other factors affecting injury-related death stemming from biological or physiological difference. For example, mortality following accidental injury may be increased for women compared to men, due to their typically smaller frame, which affects the risk of some types of internal injuries and fatality (WHO, 2002a).

Gender and violent death

Gender is particularly significant in explaining why men are more likely than women to die from both accidental and non-accidental causes. The factors involved include exposure to risk through gendered divisions in labour and paid employment, access to resources, and social constructions of gender and masculinity.

Gender, occupation, resources and violent death Major differences between men and women in terms of their employment status, income and wealth, and access to other material resources are significant in explaining risks of accidental death in particular. Road traffic accidents are the major cause of accidental death for both men and women around the world, but more men than women die from injuries caused by motor vehicles, reflecting gendered patterns in car ownership and use of vehicles (WHO, 2002a). Globally, more men than women own cars and have driving licences, men drive more often than women, and men are more likely to be driving at night or at other times when visibility is poor, while men also drive more often after drinking alcohol (WHO, 2002a; Lourens et al., 1999). In countries where safety helmets are not mandatory with motorcycles and mopeds, women are more likely to choose to wear them than men, and this too contributes to differences in road traffic fatalities (WHO, 2002a).

There are differences in the kinds of paid work men and women do which also help to explain men's higher risk of both accidental and non-accidental death, particularly in lower social classes. Historically, male manual work has been concentrated in occupations with higher fatality rates than women's manual labour – manufacturing, construction and distribution or transport work. While the proportion of the male workforce employed in these sectors has declined to some extent in recent years in developed countries, many more men than women continue to be employed in dangerous industries, and the high male accident mortality rate reflects this gendered occupational segregation (Courtenay, 2000). In the UK, for example, the great majority of workers in the construction industry, mining, transport and agriculture are men (ONS, 1997). While some of these are now relatively minor sectors of employment in the UK, the total number of men employed in these four industries is just under 2 million, and men outnumber women in these industries by about four to one. In addition, where women are employed in these industries, they largely work in jobs where the risk of fatal injury is substantially lower.

Similarly, in the USA, more men work in dangerous occupations – in timber cutting, fishing, mining, construction, truck driving, farming and forestry, as well in the police force and in fire fighting (Courtenay, 2000). Not surprisingly, more men are injured at work in the United States, and nearly all fatal injuries at work are suffered by men, with particularly high risks of death among Hispanic and Latino men (NCHS, 2004; Courtenay, 2000). There are high fatality rates among male workers in the construction industry and in agriculture, due to deaths from falls, vehicle accidents, machinery injury and electrocution (Lipscomb et al., 2000). Operating or driving a crane is a particularly risky male occupation, with high mortality from falls and electrocution from overhead cables (Davis and Brissie, 2000). Similarly, in Australia, male work-related deaths are higher than those of women, with high risks in the same kinds of male-dominated industries (Connell, 2000). Fatal workplace accidents are more common in younger men, reflecting their relative lack of experience, their greater likelihood of working in an unsafe environment due to their lower status in the workplace, and insufficient training and supervision (Courtenay, 2000). In addition, men suffer greater risks of fatal accidents at work because of the way in which work is structured, particularly the speed of work and hours at work. More men work shifts, for example, and this is associated with higher levels of fatal injury as a result of disturbed sleep patterns and poorer concentration (Akerstedt et al., 2002).

However, although men's increased risk of accident mortality is associated with the jobs they are likely to do, not all men are equally at risk of accidental death at work, and occupational classes differ in the dangers to which they are exposed. Fatal industrial accidents are rare among white-collar workers compared with manual labourers, for example. The higher mortality rates for black and minority men for accidental and non-accidental injury are similarly associated with structural factors – minority men and women are both more likely to be employed in sectors such as the service industry, where the risk of homicide is greater, and also in areas of work which are less unionized or where less attention is paid to safety measures (Richardson et al., 2004).

The greater risk of fatal work-related injury among men is also associated with men's failure to use safety measures, and to their risk taking in the workplace. This behaviour needs to be contextualized in terms of structural barriers which make it harder to follow safety advice – where safety measures or doing the job in a risk-free way would slow the pace of work and reduce pay, for example. However, men's risky work practices also relate to constructions of masculinity. Connell (2000) suggests that in an economic and social system in which men's role as 'breadwinner' is closely linked with their earning capacity and their ability to labour, 'working men may embrace the processes that consume their bodies, as their way of "doing" masculinity, and claiming some self-respect in the damaging world of wage-labour' (Connell, 2000: 188). The historical tradition of 'strong' male workers in working-class culture, and their modern-day equivalents who spurn safety equipment, who use stimulants to get through the day, or who lift too-heavy weights, embody masculinity in ways which damage their health, through increased risks of accidental injury in the present, and cumulative musculo-skeletal damage in the future. Thus men's workplace mortality might be explained by masculinity in the workplace, which maps on to an economic system that encourages (some) working men to take unsafe short cuts or ignore safety mechanisms to increase pay and profit.

What about women's deaths as a result of work-related injury? On the whole, women are less at risk of accidental death at work, but the risks also vary for women by occupation and location. In the USA, women workers have a much lower mortality rate compared with male workers, but most of the female deaths come from two traditionally female occupations – retail and the service industry – and the single most common cause of death from injury at work for women is homicide (Jenkins, 1996). Men are more likely than women to die from work-related homicide, in particular in police and detective work, where 97 per cent of fatalities are male officers, but homicide contributes a lower proportion of male work-related deaths because of all the other risks that men experience in the workplace (Courtenay, 2000). For women, however, homicide is the major threat facing them when they go to work. Women's unpaid work outside the formal labour market also helps to explain their risk of some forms of violent death. Women are at greater risk of dying in fires, for example, because most fatal fires occur in domestic settings, where women spend more of their time in unpaid work as a result of the gendered distribution of responsibility for domestic labour and child care.

Gender, behaviour and violent death Discursive constructions of masculinity and femininity are particularly important in the distribution of injury-related deaths related to other aspects of risk-taking behaviour, although class, poverty and social exclusion, racism and other discrimination also form part of the explanation of accidental and non-accidental injury.

Doing gender may involve acting in ways which are more or less dangerous for health and survival. Masculinity for some younger men, for example, may call for participation in dangerous acts, particularly collective acts which increase the risk of fatal injury, including joyriding, driving too fast, driving while drunk, gang violence and the use of illicit drugs (Abdel-Aty and Abdelwahab, 2000). Some risky activities are publicly approved or endorsed – competitive sport, for example – while others are approved within peer groups and are a means of negotiating a masculine identity, or entering and maintaining a position within a peer group.

These discourses are also racialized. Staples (1995) has described young black men in America as an 'endangered species', due to their high risk of homicide in the context of gun use, illicit drugs and gang membership. The risks of homicide in the USA are greater in urban areas for both black and white men, particularly in areas with high levels of poverty, overcrowding and educational disadvantage, and while the disproportionate number of black males living in deprived urban areas in the USA helps to explain their higher homicide mortality rate (Cubbin et al., 2000), these structural factors are also associated with particular expressions of black masculinity in which alternative routes to manhood – including participation in substance misuse, crime and gang violence – are given prominence (Jefferson, 1998).

Although rates of accidental and non-accidental fatalities are higher among young men, it is not only in youth that expressions of masculinity may increase the risk of violent death. For example, the greater risk of fatal injury at work associated with alcohol use among working-class men also reflects cultural constructions of male behaviour (Makela et al., 1997). Doing masculinity in later life may also increase the risk of accidental and non-accidental injury through reckless driving, and drinking and driving, for example, as well as work-related injury through behaviour which continues to 'act tough' and deny weakness (Connell, 2000; Shinar et al., 2001).

Deaths resulting from conflict and war epitomize the degree to which masculinity may pose the risk of premature death. The very high proportion of conflict fatalities which are male reflects the greater participation of men in armed services, military populations and guerrilla forces, but also a construction of masculinity and femininity which maintains the firing line as a male preserve and restricts women's participation in active duty (Goldstein, 2001). However, women's risks of fatal injury in conflict situations, as a result of sexual and physical violence, transport accidents and disease, follow from their location as civilians, their responsibility for caring work, and their construction as sexually available or as part of the resisting 'body' to be overcome or subjugated by invading forces.

A number of explanations of the male dominance in statistics for violent death – whether accidental or non-accidental – have focused on issues relating to masculinity and male gender construction. This focus encapsulates different ways of viewing gender as an explanation – ranging from relatively simple ideas that men are encouraged by gender processes of socialization to behave in aggressive or risk-taking ways, to arguments highlighting the structural causes of men's risk of violent death, including employment-related factors, to the suggestion that masculinities are discursively constructed and enacted by men, and that some of these masculinities are more dangerous to men's health.

Conclusion

This chapter has explored the ways in which women and men die and the various influences on the risk of mortality which relate to sex, gender and other factors. While both men and women die, there are important differences in the risk of premature death and in the risk of some kinds of death, which together explain the gap between women and men in life expectancy at birth and throughout the life course.

7 Conclusion

Introduction

What, then, do we know about the health of women and men? This book began with the suggestion that both sex and gender are important in our understanding of women's and men's health, and that we need a model of health differences which is able to reflect the very complex patterns of differences and similarities between women and men. In addition, a number of studies have demonstrated that the description of health inequalities between women and men implied by the gender paradox – that women live longer than men but experience more ill health during their lives – is too simplistic, particularly for women and men in more developed parts of the world. Models of health which have been used in the past no longer accurately represent the experiences of either women or men. Instead, figures for morbidity and mortality show us that sometimes men are worse off, sometimes women, and the details of differences between women and men, in terms of both health conditions and which men and which women suffer poorer health or reduced life expectancy, matter a lot. This last chapter pulls together the various points made earlier about the health of women and men, in order that we might move further towards a model of sex and gender influences on health.

The health of men and women

Many of the earlier chapters raised questions about the accuracy of data on health and the need to remain aware of potential bias, particularly in relation to gender, which may affect comparisons made between women and men. These concerns are important in self-reported data, where gender and other differences may affect ideas about health and willingness to report ill health, and they are also important in data based on use of health care, which is affected by gender differences in access to resources and in beliefs about health, as well as other factors. However, mortality data suggest that women have an advantage over men in terms of life expectancy in nearly every country around the world. The size of this advantage varies between countries, between populations within countries, and has varied over time – all of which suggests that sex-related factors and gender both play a part. Women also appear to enjoy an advantage over men when it comes to healthy life expectancy – the period of time spent in full health. The gap between women and men is narrower for healthy life expectancy than it is for total life expectancy, meaning that women lose some of their advantage over men once we look at their chances of living a life without illness or disability, but women largely seem to enjoy a greater proportion of their lives in full health compared with men.

When it comes to how men and women feel about their health, the gap narrows again. Women and men are, on the whole, very similar when it comes to self-reported health status, although often men report better health. While there are variations in this pattern, especially in relation to ethnicity, there are perhaps surprisingly few differences between women and men in their subjective accounts of health experience, particularly when these data are compared with findings on healthy life expectancy.

However, women do use health care more than men in countries where access is relatively easy, particularly where the decision to consult a health professional is not dependent on approval of other members of the household or financial outlay. Some of this relates to reproductive health needs, but women also consult more often for other conditions, especially for minor illnesses, and for mental health difficulties. Again, this would appear to be at odds with the findings on the gap between women and men in their healthy life expectancy.

Perhaps most revealing in terms of health are the differences between women and men in their experience of specific conditions, rather than generalized data about overall health and death. So we need to consider the health of women and men more closely, looking at specific conditions and diseases, partly because the gap between them varies according to what we are looking at, but also because the reasons for the gap differ. With mortality, for example, women and men largely die of the same diseases and conditions, and what matters in terms of our understanding of sex and gender as influences on health is the risk of death at particular ages and from particular causes.

While men are more likely than women to die from cardiovascular diseases, women's mortality from these conditions increases later in life and, overall, similar numbers of women and men die as a result of heart disease. Cancer mortality also accounts for similar numbers of deaths for women and men, but worldwide more men die of cancer related to health lifestyle factors, particularly lung and liver cancer, while women's cancer deaths are primarily associated with reproductive organs. Although health behaviours, including diet and alcohol use, may play a part in breast, ovarian, womb and cervical cancers, these cancers are sex-specific, and sexual and reproductive history are also important. There are further differences in patterns of morbidity. Both women and men suffer from poor mental health and, overall, there are fewer differences than might be thought in their risk of mental illness. However, more women suffer from depression, while men are more vulnerable to disorders associated with alcohol and substance misuse. Similarly, both women and men suffer from painful chronic conditions such as arthritis, but there are differences between them in which illnesses are experienced and in their severity. In order to explain these differences between women and men, we need to consider the ways in which sex and gender affect vulnerability to a disease or health condition, and the ways in which gender also affects diagnosis, access to health services, use made of services, and treatment offered.

Explaining the differences

If the differences between women and men in health experience and the risk of mortality are complex and specific, rather than general, what is the value of explanations resting on such large-scale concepts as 'sex' and 'gender'? Although different conditions can be explained with reference to specific aspects of biology and gender relations, is it still possible to map these influences and the interactions between them on the larger scale?

Table 7.1 suggests a model which might explain the health of women and men, which incorporates both sex and gender, but which also develops gender influences into three interrelated areas. The second column in table 7.1 focuses on the ways in which sex or biology might affect vulnerability to different conditions, and the impact of disease on health status. Differences between women and men in their reproductive, genetic and hormonal make-up influence their vulnerability to specific conditions, and also influence how that condition

Table 7.1 Modelling the relationship between sex, gender and health

	Sex	Gender		
		Structural/material factors	**Gender discourses**	**Treatment and research**
Definition	Biological factors including genetic, reproductive and hormonal differences.	Gender differences in access to resources, sexual division of paid and unpaid labour.	Constructions of femininity and masculinity including hegemonic and other gender discourses.	Extent to which treatment is gender-blind/neutral or sensitive, gender bias in research, and gendered dimensions of medical knowledge and education.
Examples				
Lung cancer	Women may have greater genetic susceptibility due to differences in gene expression relating to 'x' gene. Hormonal factors interact with impact of smoking.	Gender differences in material resources and access to tobacco increase men's smoking. Gender differences in exposure to stress and alternative coping strategies. Gender division of labour increases risks for men (e.g. occupational carcinogens) and women (e.g. domestic labour in some countries, cooking over coal fires). Parenting roles, especially in poverty.	Gender discourses and sanctioning of smoking behaviour for men. Associations between women's smoking and modernity/independence/beauty fed by tobacco-marketing strategies.	Cessation strategies need to identify gender differences in smoking career and smoking behaviour. Research needed on biological factors (e.g. sex differences in nicotine clearance) and gender factors (e.g. impact of advertising on smoking trajectory).

Suicide	Little evidence of sex/biological factors.	Poverty and stress. Access to particular (violent) methods. Occupational risk (e.g. professions which increase access to means).	Masculinity – risk taking, emotional expression, help-seeking behaviour. Suicide sanctioned for men.	Gender-blind health services: men's mental health problems less often recognized.
HIV/AIDS	Sex differences in vulnerability to transmission in heterosexual intercourse. Viral load differs. Sex-linked factors in responses to treatment.	Poverty. Occupational risks – sex-workers. Risks associated with migration, insecurity, conflict situations.	Gendered expectations of age at marriage, sexual relationships, sexual experience, penetrative intercourse, safe sex and risk taking.	Differences between women and men in access to treatment and ability to follow regime. Research on sex/gender differences focuses on modes of transmission from mother to child.
Arthritis	Sex differences in both vulnerability to disease and symptoms; sex differences in pain and responses to treatment.	Arthritis impacts on paid employment and caring work for men and women.	Gender differences in pain response and strategies – women more able to report pain and seek help.	Treatment strategies may vary in context of familial/occupational responsibilities, which are gendered.

Table 7.1 (continued)

	Sex		Gender	
Solutions	Biological/sex differences may mean different treatment interventions: use of different diagnostic tests, screening programmes, analgesics or therapies.	Attention to gender differences in access to resources and responsibilities.	Attention to gender-specific aspects of performance, including risk taking and healthy behaviour.	Gender-sensitive research to include sufficient numbers of women and men. Gender-sensitive delivery of health care – access, location, over-the-counter and external costs; gender-sensitive training for health professionals, and evaluation of services–specific and general. Gender-sensitive public health policy – e.g. health promotion which addresses specific needs of (different) men and women. Medical curriculum to reflect both sex and gender influences on health of both women and men.

takes hold. However, for most health conditions other factors also affect the chance of developing that disease – exposure to different carcinogens, for example. The third and fourth columns in table 7.1 suggest that different aspects of gender relations affect vulnerability to specific conditions in different ways, either by increasing exposure to structural risk factors, for example, or by affecting behaviour which in turn modifies risk. The fifth column similarly relates to gender relations, but reflects different influences on the health of women and men, particularly those relating to health care. Of course, in reality these influences overlap far more than can be shown in a two-dimensional table. For example, sex differences between women and men may reduce women's vulnerability to malaria compared with that of men, although during pregnancy their risk increases. Structural inequalities between women and men may increase women's exposure to the risk of malaria when they are denied access to preventive measures such as mosquito nets, when their paid or unpaid labour increases their risk of being bitten, and when they are denied access to medical care. Gendered discourses may also impede women's treatment, when tropical diseases are stigmatized, for example, or where women are not permitted to visit health care practitioners unless accompanied by a male. In addition, gender-insensitive health care may interpret women's health needs primarily in relation to reproduction and fail to act on women's other health problems, so that their disease will not be diagnosed.

The interactions between these different factors are hugely significant in health outcomes for men and women, but other factors – ethnicity, socio-economic class and sexuality, for example – also exert an influence on health. This book has focused on sex and gender as influences on health, but throughout we have seen the ways in which health also varies, for both women and men, particularly in relation to social class and ethnicity. Figures for morbidity, measured in various ways, and for mortality reveal poorer health among those from lower socio-economic groups compared with those in higher groups, and among those from black and minority ethnic groups compared with white and white European populations. These differences reflecting class and ethnicity are as marked as differences between women and men – possibly more so. For some writers, social class and access to material and social resources are key explanations for health inequalities between men and women, and between ethnic groups. That is, women's experiences of ill health are seen as owing a lot to their social class, their position in the labour market – in lower-status, poorly paid jobs with fewer benefits – and their greater reliance on state sources of income maintenance due to caring responsibilities. The poorer health of minority groups is similarly argued to reflect their over-representation in lower social classes and their increased risk of poverty compared with white populations. Socio-economic status also affects access to health care, which further explains differences between women and men, and between people from different ethnic groups.

While these differences are important, they do not explain all of the variation between women and men, however. Part of men's higher risk of mortality in comparison with women, for example, can be related to occupational status and the risks associated with some forms of employment, but gender remains important in explanations of other risk factors – health lifestyles in particular – and also in the way in which services are delivered.

Rather than trying to rank different aspects of inequality in terms of their health impact, we need to appreciate the way in which both health through the life course and the risk of premature death are the product of many influences, both external and internal, and especially the intersection of these major sources of inequality. In addition to the material consequences of inequality, we need also to consider 'biological expressions of social inequality' (Krieger, 2001: 693) – that is, the way in which the body takes on or literally incorporates social inequalities, including those of gender, social class and race or ethnicity, with consequent outcomes for health. Thus discrimination, stress and the awareness of being in a subordinate position also carry consequences for health, and this helps to explain why patterns of disease and health reflect different kinds of inequality, and the part played by multiple experiences of such subordination (Krieger, 2001; Zierler and Krieger, 1997):

> Being a working class white woman is qualitatively different from being the first woman in a Filipino immigrant family to attain a college education or being an African American woman who grew up with Jim Crow or being a white woman who is a business executive. Evaluating these differences means more than simply adding one-dimensional terms like *race/ethnicity* or *social class* to a long list of other variables in a multi-variate analysis and looking for other additive or multiplicative effects. It instead requires asking questions about deprivation, privilege, discrimination, and aspirations, to permit characterizing people more fully, and as more than the sum or product of their parts. (Krieger and Zierler, 1995: 253)

Thus, wider inequalities are also significant in the ways in which individual men and women experience health, and their risks of premature death. However, instead of following an 'additive' approach which attempts to sum the impact of each additional factor, we need to unpick these influences separately, while also remaining conscious of the interactions between various forms of subordination and discrimination, and various influences, at the individual and societal level.

Men's health or women's health?

The second theme which underpins this book is the tension between men's health and women's health, both in academic research and in health policy. The recent increased interest in men's health studies has produced a number of articles and books highlighting inequalities in health from men's perspective. Many of these papers focus on gender influences on men's health, rather than on biological or sex-linked factors, particularly the cost of masculinity to men's health. One response to this growing field of study has been a debate in the women's health movement over the meaning of gender equity in terms of health – particularly over whether to strive for equity in service delivery or equity in outcome. At heart, this is a struggle over scarce resources and public health prominence.

One of the key arguments in relation to men's health focuses on the lack of attention that men pay to their own health, and the need to find a way to encourage men to understand their bodies and to take measures to reduce the risks they currently experience due to their unhealthy behaviour and their failure to use health services. This has led to calls for more research on men's health behaviour and the provision of services which are tailored to men's needs and their reluctance to seek help – the provision of facilities in bars or in the workplace, for example. This is not contentious in itself, though the call for women to teach men how to look after their health is (see Rumm and Johnson, 2002, for example). Similarly, the call for interdisciplinary approaches to men's health is not only appropriate, but is something that is needed in women's health as well. A focus on men's health alone is problematic, however, in the same way that a focus on women's health alone is problematic – when such a focus threatens the provision of health care for the other, or when it demands sole attention. The risks that women continue to experience around the world because of poor reproductive health care, exposure to HIV and AIDS, from sexual violence and lack of sexual, reproductive and economic rights, are of major significance for our understanding of global patterns of health. Similarly, men's risk of premature death from violence, injury, and occupational hazards combined with poor health due to health lifestyles also matter in global patterns of health. But these need to be treated as interrelated, because gender affects both men and women, because many of these risks are experienced by women and men jointly, and because together they make up a complex whole.

In addition, other differences are often more significant in global patterns of health than differences between women and men, particularly the gap between people living in more developed countries and those living in less developed countries, where health is also shaped by poverty, malnutrition, lack of security, enforced migration, lack of protection in the workplace, and health treatment which is of poor quality and unavailable to large parts of the population.

Solutions in terms of policy and research need to pay detailed attention to difference at all levels – in terms of patterns of disease, risk factors, delivery of health care, and medical knowledge. Returning to table 7.1, the solutions to inequalities in health between women and men vary in relation to different conditions, but broadly encompass medical care which understands and reacts to sex-specific differences and which is also cognizant of gender; gender-sensitive health policy which includes the delivery of specific as well as general services; and the need for gendered understandings of health to be absorbed into research and medical education.

If we want to explore the ways in which health might be improved for either men or women, we can also look at those aspects of men's and women's lives which appear to increase their chances of good health. Men's access to economic resources, and their relative lack of caring and domestic responsibilities, help to explain their opportunities for good health, while feminine discourses – as opposed to those related to masculinity – can have a positive health effect through an emphasis on positive health lifestyles. When it comes to changing gender inequalities in health, two columns in table 7.1 suggest solutions which address gendered differences in resources and discursive constructions of gender. These are, of course, largely beyond the scope of health policy, though we should bear in mind that medical knowledge and health delivery affect gendered discourses, while the way in which health care is provided can increase poverty as well as affect the use made of health services. But reducing gendered structural inequalities, including poverty, social exclusion and occupational hazards, would improve the health of both women and men. Similarly, shifts in gendered discourses associated with specific kinds of behaviour could improve the health of both women and men.

Conclusion

At the start of this book it was suggested that while women's health had a long history in terms of research and writing, men's health was a relatively new area of study which focused particularly on men's prospects of premature death and on men's behaviour as a key factor in that risk. A Medline search, for example, revealed a broader understanding of women's health – beyond reproductive matters – and also that gender was commonly used as a keyword in papers on women's health. The same search on Medline suggested that the world of men's health was narrower, with a particular focus on sexual health among gay men, sexually transmitted diseases and men's unhealthy practices. If we enter these terms into a general on-line search engine, however, women's health reveals around 46 million web pages, compared with nearly 80 million pages referring to men's health – a surprising reversal which reflects the very rapid increase in men's health as a popular discourse in recent years in particular. The content of these pages – and what is meant in general by women's health or men's health – is perhaps rather more predictable. Web pages relating to women's health include primarily sites on sexual and reproductive health, reproductive rights, including abortion, and exercise and beauty. The content of men's health websites also includes men's sexual and reproductive health issues, though not their reproductive rights, together with pages about body-building, fitness and appearance. In other words, for all the discussion about broad and subtle differences in health experience, in general discourse similar themes dominate the meaning of health for women and men – those about reproductive difference and those about the body and the presentation of the self.

Where, then, do we go from here? Two conclusions can be drawn from the literature on men's health and women's health. The first is that these are complex matters, reflecting a wide range of influences, which include sex and gender but which go beyond these. The second is that the complexity of these patterns, and the existence of other influences, while making it difficult for those who want neat and tidy models of health, are also the reason why we need to look continuously at the health of both women and men, as they are and as they are discursively constructed, if we want to understand the part played by sex and gender in mortality and experiences of health and illness.

References

Abbott, P. and E. Williamson (1999). Women, health and domestic violence. *Journal of Gender Studies* 8 (1): 83–102.

Abdel-Aty, M. and H. Abdelwahab (2000). Exploring the relationship between alcohol and the driver characteristics in motor vehicle accidents. *Accident Analysis and Prevention* 32: 473–82.

AbouZahr, C. and T. Wardlaw (2001). Maternal mortality at the end of a decade: signs of progress? *Bulletin of the World Health Organization* 79 (6): 561–8.

Affleck, G., H. Tennen, et al. (1999). Everyday life with osteoarthritis or rheumatoid arthritis: independent effects of disease and gender on daily pain, mood, and coping. *Pain* 83 (3): 601–9.

Afsana, K. (2004). The tremendous cost of seeking hospital obstetric care in Bangladesh. *Reproductive Health Matters* 12 (24): 171–80.

Ahmed, S. M., A. M. Adams, et al. (2003). Changing health-seeking behaviour in Matlab, Bangladesh: Do development interventions matter? *Health Policy & Planning* 18 (3): 306–15.

AIHW (2004). *Australia's Health 2004: The Ninth Biennial Health Report of the Australian Institute of Health and Welfare.* Canberra: Australian Institute of Health and Welfare.

Akbar Zaidi, S. (1996). Gender perspectives and quality of care in underdeveloped countries: disease, gender and contextuality. *Social Science & Medicine* 43 (5): 721–30.

Akerstedt, T., P. Fredlund, et al. (2002). A prospective study of fatal occupational accidents – relationship to sleeping difficulties and occupational factors. *Journal of Sleep Research* 11: 69–71.

Alcohol Alert (1999). *Are Women More Vulnerable to Alcohol's Effects?* New York: National Institute on Alcohol Abuse and Alcoholism.

Ali, A., B. Toner, et al. (2000). Emotional abuse, self-blame and self-silencing in women with irritable bowel syndrome. *Psychosomatic Medicine* 62: 76–82.

Aliaga, C. (2002). *Les Femmes plus attentives à leur sante que les hommes.* Paris: INSEE.

Allahbadia, G. (2002). The 50 million missing women. *Journal of Assisted Reproduction and Genetics* 19 (9): 411–16.
Alt, R. L. (2002). Where the boys are not: a brief overview of male preventive health. *Wisconsin Medical Journal* 101 (4): 22–7.
Amazigo, U. (1998). *Women's Health and Tropical Diseases: A Focus on Africa.* Report of an expert group meeting on health, United Nations, the Division for the Advancement of Women, United Nations Department of Economic and Social Affairs (DAW/DESA), the World Health Organisation (WHO), and the United Nations Population Fund (UNFPA).
Annandale, E. and K. Hunt (2000). *Gender Inequalities in Health.* Milton Keynes: Open University Press.
Aoun, S. and L. Johnson (2002). Men's health promotion by general practitioners in a workplace setting. *Australian Journal of Rural Health* 10 (6): 268–72.
Arber, S. and H. Cooper (1999). Gender differences in health in later life: the new paradox? *Social Science & Medicine* 48: 61–76.
Ashley, M. J. (1997). Smoking and diseases of the gastrointestinal system: an epidemiological review with special reference to sex differences. *Canadian Journal of Gastroenterology* 11 (4): 345–52.
ASSO (2005). *Obesity in Australian Adults: Prevalence Data.* Sydney: Australian Society for the Study of Obesity.
Astbury, J. (1999). *Gender and Mental Health.* Melbourne: Key Centre for Women's Health.
Audini, B. and P. Lelliott (2002). Age, gender and ethnicity of those detained under Part II of the Mental Health Act 1983. *British Journal of Psychiatry* 180: 222–6.
AusStats (2002). *National Health Survey.* Canberra: Australian Bureau of Statistics.
Baghadi, G. (2005). Gender and medicines: an international public health perspective. *Journal of Women's Health* 14 (1): 82–6.
Bagnardi, V., M. Blangiardo, et al. (2001). A meta-analysis of alcohol drinking and cancer risk. *British Journal of Cancer* 85 (11): 1700–5.
Bailey, J. V., J. Kavanagh, et al. (2000). Lesbians and cervical screening. *British Journal of General Practice* 50 (455): 481–2.
Bajekal, M., P. Primatesta, et al. (2003). *Health Survey for England 2001.* London: Department of Health.
Baker, D., K. North, et al. (1999). Does employment improve the health of lone mothers? *Social Science & Medicine* 49: 121–31.
Bammer, G. and L. Strazdins (2004). Women, work and musculoskeletal health. *Social Science & Medicine* 58 (6): 997–1005.
Bancroft, A., S. Wiltshire, et al. (2003). 'It's like an addiction first thing . . . afterwards it's like a habit': daily smoking behaviour among people living in areas of deprivation. *Social Science & Medicine* 56 (6): 1261–7.
Banks, I. (2001). No man's land: men, illness and the NHS. *British Medical Journal* 323: 1058–60.

Barlow, J., L. Cullen, et al. (1999). Does arthritis influence perceived ability to fulfill a parenting role? Perceptions of mothers, fathers and grandparents. *Patient Education and Counseling* 37: 141–51.

Barrett, S. E. and H. Roberts (1978). *Doctors and their Patients: The Social Control of Women in General Practice*. In S. C. Smart and B. Smart (eds), *Women, Sexuality and Social Control*, London: Routledge & Kegan Paul.

Bartley, M., A. Sacker, et al. (1999). Social position, social roles and women's health in England: changing relationships 1984–1993. *Social Science & Medicine* 48: 99–115.

Bates, I., C. Fenton, et al. (2004). Vulnerability to malaria, tuberculosis, and HIV/AIDS infection and disease. Part 1: Determinants operating at individual and household level. *The Lancet Infectious Diseases* 4 (5): 267–77.

Bauermeister, J. and A. Carballo-Dieguez (2004). 'Barebacking': intentional condomless anal sex in HIV-risk contexts. Reasons for and against it. *Journal of Homosexuality* 47 (1): 1–16.

Beauboeuf-Lafontant, T. (2003). Strong and large black women?: exploring relationships between deviant womanhood and weight. *Gender Society* 17 (1): 111–21.

Benjamins, M., R. Hummer, et al. (2004). Self-reported health and adult mortality risk: an analysis of cause-specific mortality. *Social Science & Medicine* 59: 1297–1306.

Benyamini, Y. and E. L. Idler (1999). Community studies reporting association between self-rated health and mortality: additional studies, 1995 to 1998. *Research on Aging* 21: 392–440.

Benzeval, M. (1998). The self-reported health status of lone parents. *Social Science & Medicine* 46: 1337–53.

Berer, M. and T. Sundari Ravindran (1999). *Safe Motherhood Initiatives: Critical Issues*. UK: Blackwell Science.

Bergart, A. M. (2000). The experience of women in unsuccessful infertility treatment: what do patients need when medical intervention fails? *Social Work in Health Care* 30 (4): 45–69.

Berrigan, D., K. Dodd, et al. (2003). Patterns of health behavior in U.S. adults. *Preventive Medicine* 36 (5): 615–23.

Bhardwaj, A. (2001). Growing up young, Asian and female in Britain: a report on self-harm and suicide. *Feminist Review* 68 (1): 52–67.

Bhopal, R. (2001). *Ethnicity and Race as Epidemiological Variables*. In H. McBeth and P. Shetty (eds), *Ethnicity and Health*, London: Taylor & Francis.

Bhui, K., M. Chandran, et al. (2002). Mental health assessment and South Asian men. *International Review of Psychiatry* 14: 52–9.

Biddulph, S. (1995). Healthy masculinity starts in boyhood. *Australian Family Physician* 24 (11): 2047–50.

Biji, R., A. Ravelli, et al. (1998). Prevalence of psychiatric disorder in the general population: results of the Netherlands Mental Health Survey and Incidence Study (NEMESIS). *Social Psychiatry and Psychiatric Epidemiology* 33: 587–95.

Bildt, C. and H. Michelsen (2002). Gender differences in the effects from working conditions on mental health: a 4 year follow-up. *International Archives of Occupational & Environmental Health* 75 (4): 252–8.

Bird, C. E. and R. P. Rieker (1999). Gender matters: an integrated model for understanding men's and women's health. *Social Science & Medicine* 48: 745–55.

Biswas, L., B. Manna, et al. (1997). Sexual risk factors for cervical cancer among rural Indian women: a case-control study. *International Journal of Epidemiology* 26 (3): 491–5.

Black, J. and D. Debelle (1995). Female genital mutilation in Britain. *British Medical Journal* 310: 1590–92.

Blair-West, G., C. Cantor, et al. (1999). Lifetime suicide risk in major depression: sex and age determinants. *Journal of Affective Disorders* 55: 171–8.

Blake, M., M. Ince, et al. (2005). Inclusion of women in cardiac research: current trends and need for reassessment. *Gender Medicine* 2 (2): 71–5.

Blaxter, M. (1990). *Health and Lifestyles.* London: Tavistock/Routledge.

Bonnar, J. and B. L. Sheppard (1996). Treatment of menorrhagia during menstruation: randomised controlled trial of ethamsylate, mefenamic acid, and tranexamic acid. *British Medical Journal* 313: 579–82.

Booth, C. and N. Owens (2000). Silent suicide: suicide among people not in contact with mental health services. *International Review of Psychiatry* 12 (1): 27–30.

Bordo, S. (1993). *Unbearable Weight: Feminism, Western Culture and the Body.* Berkeley and Los Angeles: University of California Press.

Boswell, G. and F. Poland (2002). *Women's Minds, Women's Bodies: Interdisciplinary Approaches to Women's Health.* Basingstoke: Palgrave Macmillan.

Boyle, P., D. Exeter, et al. (2005). Suicide gap among young adults in Scotland: population study. *British Medical Journal* 330: 175–6.

Bradley, L. and G. Alarcon (1999). Sex-related influences in fibromyalgia. In B. D. Fillingim (ed.), *Sex, Gender and Pain*, Seattle: IASP Press.

Bremner, J., S. Southwick, et al. (1996). Chronic PTSD in Vietnam combat veterans: course of illness and substance abuse. *American Journal of Psychiatry* 153 (3): 369–75.

Brems, C., D. G. Fisher, et al. (1998). Physicians' assessment of drug use and other HIV risk behavior: reports by female drug users. *Drugs and Society* 13 (1/2): 145–59.

Brod, H. and M. Kaufman (1994). *Theorizing Masculinities.* Thousand Oaks, Calif.: Sage.

Broom, D. (1999). The genders of health. Paper Presented at the Conference Gender, Health and Healing: Reflections on the Public-Private Divide, University of Warwick, 23–4 April 1999.

Brown, A. E., K. E. Sadler, et al. (2004). Recent trends in HIV and other STIs in the United Kingdom: data to the end of 2002. *Sexually Transmitted Infections* 80: 159–66.

Brugh, V. and L. Lipshultz (2004). Male factor infertility: evaluation and management. *Medical Clinics of North America* 88: 367–85.

Burr, J. and T. Chapman (2004). Contextualising experiences of depression in women from South Asian communities: a discursive approach. *Sociology of Health & Illness* 26 (4): 433–52.

Busfield, J. (1983). Gender, mental health and psychiatry. In M. Evans and C. Ungerson (eds), *Sexual Divisions: Patterns and Processes*, London: Tavistock.

Busfield, J. (2002). Disordered minds: women, men and unreason in thought, emotion and behaviour. In G. Boswell and F. Poland (eds), *Women's Minds, Women's Bodies: Interdisciplinary Approaches to Women's Health*, Basingstoke: Macmillan.

Byles, J. and Women's Health Australia Researchers (1999). Over the hill and picking up speed: older women of the Australian Longitudinal Study on Women's Health. *Australasian Journal on Ageing* 18 (3 supplement): 5–62.

Calin, A., S. Brophy, et al. (1999). Impact of sex on inheritance of ankylosing spondylitis: a cohort study. *The Lancet* 354: 1687–98.

Cameron, E. and J. Bernardes (1998). Gender and disadvantage in health: men's health for a change. *Sociology of Health and Illness* 20 (5): 673–93.

Campos, P. (2004). *The Obesity Myth: Why America's Obsession with Weight is Hazardous to your Health*. New York: Gotham Books.

Canetto, S. S. and I. Sakinofsky (1998). The gender paradox in suicide. *Suicide and Life Threatening Behaviour* 28 (1): 1–23.

Capraro, R. (2000). Why college men drink: alcohol, adventure and the paradox of masculinity. *Journal of American College Health* 48: 307–15.

CDC (2002). *Suicide and Attempted Suicide – China 1990–2002*. Washington: Centre for Disease Control.

CDC (2003). *HIV/AIDs Surveillance Report*. Washington: Centre for Disease Control.

CDC (2004) *Suicide Fact Sheet*. Washington: Centre for Disease Control.

Chandola, T. and C. Jenkinson (2000). Validating self-rated health in different ethnic groups. *Ethnicity and Health* 5 (2): 151–9.

Chang, L. and M. M. Heitkemper (2002). Gender differences in irritable bowel syndrome. *Gastroenterology* 123 (5): 1686–1701.

Chapple, A., M. Ling, et al. (1998). General practitioners' perceptions of the illness and behaviour needs of SA women with menorrhagia. *Ethnicity and Health* 3: 81–93.

Charles, N. and V. Walters (1998). Age and gender in women's accounts of their health: interviews with women in South Wales. *Sociology of Health and Illness* 20 (3): 331–50.

Chaudron, L. and E. Caine (2004). Suicide among women: a critical review. *Journal of American Medical Women's Association* 59: 125–34.
Chen,Y., S. Subramanian, et al. (2005). Women's status and depressive symptoms: a multilevel analysis. *Social Science & Medicine* 60: 49–60.
Cheng, A. and C. Lee (2000). Suicide in Asia and the Far East. In K. Hawton and Van Heeringar, K. (eds), *The International Handbook of Suicide and Attempted Suicide*, Chichester: Wiley.
Chun, H., L. Doyal, et al. (2005). The health of women and men in Korea. Paper presented at School for Policy Studies Seminar, University of Bristol, March 2005.
<cia.gov> (2005). CIA – the World factbook – Côte d'Ivoire, CIA.
CIHR (2000). *Sex, Gender and Women's Health.* Montreal: Canadian Institute for Health Research.
Clarke, A. E. (2003). IV. The more things change, the more they [also] remain the same. *Feminism & Psychology* 13 (1): 34–9.
Cohn, S. and R. Clark (2003). Sexually transmitted diseases, HIV and AIDs in women. *Medical Clinics of North America* 87: 971–95.
Collins, K., C. Schoen, et al. (1999). *Health Concerns across a Woman's Lifespan.* The Commonwealth Fund.
Connell, R. (2000). *The Men and the Boys.* Berkeley: University of California Press.
Cooper, H. and S. Arber (2002). Ethnicity and inequalities in older women's health. In G. Boswell and F. Poland (eds), *Women's Minds, Women's Bodies: Interdisciplinary Approaches to Women's Health.* Basingstoke: Palgrave Macmillan.
Corea, G., R. Klein, et al. (1987). *Man-Made Women: How New Reproductive Technologies Affect Women.* Bloomington: Indiana University Press.
Costello, A., D. Orsrin, et al. (2004). Reducing maternal and neonatal mortality in the poorest communities. *British Medical Journal* 329: 1166–8.
Courtenay, W. H. (2000). Constructions of masculinity and their influence on men's well-being: a theory of gender and health. *Social Science & Medicine* 50: 1385–1401.
Craft, N. (1997). Women's health: life span: conception to adolescence. *British Medical Journal* 315: 1227–30.
Crampin, A. C., J. R. Glynn, et al. (2004). Tuberculosis and gender: exploring the patterns in a case control study in Malawi. *International Journal of Tuberculosis & Lung Disease* 8 (2): 194–203.
Crawford, M. and M. Prince (1999). Increasing rates of suicide in young men in England during the 1980s: the importance of social context. *Social Science & Medicine* 49 (10): 1419–23.
Crossley, M. L. (2004). Making sense of 'barebacking': gay men's narratives, unsafe sex and the 'resistance habitus'. *British Journal of Social Psychology* 43 (2): 225–44.
Cubbin, C., L. Pickle, et al. (2000). Social context and geographic patterns of

homicide among US Black and White males. *American Journal of Public Health* 90 (4): 579–87.

Cummings, J. H. and S. A. Bingham (1998). Diet and the prevention of cancer. *British Medical Journal* 317: 1636–40.

Curtis, S. and K. Lawson (2000). Gender, ethnicity and self-reported health: the case of African-Caribbean populations in London. *Social Science & Medicine* 50: 365–85.

Cyranowski, J. M., E. Frank, et al. (2000). Adolescent onset of the gender difference in lifetime rates of major depression: a theoretical model. *Archives of General Psychiatry* 57 (1): 21–7.

daSilva, J. and G. Hall (1992). The effects of gender and sex hormones on outcome in rheumatoid arthritis. *Baillieres Clinical Rheumatology* 6 (1): 193–219.

Davey Smith, G., D. Dorling, et al. (1999). *The Widening Health Gap – What are the Solutions? Critical Public Health* 9 (2): 151–70.

Davies, J., B. McCrae, et al. (2000). Identifying male college students' perceived health needs, barriers to seeking help and recommendations to help men adopt healthier lifestyles. *Journal of American College Health* 48: 259–67.

Davis, C. and M. Katzman (1998). Chinese men and women in the United States and Hong Kong: body and self-esteem ratings as a prelude to dieting and exercise. *International Journal of Eating Disorders* 23 (1): 99–102.

Davis, D. (1996). The cultural construction of the premenstrual and menopause syndromes. In C. Sargent and C. Brettall (eds), *Gender and Health: An International Perspective*, London, Prentice-Hall.

Davis, G. and R. Brissie (2000). A review of crane deaths in Jefferson County, Alabama. *Journal of Forensic Science* 45 (2): 392–6.

De Casanova, E. (2004). 'No Ugly Women': concepts of race and beauty among adolescent women in Ecuador. *Gender & Society* 18 (3): 287–308.

DeCosse, J. J., S. S. Ngoi, et al. (1993). Gender and colorectal cancer. *European Journal of Cancer Prevention: The Official Journal of the European Cancer Prevention Organisation* 2 (2): 105–15.

Delvaux, M., P. Denis, et al. (1997). Sexual abuse is more frequently reported by IBS patients than by patients with organic digestive diseases or controls: results of a multicentre inquiry, French Club of Digestive Motility. *European Journal of Gastroenterology and Hepatology* 9 (4): 345–52.

Denton, M. and V. Walters (1999). Gender differences in structural and behavioural determinants of health: an analysis of the social production of health. *Social Science & Medicine* 48: 1221–35.

Denton, M., S. Prus, et al. (2004). Gender differences in health: a Canadian study of the psychosocial, structural and behavioural determinants of health. *Social Science & Medicine* 58 (12): 2585–2600.

DHS (1999). *Zimbabwe: Demographic and Health Survey*. Calverton, USA: Marco International.

DHS (2000). *Rwanda: Demographic and Health Survey*. ORC-Marco Demographic and Health Surveys. Calverton, USA: Marco International.

Dibble, S. L., S. A. Roberts, et al. (2004). Comparing breast cancer risk between lesbians and their heterosexual sisters. *Women's Health Issues* 14 (2): 60–8.

Dieppe, P. (1999). Osteoarthritis: time to shift the paradigm. *British Medical Journal* 318: 1299–1300.

DOH (2003). *Hospital Episode Statistics*. London: Department of Health.

DOH (2004). *Choosing Health: Making Healthier Choices Easier*. London: Government Statistical Service.

Donovan, B. (2002). Rising prevalence of genital Chlamydia trachomatis infection in heterosexual patients at the Sydney Sexual Health Centre, 1994 to 2000. *Communicable Diseases Intelligence* 26 (1): 51–4.

Doyal, L. (1995). *What Makes Women Sick? The Politics of Women's Health*. Basingstoke: Macmillan.

Doyal, L. (1998). *Women and Health Services: An Agenda for Change*. Buckingham: Open University Press.

Doyal, L. (2000a). Gender equity in health: debates and dilemmas. *Social Science & Medicine* 51: 931–9.

Doyal, L. (2000b). A preliminary conceptual framework: sex, gender and health. *Bulletin Medicus Mundi* 77. <http://www.medicusmundi.ch/mms/services/bulletin/bulletin200002/kap02/02doyal.html>.

Doyal, L. (2002). *Health and Work of Older Women: A Neglected Issue*. London: Pennell Initiative for Women's Health TUC.

Doyal, L. (2004). *Integrating Gender Considerations into Health Policy Development: UK Case Study on Coronary Heart Disease*. Geneva: WHO.

Doyal, L. and J. Anderson (2005). 'My fear is to fall in love again': how HIV-positive African women survive in London. *Social Science & Medicine* 60: 1729–38.

Drever, F., T. Doran, et al. (2004). Exploring the relationship between class, gender and self-rated general health using the new socio-economic classification: a study using data from the 2001 census. *Journal of Epidemiology and Community Health* 58: 590–6.

Duncan, B. and G. Hart (1999). Sexuality and health: the hidden costs of screening for Chlamydia trachomatis. *British Medical Journal* 318: 931–3.

Dunnell, K., J. Fitzpatrick, et al. (1999). Making use of official statistics in research on gender and health status: recent British data. *Social Science & Medicine* 48: 117–27.

Early, R. (2001). Men as consumers of maternity services: a contradiction in terms. *International Journal of Consumer Studies* 25 (2): 160–71.

Ehrmin, J. (2002). 'That numbing feeling of not feeling' – numbing the pain for substance-dependent African American women. *Qualitative Health Research* 12 (6): 780–91.

Eliason, M. and R. Schope (2001). Does 'Don't Ask Don't Tell' apply to health care? Lesbian, gay and bisexual people's disclosure to health care providers. *Journal of the Gay and Lesbian Medical Association* 5 (4): 125–34.

Emslie, C., K. Hunt, et al. (1999). Problematizing gender, work and health: the relationship between gender, occupational grade, working conditions and minor morbidity in full-time bank employees. *Social Science & Medicine* 48: 33–48.

Emslie, C., R. Fuhrer, et al. (2002). Gender differences in mental health: evidence from three organisations. *Social Science & Medicine* 54: 621–4.

Epstein, S. (2004). Bodily differences and collective identities: the politics of gender and race in biomedical research in the United States. *Body and Society* 10 (2–3): 183–203.

Erens, B., P. Primatesta, et al. (1999). *Health Survey for England: The Health of Minority Ethnic Groups*. London: The Stationery Office.

Eriksson, I. and A. L. Undén (2001). Self-rated health: comparisons between three different measures: results from a population study. *International Journal of Epidemiology* 30 (2): 326–33.

EUROSTAT (2003). *Health Statistics: Atlas on Mortality in the European Union*. Luxemburg: European Commission.

Fernquist, R. (2004). Does single motherhood protect against Black female suicide? *Archives of Suicide Research* 8 (2): 163–71.

Ferraro, K. and M. Farmer (1999). Utility of health data from social surveys: is there a gold standard for measuring morbidity? *American Sociological Review* 64 (2): 303–15.

Ferrie, J. E., M. J. Shipley, et al. (2005). Self-reported job insecurity and health in the Whitehall II Study: potential explanations of the relationship. *Social Science & Medicine* 60: 1593–1602.

Ferris, D. G., S. Batish, et al. (1996). A neglected lesbian health concern: cervical neoplasia. *Journal of Family Practice* 43 (6): 581–4.

Fertig, J. B. and J. P. Allen (1996). Health behavior correlates of hazardous drinking by Army personnel. *Military Medicine* 161 (6): 352–5.

Fidler, H., A. Hartnett, et al. (2000). Sex and familiarity of colonoscopists: patient preferences. *Endoscopy* 32 (6): 481–2.

Field, D., J. Hockey, et al. (1997). Making sense of difference: death, gender and ethnicity in modern Britain. In D. Field, J. Hockey and N. Small (eds), *Death, Gender and Ethnicity*, London: Routledge.

Fikree, F. F. and O. Pasha (2004). Role of gender in health disparity: the South Asian context. *British Medical Journal* 328 (7743): 823–6.

Fillingim, B. D. (1999). Sex, gender and pain: a biopsychosocial framework. In B. D. Fillingim (ed.), *Sex, Gender and Pain*, Seattle: IASP Press.

Fodor, J. and R. Tzerovska (2004). Coronary heart disease: is gender important? *Journal of Men's Health and Gender* 1 (1): 32–7.

Foster, P. (1995). *Women and the Health Care Industry: An Unhealthy Relationship?* Buckingham: Open University Press.

Francome, C. (2000). *Improving Men's Health*. Enfield: Middlesex University Press.

Friedman, A. (1998). Substance use/abuse as a predictor to illegal and violent behaviour: a review of the relevant literature. *Aggression and Violent Behaviour* 3 (4): 339–55.

Frisch, M., E. Smith, et al. (2003). Cancer in a population-based cohort of men and women in registered homosexual partnerships. *American Journal of Epidemiology* 157: 966–72.

Frumkin, H. (1999). Across the water and down the ladder: occupational health in the global economy. *Occupational Medicine* 14 (3): 637–63.

Furnham, A. and S. Adam-Saib (2001). Abnormal eating attitudes and behaviours and perceived parental control: a study of white British and British-Asian school girls. *Social Psychiatry and Psychiatric Epidemiology* 36 (9): 462–70.

Ganju, D., S. Jejeebhoy, et al. (2004a). *The Adverse Health and Social Outcomes of Sexual Coercion: Experiences of Young Women in Developing Countries*. New Delhi: Population Council.

Ganju, D., S. Jejeebhoy, et al. (2004b). *Sexual Coercion: Young Men's Experiences as Victims and Perpetrators*. New Delhi: Population Council.

Gannon, K., L. Glover, et al. (2004). Masculinity, infertility, stigma and media reports. *Social Science & Medicine* 59: 1169–75.

Garcia-Moreno, C. and C. Watts (2000). Violence against women: its importance for HIV/AIDS. *AIDS* 14 (supplement 3): s253–65.

GHS (2004). *Living in Britain: Results from the 2002 General Household Survey*. London: The Stationery Office.

Gijsbers Van Wijk, K. P. Van Vliet, et al. (1996). Gender perspectives and quality of care: towards appropriate and adequate health care for women. *Social Science & Medicine* 43 (5): 707–20.

Giovannucci, E., A. Ascherio, et al. (1993). A prospective cohort study of vasectomy and prostate cancer in US men. *Journal of the American Medical Association* 269 (7): 873–7.

Glasgow, R. E. et al. (1993). Participation in worksite health promotion: a critique of the literature and recommendations for future practice. *Health Education Quarterly* 20 (3): 391–408.

Gogna, M., M. Romero, et al. (2002). Abortion in a restrictive legal context: the views of obstetrician-gynaecologists in Buenos Aires, Argentina. *Reproductive Health Matters* 10 (19): 128–37.

Goldacre, M., V. Seagroatt, et al. (1993). Suicide after discharge from psychiatric inpatient care. *The Lancet* 342 (8866): 283–6.

Goldstein, J. (2001). *War and Gender: How Gender Shapes the War System and Vice Versa*. Boston: Cambridge University Press.

Graham, H. (1984). *Women, Health and the Family*. Brighton: Wheatsheaf.

Graham, H. (2000). Socio-economic change and inequalities in men and women's health in the UK. In E. Annandale and K. Hunt (eds), *Gender Inequalities in Health*, Milton Keynes: Open University Press.

Graham, H. and G. Der (1999). Patterns and predictors of tobacco consumption among women. *Health Education Research* 14 (5): 611–18.

Green, J. (1997). *Risk and Misfortune: The Social Construction of Accidents.* London: University College Press.

Griffiths, S. (1996). Men's health. *British Medical Journal* 312: 69–70.

Gritz, E., I. Nielsen, et al. (1996). Smoking cessation and gender: the influence of physiological, psychological and behavioural factors. *Journal of American Medical Women's Association* 51 (1 & 2): 35–42.

Grogan, S., R. Evans, et al. (2004). Femininity and muscularity: accounts of seven women body builders. *Journal of Gender Studies* 13 (1): 49–61.

Grundy, E., D. Mayer, et al. (2004). Living arrangements and place of death of older people with cancer in England and Wales: a record linkage study. *British Journal of Cancer* 91: 907–12.

Gunnell, D. (2000). The epidemiology of suicide. *International Review of Psychiatry* 12: 21–6.

Gunnell, D. J., T. J. Peters, et al. (1995). Relation between parasuicide, suicide, psychiatric admissions, and socioeconomic deprivation. *British Medical Journal* 311: 226–30.

Hagoel, L., L. Ore, et al. (2002). Clustering women's health behaviors. *Health Education and Behavior* 29 (2): 170–82.

Hankin, B., L. Abramson, et al. (1998). Development of depression from preadolescence to young adulthood: emerging gender differences in a ten-year longitudinal study. *Journal of Abnormal Psychology* 107 (1): 128–40.

Hann, C. (1995). Screening women for cancer: a time for reappraisal. *Critical Social Policy* 15 (2/3, issues 44/5): 183–92.

Hanson, K. (1999). Measuring up: gender, burden of disease and priority setting techniques in the health sector. Harvard Center for Population and Development Studies, Working Paper Series Number 99.12.

Harris, B., Lovett L., et al. (1994). Maternity blues and major endocrine changes: Cardiff puerperal mood and hormone study II. *British Medical Journal* 308: 949–53.

Harris, T. (2003). Depression in women and its sequelae. Review article. *Journal of Psychosomatic Research* 54 (2): 103–12.

Harrison, A., E. T. Montgomery, et al. (2000). Barriers to implementing South Africa's Termination of Pregnancy Act in rural KwaZulu/Natal. *Health Policy and Planning* 15 (4): 424–31.

Hart, N. (1987). Sex, gender and survival: inequalities of life chances between European men and women. In J. Fox (ed.), *Health Inequalities in European Countries,* Aldershot: Gower.

Haslam, D. (2004). Male central obesity. *Journal of the Royal Society for the Promotion of Health* 124 (5): 209–10.

Hassan, R. (1996). *Social Factors in Suicide in Australia.* Trends and Issues Report 52. Canberra: Australian Institute of Criminology.

Haugen, A. (2002). Women who smoke: are women more susceptible to tobacco-induced lung cancer? *Carcinogenesis* 23 (2): 227–9.

Hawton, K. (2000). Sex and suicide: gender differences in suicidal behaviour. *British Journal of Psychiatry* 177: 484–5.

Hayes, B. C. and P. M. Prior (2003). *Gender and Health Care in the UK: Exploring the Stereotypes.* Basingstoke and New York: Palgrave-Macmillan.

Health Systems Trust (2004). *Health Statistics: Obesity, Health Systems Trust South Africa.* Durban.

Hegarty, K., J. Gunn, et al. (2004). Association between depression and abuse by partners of women attending general practice: descriptive, cross sectional survey. *British Medical Journal* 328: 621–4.

Heitkemper, M., M. Jarrett, et al. (2003). Impact of sex and gender on irritable bowel syndrome. *Biological Research for Nursing* 5 (1): 56–65.

Helgeson, V. (1995). Masculinity, men's roles, and coronary heart disease. In D. Sabo and D. F. Gordon (eds), *Men's Health and Illness: Gender, Power and the Body*, London: Sage.

Hemenway, D., T. Shinoda-Tagawa, et al. (2002). Firearm availability and female homicide victimization rates among 25 populous high-income countries. *Journal of American Women's Medical Association* 57 (2): 100–4.

Henson, K. and J. Krasas-Rogers (2001). 'Why Marcia you've changed!' Male clerical temporary workers doing masculinity in a feminized occupation. *Gender & Society* 15 (2): 218–38.

Herbert, R. and P. Landrigan (2000). Work-related death: a continuing epidemic. *American Journal of Public Health* 90 (4): 541–5.

Higgitt, A. (2000). Suicide reduction: policy context. *International Review of Psychiatry* 12: 15–20.

Hill Collins, P. (1990). *Black Feminist Thought: Knowledge, Consciousness, and the Politics of Empowerment.* Boston: Unwin Hyman.

Hippisley-Cox, J., M. Pringle, et al. (2001). Sex inequalities in ischaemic heart disease in general practice: cross sectional survey. *British Medical Journal* 322: 832.

Hochman, J. S. and J. Tamis-Holland (2002). Acute coronary syndromes: does sex matter? *Journal of American Medical Association* 24 (288): 3124–9.

Houghton, L. A., N. A. Jackson, et al. (2000). Do male sex hormones protect from irritable bowel syndrome? *American Journal of Gastroenterology* 95 (9): 2296–2300.

HPA (2003). *Renewing the Focus: HIV and Other Sexually Transmitted Infections in the United Kingdom in 2002.* London: Health Protection Agency.

HRSA (2004). *Women's Health USA 2004.* Rockville, Md.: US Department of Health and Human Services, Health Resources and Services Administration.

Huber, T. J., C. Tettenborn, et al. (2005). Sex hormones in psychotic men. *Psychoneuroendocrinology* 30: 111–14.

Hughes, C. and A. Evans (2003). Health needs of women who have sex with women. *British Medical Journal* 327: 939–40.

Hunt, K. (2002). A generation apart? Gender-related experiences and health in women in early and late mid-life. *Social Science & Medicine* 54: 663–676.

Hunt, K. and E. Annandale (1999). Relocating gender and morbidity: examining men's and women's health in contemporary Western societies. Introduction to special issue on gender and health. *Social Science & Medicine* 48 (1): 1–5.

Hunt, K., G. Ford, et al. (1999). Are women more ready to consult than men? Gender differences in family practitioner consultation for common chronic conditions. *Journal of Health Services Research and Policy* 4 (2): 96–100.

Hunter, M. (1996). Depression and the menopause. *British Medical Journal* 313: 1217–18.

Hussein, J., J. Bellb, et al. (2004). The skilled attendance index: proposal for a new measure of skilled attendance at delivery. *Reproductive Health Matters* 12 (24): 160–70.

Hynes, H. (2004). On the battlefield of women's bodies: an overview of the harm of war to women. *Women's Studies International Forum* 27: 431–45.

IASO (2004). *About Obesity*. London: International Association for the Study of Obesity.

Ilic, M., H. Vlajinac, et al. (1996). Case-control study of risk factors for prostate cancer. *British Journal of Cancer* 74: 1682–6.

Ingram, D. and S. Hutchinson (2000). Double binds and the reproductive and mothering experiences of HIV-positive women. *Qualitative Health Research* 10 (1): 117–32.

Inhorn, M. C. and L. Whittle (2001). Feminism meets the 'new' epidemiologies: toward an appraisal of antifeminist biases in epidemiological research on women's health. *Social Science & Medicine* 53: 553–567.

James, S., S. Reddy, et al. (2004). Young people, HIV/AIDS/STIs and sexuality in South Africa: the gap between awareness and behaviour. *Acta Paediatrica* 93 (2): 264–9.

Jansson, L. and R. Holmdahl (1998). Estrogen-mediated immunosuppression in autoimmune diseases. *Inflammation Research* 47 (7): 290–301.

Jefferson, T. (1998). Muscle, 'hard men' and 'iron Mike' Tyson: reflections on desire, anxiety and the embodiment of masculinity. *Body and Society* 4 (1): 77–98.

Jemal, A., W. D. Travis, et al. (2003). Lung cancer rates convergence in young men and women in the United States: analysis by birth cohort and histologic type. *International Journal of Cancer* 105 (1): 101–7.

Jenkins, E. (1996). Homicide against women in the workplace. *Journal of American Medical Women's Association* 51 (3): 118–19.

Jenkins, R., W. Gulbinat, et al. (2004). The Mental Health Country Profile:

background, design and use of a systematic method of appraisal. *International Review of Psychiatry* 16 (1–2): 31–47.
Jewitt, C. (1997). Images of men: male sexuality in sexual health leaflets and posters for young people. *Sociological research online* 2 (2).
Jones, C. O. H. and H. A. Williams (2004). The social burden of malaria: what are we measuring? *American Journal of Tropical Medicine and Hygiene* 71 (2 suppl.): 156–61.
Judelson, D. (1994). Coronary heart disease in women: risk factors and prevention. *Journal of American Medicine Women's Association* 49 (6): 186–91.
Jylhä, M., J. Guralnik, et al. (1998). Is self-rated health comparable across cultures and genders? *Journal of Gerontology* 53 (3): S144–52.
Kandrack, M., K. Grant, et al. (1991). Gender differences in health related behaviour: some unanswered questions. *Social Science & Medicine* 32 (5): 579–90.
Karim, S., K. Saeed, et al. (2004). Pakistan mental health country profile. *International Review of Psychiatry* 16 (1–2): 83–92.
Kavanagh, A. M. and D. H. Broom (1997). Women's understanding of abnormal cervical smear test results: a qualitative interview study. *British Medical Journal* 314: 1388–91.
Keefe, F. J., G. Affleck, et al. (2004). Gender differences in pain, coping, and mood in individuals having osteoarthritic knee pain: a within-day analysis. *Pain* 110 (3): 571–7.
Keefe, F. J., J. Lefebvre, et al. (2000). The relationship of gender to pain, pain behaviour and disability in osteoarthritis patients: the role of catastrophizing. *Pain* 87 (3): 325–34.
Keene, J. (2002). Women, drugs and alcohol. In G. Boswell and F. Poland (eds), *Women's Minds, Women's Bodies: Interdisciplinary Approaches to Women's Health*, Basingstoke: Palgrave Macmillan.
Keller, S. M., M. G. Vangel, et al. (2002). The influence of gender on survival and tumor recurrence following adjuvant therapy of completely resected stages II and IIIa non-small cell lung cancer. *Lung Cancer* 37 (3): 303–9.
Kelley, M., J. Steele, et al. (2000). *Adult Dental Health Survey: Oral Health in the United Kingdom 1998*. London: The Stationery Office.
Keohavong, P., Q. Lan, et al. (2003). K-ras mutations in lung carcinomas from nonsmoking women exposed to unvented coal smoke in China. *Lung Cancer* 41(1): 21–7.
Kerimova, J., S. Posner, et al. (2003). High prevalence of self-reported sexual intercourse among internally displaced women in Azerbaijan. *American Journal of Public Health* 93 (7): 1067–70.
Kessing, L. (1998). Recurrence in affective disorder II. Effect of age and gender. *British Journal of Psychiatry* 172: 29–34.
Khan, A., C. Garnder, et al. (2002). Gender differences in the symptoms of

major depression in opposite-sex dizygotic twin pairs. *American Journal of Psychiatry* 159 (8): 1427–29.
Khandelwal, S., P. Sharan, et al. (1995). Eating disorders: an Indian perspective. *International Journal of Social Psychiatry* 41 (2): 132–46.
King, M., E. McKeown, et al. (2003). Mental health and quality of life of gay men and lesbians in England and Wales: controlled, cross-sectional study. *British Journal of Psychiatry* 183: 552–8.
Klausner, J., W. McFarland, et al. (2001). Knock-knock: a population-based survey of risk behavior, health care access, and Chlamydia trachomatis infection among low-income women in the San Francisco Bay area. *Journal of Infectious Diseases* 183: 1087–92.
Klein, D. and B. Walsh (2003). Eating disorders. *International Review of Psychiatry* 15: 205–16.
Klitzman, R. L. and J. D. Greenberg (2002). Patterns of communication between gay and lesbian patients and their health care providers. *Journal of Homosexuality* 42 (4): 65–75.
Knodel, J. and M. Ofstedal (2003). Gender and aging in the developing world: where are the men? *Population and Development Review* 29 (4): 677–98.
Kogan, M., M. Kotelchuck, et al. (1994). Racial disparities in reported prenatal care advice from health care providers. *American Journal of Public Health* 84 (1): 82–8.
Koster-Oyekan, W. (1998). Why resort to illegal abortion in Zambia? Findings of a community-based study in Western Province. *Social Science and Medicine* 46: 1303–12.
Kposowa, A. J. (2001). Unemployment and suicide: a cohort analysis of social factors predicting suicide in the US National Longitudinal Mortality Study. *Psychological Medicine* 31: 127–38.
Kravdal, O. (1995). Is the relationship between childbearing and cancer incidence due to biology or lifestyle? Examples of the importance of using data on men. *International Journal of Epidemiology* 24 (3): 477–84.
Krieger, N. (2001). A glossary for social epidemiology. *Journal of Epidemiology and Community Health* 55: 693–700.
Krieger, N. (2003). Genders, sexes and health: what are the connections – and why does it matter? *International Journal of Epidemiology* 32: 652–7.
Krieger, N. (2005) Embodiment: a conceptual glossary for epidemiology. *Journal of Epidemiology and Community Health* 59: 350–5.
Krieger, N. and E. Fee (1994). Man-made medicine and women's health: the biopolitics of sex/gender and race/ethnicity. In E. Fee and N. Krieger (eds), *Women's Health, Politics and Power*, New York: Baywood Publishing.
Krieger, N. and P. H. Zierler (1995). Accounting for the health of women. *Current Issues in Public Health* 1: 251–6.
Krieger, N., J. Chen, et al. (2003). Choosing area-based socioeconomic measures to monitor social inequalities in low birth weight and childhood

lead poisoning: the Public Health Disparities Geocoding Project (US). *Journal of Epidemiology and Community Health* 57: 186–99.

Krug, E., G. Sharma, et al. (2000). The global burden of injuries. *American Journal of Public Health* 90 (4): 523–6.

Lahelma, E., S. Arber, et al. (2002). Multiple roles and health among British and Finnish women: the influence of socioeconomic circumstances. *Social Science & Medicine* 54 (5): 727–40.

Lahita, R. (2000). Gender and the immune system. *Journal of Gender Specific Medicine* 3 (7): 19–22.

Lakkis, J., L. A. Ricciardelli, et al. (1999). Role of sexual orientation and gender-related traits in disordered eating. *Sex Roles: A Journal of Research* 41 (1/2): 1–16.

Lang, T. (2001). Food Justice: An End to Food Poverty, <http://www.joeshort.net/foodjustice/timlang.html>.

Lang, T. and M. Heaseman (2004). *Food Wars: The Battle for Mouth, Minds and Markets.* London: Earthscan Publications Ltd.

Lawrence, S. C. and K. Bendixen (1992). His and hers: male and female anatomy in anatomy texts for U.S. medical students, 1890–1989. *Social Science & Medicine* 35 (7): 925–34.

Laws, S., V. Hey, et al. (1985). *Seeing Red: The Politics of Premenstrual Tension.* London: Hutchinson.

Lee, C. and R. G. Owens (2002). *The Psychology of Men's Health.* Buckingham: Open University Press.

Lee, E. and E. Jackson (2002). The pregnant body. In M. Evans and E. Lee (eds), *Real Bodies: A Sociological Introduction,* Buckingham: Philadelphia/Open University Press.

Legato, M. (1997). Gender-specific aspects of obesity. *International Journal of Fertility and Women's Medicine* 42 (3): 184–97.

Legato, M. (2003). Beyond women's health: the new discipline of gender-specific medicine. *Medical Clinics of North America* 87: 917–37.

Lehman, S. (2003). Psychiatric disorders in older women. *International Review of Psychiatry* 15: 269–79.

Leon, D. and G. Walt (2001). *Poverty, Inequality and Health: An International Perspective.* Oxford: Oxford University Press.

LeResche, L. (1999). Epidemiological perspectives on sex differences in pain. In B. D. Fillingim (ed.), *Sex, Gender and Pain,* Seattle: IASP Press.

LeRoi, A., C. Bernier, et al. (1995). Prevalence of sexual abuse among patients with functional disorders of the lower gastro-intestinal tract. *International Journal of Colorectal Disease* 10 (4): 200–6.

Lethbridge-Ccjku, M., J. S. Schiller, et al. (2004). *Summary Health Statistics for US Adults: National Health Interview Survey.* Washington: National Centre for Health Statistics.

Levi, F., F. Lucchini, et al. (1999). Trends in mortality from cancer in the European union 1955–1994. *The Lancet* 354: 742–3.

Lewis, G., J. Drife, et al. (2001). Why Mothers Die 1997–1999: *The Fifth Report of the Confidential Enquiries into Maternal Deaths in the United Kingdom.* London: CEMD.

Liang, W., M. Shediac-Rizkallah, et al. (1999). A population-based study of age and gender differences in patterns of health-related behaviours. *American Journal of Preventive Medicine* 17 (1): 8–17.

Lipscomb, H., J. Dement, et al. (2000). Deaths from external causes of injury among construction workers in North Carolina, 1988–1994. *Applied Occupational and Environmental Hygiene* 15 (7): 569–80.

Lloyd, T. (2002). *Boys' and Young Men's Health: What Works?* London: Working with Men/Health Development Agency.

Lock, M. (1998). Anomalous ageing: managing the postmenopausal body. *Body and Society* 4 (1): 35–61.

Locke, C. (2002). Discursive challenges: reproductive rights and women's health in developing countries. In G. Boswell and F. Poland (eds), *Women's Minds, Women's Bodies: Interdisciplinary Approaches to Women's Health,* Basingstoke: Palgrave Macmillan.

Logio, K. (2003). Gender, race, childhood abuse, and body image among adolescents. *Violence Against Women* 9 (8): 931–54.

Lorant, V., D. Deliege, et al. (2003). Socio-economic inequalities in depression: a meta-analysis. *American Journal of Epidemiology* 157 (2): 98–112.

Lorber, J. (1997). *Gender and the Social Construction of Illness.* Thousand Oaks, Calif.: Sage.

Lourens, P. F., J. A. Viessers, et al. (1999). Annual mileage driving violations, and accident involvement in relation to drivers' sex, age, and level of education. *Accident Analysis and Prevention* 31 (5): 593–7.

Lovejoy, M. (2001). Disturbances in the social body: differences in body image and eating problems among African American and White women. *Gender & Society* 15 (2): 239–61.

Lowndes, C. M. and K. A. Fenton (2004). Surveillance systems for STIs in the European Union: facing a changing epidemiology. *Sexually Transmitted Infections* 80 (4): 264–71.

LSC (2003). Culture, Age, Gender and Smoking, Liberty Science Centre: <http://www.lsc.org/tobacco/health/culutre.html>.

Luo, R., B. Wu, et al. (1996). Indoor burning coal air pollution and lung cancer – a case-control study in Fuzhou, China. *Lung Cancer* 14 (1): S113–19.

Lupton, D. (1999). *Risk and Sociocultural Theory: New Directions and Perspectives.* Cambridge: Cambridge University Press.

Lupton, D. and L. Barclay (1997). *Constructing Fatherhood: Discourses and Experiences.* London: Sage.

Luy, M. (2003). Causes of male excess mortality: insights from cloistered populations. *Population and Development Review* 29 (4): 647–76.

Macintyre, S. (2001). Inequalities in health: is research gender blind? In

D. Leon and G. Walt (eds), *Poverty, Inequality and Health: An International Perspective*, Milton Keynes: Open University Press.
Macintyre, S. and K. Hunt (1997). Socio-economic position, gender and health. How do they interact? *Journal of Health Psychology* 2 (3): 315–34.
Macintyre, S. and C. Pritchard (1989). Comparisons between the self-assessed and observer-assessed presence and severity of colds. *Social Science & Medicine* 29 (11): 1243–8.
Macintyre, S., G. Ford, et al. (1999). Do women 'over-report' morbidity? Men's and women's responses to structured prompting on a standard question on long-standing illness. *Social Science & Medicine* 48: 89–98.
Macintyre, S., K. Hunt, et al. (1996). Gender differences in health: are things really as simple as they seem? *Social Science & Medicine* 42 (4): 617–24.
MacKay, J. (1996). Women and tobacco: international issues. *Journal of the American Medical Association* 51 (1 & 2): 48–51.
Makela, P., T. Valkonen, et al. (1997). Contribution of deaths related to alcohol use to socioeconomic variation in mortality: register-based follow-up study. *British Medical Journal* 315: 211–16.
Malson, H. M. and J. M. Ussher (1997). Beyond this mortal coil: femininity, death and discursive constructions of the anorexic body. *Mortality* 2 (1): 43–61.
Malterud, K. and I. Okkes (1998). Gender differences in general practice consultations: methodological challenges in epidemiological research. *Family Practice* 15 (5): 404–10.
Mamo, L. and J. Fishman (2001). Potency in all the right places: Viagra as a technology of the gendered body. *Body and Society* 7 (4): 13–35.
Manderson, L. (1999). Social meanings and sexual bodies: gender, sexuality and barriers to women's health care. In T. Pollard and S. Brin Hyatt (eds), *Sex, Gender and Health*, Cambridge: Cambridge University Press.
Mant, D. and C. Silagy (1998). The epidemiology of men's health. In T. O'Dowd and D. Jewell (eds), *Men's Health*, Oxford, Oxford University Press.
Marmot, M. and M. Bobak (2000). International comparators and poverty and health in Europe. *British Medical Journal* 321: 1124–28.
Marrazzo, J. M. and K. Stine (2004). Reproductive health history of lesbians: implications for care. *American Journal of Obstetrics and Gynecology* 190 (5): 1298–1304.
Marsh, B. (2004). The ladette takeover. *The Mail on Sunday*, London.
Marshall, B. and S. Katz (2002). Forever functional: sexual fitness and the ageing male body. *Body and Society* 8 (4): 43–70.
Martin, R., C. Lemos, et al. (2004). Gender disparities in common sense models of illness among myocardial infarction victims. *Health Psychology* 24 (3): 345–53.
Mather, H. M., N. Chaturvedi, et al. (1998). Mortality and morbidity from diabetes in South Asians and Europeans: 11 year follow-up of the Southall Diabetes Survey, London, UK. *Diabetes Medicine* 15 (1): 53–9.

Matthey, S., B. Barnett et al. (2001). Validation of the Edinburgh Postnatal Depression Scale for men, and comparison of item endorsement with their partners. *Journal of Affective Disorders*, 64 (2–3): 175–84.

Mayer, E. A., B. Naliboff, et al. (1999). Review article: gender-related differences in functional gastrointestinal disorders. *Alimentary Pharmacology and Therapeutics* 13, suppl. 2: 65–9.

McAllister, M. (2003). Multiple meanings of self harm: a critical review. *International Journal of Mental Health Nursing* 12 (3): 177–85.

McBeth, H. (2001). Defining the ethnic group. H. McBeth and P. Shetty (eds), *Health and Ethnicity*, London: Taylor & Francis.

McCabe, M. P. and L. A. Ricciardelli (2004). Body image dissatisfaction among males across the lifespan: a review of past literature. *Journal of Psychosomatic Research* 55 (6): 675–85.

McCormick, A., D. Fleming, et al. (1995). *Morbidity Statistics from General Practice: Fourth National Study 1991–1992*. London: HMSO.

McCullough, M. and J. Laurenceau (2004). Gender and the natural history of self-rated health: a 59 year longitudinal study. *Health Psychology* 23 (6): 651–5.

McKenzie, K., M. Serfaty, et al. (2003). Suicide in ethnic minority groups. *British Journal of Psychiatry* 183: 100–1.

McKinley, J. (1996). Some contributions from the social system to gender inequalities in heart disease. *Journal of Health and Social Behavior* 37: 1–26.

McMichael, A. J. and R. Beaglehole (2000). The changing global context of public health. *The Lancet* 356: 495–9.

McNair, L. and C. Prather (2004). African American women and AIDS: factors influencing risk and reaction to HIV disease. *Journal of Black Psychology* 30 (1): 106–23.

McNair, R. (2003). Outing lesbian health in medical education. *Women's Health* 37 (4): 89–103.

McNulty, P. A. (2001). Prevalence and contributing factors of eating disorder behaviors in active duty service women in the Army, Navy, Air Force, and Marines. *Military Medicine* 166 (1): 53–8.

Meischke, H., M. Larson, et al. (1998). Gender differences in reported symptoms for acute myocardial infarction: impact on prehospital delay time interval. *American Journal of Emergency Medicine* 17 (4): 363–6.

Mendelsohn, K. D., L. Z. Nieman, et al. (1994). Sex and gender bias in anatomy and physical diagnosis text illustrations. *Journal of the American Medical Association* 272 (16): 1267–70.

Men's Health Forum (2002). Men's Health Week. *Men's Health Forum Update*, July 2002.

Messing, K., L. Punnett, et al. (2003). Be the fairest of them all: challenges and recommendations for the treatment of gender in occupational health research. *American Journal of Industrial Medicine* 43 (6): 618–29.

MIND (2002). *Men's Mental Health*. London: MIND.
Miranda, J. and B. Green (1999). The need for mental health services research focusing on poor young women. *Journal of Mental Health Policy* 2: 73–80.
Mitchell, A. and K. Herring (1998). *What the Blues is all about: Black Women Overcoming Stress and Depression*. New York: Perigree.
Monaghan, L. (2001). *Bodybuilding, Drugs and Risk*. London: Routledge.
Moran, N. (1996). Lesbian health care needs. *Canadian Family Physician* 42: 879–84.
Morris, M. and A. Symonds (2004). 'We've been trained to put up with it': real women and the menopause. *Critical Public Health* 14 (3): 311–23.
Mosley, P. and Y. Kalyuzhnova (2000). Are poverty and social goals attainable in the transition region? *Development Policy Review* 18 (1): 107–20.
Moynihan, C. (1998). Theories of masculinity. *British Medical Journal* 317: 1072–5.
Moynihan, R. (2005). The marketing of a disease: female sexual dysfunction. *British Medical Journal* 330: 192–4.
Muntaner, C., W. Eaton, et al. (2004). Socio-economic position and major mental disorders. *Epidemiologic Reviews* 26: 53–62.
Murphy, R. (2003). Fertility and distorted sex ratios in a rural Chinese county: culture, state, and policy. *Population and Development Review* 29 (4): 596–626.
Murray, C. J. and A. Lopez (1997). Global mortality, disability, and the contribution of risk factors: Global Burden of Disease Study. *The Lancet* 350 (9071): 1436–42.
Nathanson, C. (1977). Sex, illness and medical care: a review of data, theory and method. *Social Science & Medicine* 11: 13–25.
National Centre in HIV Epidemiology and Clinical Research (2004). *2004 Annual Surveillance Report: HIV/AIDS, Viral Hepatitis and Sexually Transmitted Infections in Australia*. Sydney: National Centre in HIV Epidemiology and Clinical Research.
National Comparative Survey of Minority Health Care (1997). *A Comparative Survey of Minority Health: Minority Health Care Survey Highlights*. New York: The Commonwealth Fund.
NCHS (2003). *International Classification of Diseases, Tenth Revision* (ICD-10-CM), National Centre for Health and Statistics: <http://www.cdc.gov/nchs/data/icd9/draft_i10guideln.pdf>.
NCHS (2004). *Health United States 2004*. Washington: National Centre for Health Statistics.
Neumark-Sztainer, D., J. Croll, et al. (2002). Ethnic/racial differences in weight-related concerns and behaviors among adolescent girls and boys – Findings from Project EAT. *Journal of Psychosomatic Research* 53 (5): 963–74.
NIAID (2004). *HIV Infection in Women*. Rockville, Md.: National Institute of Allergy and Infectious Diseases.
Nunez, A. E. and C. Robertson (2003). Multicultural considerations in women's health. *Medical Clinics of North America* 87 (5): 939–54.

Nurminen, M. and A. Karjalainen (2001). Epidemiologic estimate of the proportion of fatalities related to occupational factors in Finland. *Scandinavian Journal of Work, Environment & Health* 27 (3): 161–213.

NZHIS (2005). *Suicide Facts: Provisional 2002 All Ages Statistics*. Wellington: New Zealand Ministry of Health.

NZMOH (2004). *A Portrait of Health*. Wellington: New Zealand Ministry of Health.

Oakley, A. (1972). *Sex, Gender and Society*. London: Temple Hill.

O'Brien, R., K. Hunt, et al. (2005). 'It's caveman stuff, but that is to a certain extent how guys still operate': men's accounts of masculinity and help-seeking. *Social Science & Medicine* 61: 503–16.

O'Brien Cousins, S. and M. M. Gillis (2005). 'Just do it . . . before you talk yourself out of it': the self-talk of adults thinking about physical activity. *Psychology of Sport and Exercise* 6 (3): 313–34.

O'Donnell, L., C. O'Donnell, et al. (2004). Risk and resiliency factors influencing suicidality among urban African American and Latino youth. *American Journal of Community Psychology* 33 (1–2): 37–49.

O'Dowd, T. and D. Jewell (1998). *Men's Health*. Oxford: Oxford University Press.

ONS (1997). *Regional Trends*. London: Office for National Statistics.

ONS (2003). *Deaths by Age, Sex and Underlying Cause, 2003 Registrations*. London: Office for National Statistics.

ONS (2004). *Focus on Health: Health Status*. London: Office for National Statistics.

ONS (2005a). General Practice Research Database, Office for National Statistics.

ONS (2005b). *Trends in Life Expectancy by Social Class 1972–2001*. London: Office for National Statistics.

Orengo, C., G. Fullerton, et al. (2004). Male depression: a review of gender concerns and testosterone therapy. *Geriatrics* 59 (10): 24–30.

Ostlin, P. (2002). Examining Work and its Effects on Health. In G. Sen et al. (eds), *Engendering/International/Health: The Challenge of Equity*, Cambridge, Mass.: MIT Press.

Oxaal, Z. and S. Cook (1998). Health and poverty gender analysis. Brighton: BRIDGE.

Ozcan, M. E. and R. Banoglu (2003). Gonadal hormones in schizophrenia and mood disorders. *European Archives of Psychiatry and Clinical Neurology* 253: 193–6.

Padayachee, A. (1998). The hidden health burden: alcohol-abusing women, misunderstood and mistreated. *International Journal of Drug Policy* 9 (1): 57–62.

Palinkas, L., D. L. Wingard, et al. (1996). Depressive symptoms in overweight and obese older adults: a test of the 'jolly fat' hypothesis. *Journal of Psychosomatic Research* 40 (1): 59–66.

Palmer, P., L. Coleman, et al. (1993). Childhood sexual experiences with

adults: a comparison of reports by women psychiatric patients and general practice attenders. *British Journal of Psychiatry* 163: 499–504.
Pamuk, E., D. Makuc, et al. (1998). *Socioeconomic Status and Health Chartbook*. Hyattsville, Md.: National Center for Health Statistics.
Pandey, M., A. Mathew, et al. (1999). Global perspective of tobacco habits and lung cancer: a lesson for third world countries. *European Journal of Cancer Prevention* 8: 271–9.
Paquette, M. C. and K. Raine (2004). Sociocultural context of women's body image. *Social Science & Medicine* 59 (5): 1047–58.
Parameshvara Deva, M. (2004). Malaysia mental health country profile. *International Review of Psychiatry* 16 (1–2): 167–76.
Patel, V. and A. Kleinman (2003). Poverty and common mental disorders in developing countries. *Bulletin of the World Health Organisation* 81 (8): 609–15.
Patel, V., M. Abas, et al. (2001). Depression in developing countries: lessons from Zimbabwe. *British Medical Journal* 322: 482.
Payne, J. (2003). The role of estrogen in mood disorders in women. *International Review of Psychiatry* 15: 280–90.
Payne, S. (1998). 'Different and dangerous': reconstructions of madness in the 1990s and the role of mental health policy. In S. Watson and L. Doyal (eds), *Engendering Social Policy*, Milton Keynes: Open University Press.
Payne, S. (2000). Poverty and mental health. Bristol: Townsend Centre for the Study of Poverty, University of Bristol. Working Paper No. 15, <http://www.bris.ac.uk/poverty/pse>.
Payne, S. (2001). 'Smoke like a man, die like a man'?: a review of the relationship between gender, sex and lung cancer. *Social Science & Medicine* 53 (8): 1067–80.
Payne, S. (2004). *Gender in Lung Cancer and Smoking Research*. Geneva: WHO.
Pearson, S. (2003). Men's use of sexual health services. *Journal of Family Planning & Reproductive Health Care* 29 (4): 190–4.
Pearson, V. (2005). A broken compact: women's health in the reform era. In L. Dittmer and G. Liu (eds), *China's Deep Reform Domestic Politics in Transition*. Lanham, Md.: Rowman & Littlefield Publishers.
Pearson, V. and L. Meng (2002). Ling's death: an ethnography of a Chinese woman's suicide. *Suicide and Life-Threatening Behaviour* 32 (4): 348–58.
Peixoto Labre, M. (2002). Adolescent boys and the muscular male body ideal. *Journal of Adolescent Health* 30 (4): 233–42.
Peterson, A. (1998). Sexing the body: representations of sex differences in Gray's Anatomy 1858 to the present. *Body and Society* 4 (1): 1–15.
Petrek, J. A., W. A. Sandberg, et al. (1985). The role of gender and other factors in the prognosis of young patients with colorectal cancer. *Cancer* 56 (4): 952–5.
Phillimore, P. (1989). *Shortened Lives: Premature Death in North Tyneside*. Bristol: School of Applied Social Studies.

Phillips, D. and F. Brooks (1998). Women patients' preferences for female or male GPs. *Family Practice* 15 (6): 543–7.

Phillips, M., X. Li, et al. (2002). Suicide rates in China 1995–1999. *The Lancet* 359 (8309): 835–40.

Phillips-Angeles, E., P. Wolfe, et al. (2004). Lesbian health matters: a pap test education campaign nearly thwarted by discrimination. *Health Promotion Practice* 5 (3): 314–25.

Piccinelli, M. and G. Wilkinson (2000). Gender differences in depression: critical review. *British Journal of Psychiatry* 177: 486–92.

Pollard, T. (1999). Sex, gender and cardiovascular disease. In T. Pollard and S. Brin Hyatt (eds), *Sex, Gender and Health*, Cambridge: Cambridge University Press.

Pollard, T. and S. Brin Hyatt (1999). Sex, gender and health: integrating biological and social perspectives. In T. Pollard and S. Brin Hyatt (eds), *Sex, Gender and Health*, Cambridge: Cambridge University Press.

Popay, J., M. Bartley, et al. (1993). Gender inequalities in health: social position, affective disorders and minor physical morbidity. *Social Science & Medicine* 36: 21–32.

Porcerelli, J., R. Cogan, et al. (2003). Violent victimization of women and men: physical and psychiatric symptoms. *Journal of American Board of Family Practitioners* 16: 32–9.

Prendergast, M. (2004). Do women possess a unique susceptibility to the neurotoxic effects of alcohol? *Journal of American Medical Women's Association* 59 (3): 225–7.

Prescott, E., M. Hippe, et al. (1998). Smoking and risk of myocardial infarction in women and men: longitudinal population study. *British Medical Journal* 316: 1043–7.

Price, J. H., A. N. Easton, et al. (1996). Perceptions of cervical cancer and PaP smear screening behavior by women's sexual orientation. *Journal of Community Health* 21 (2): 89–105.

Prieto Carron, M. (2004). Is anyone listening? Women workers in factories in central America and corporate codes of conduct. *Development* 47 (3): 101–5.

Prior, L. (1989). *The Social Organization of Death: Medical Discourse and Social Practices in Belfast*. Basingstoke: Macmillan.

Pugliesi, K. (1999). Gender and work stress: differential exposure and vulnerability. *Journal of Gender, Culture, and Health* 4 (2): 97–117.

Puras, D., A. Germanavicius, et al. (2004). Lithuania mental health country profile. *International Review of Psychiatry* 16 (1–2): 117–25.

Rahman, M. and A. Barsky (2003). Self-reported health among older Bangladeshis: how good a health indicator is it? *Gerontologist* 43 (6): 856–63.

Raine, R., A. Hutchings, et al. (2003). Is publicly funded health care really distributed according to need? The example of cardiac rehabilitation in the UK. *Health Policy* 63: 63–72.

Raleigh, V. (1996). Suicide patterns and trends in people of Indian subcontinent and Caribbean origin in England and Wales. *Ethnicity and Health* 1: 55–63.

Ramasubbu, K., H. Gurm, et al. (2001). Gender bias in clinical trials: do double standards still apply? *Journal of Women's Health and Gender-Based Medicine* 10 (8): 757–64.

Redgrave, G., K. Swartz, et al. (2003). Alcohol misuse by women. *International Review of Psychiatry* 15: 256–68.

Rees, C., M. Jones, et al. (1995). Exploring men's health in a men-only group. *Nursing Standard* 9 (43): 38–40.

Rennie, D., Y. Chen, et al. (2005). Differential effect of damp housing on respiratory health in women. *Journal of the American Medical Women's Association* 60: 45–51.

Rich-Edwards, J., N. Krieger et al. (2001). Maternal experiences of racism and violence as predictors of preterm birth: rationale and study design. *Paediatric and Perinatal Epidemiology*, 15 (s2): 124–35.

Richardson, D., D. Loomis, et al. (2004). Fatal occupational injury rates in southern and non-southern states, by race and Hispanic ethnicity. *American Journal of Public Health* 94 (10): 1756–61.

Richardson, N. (2004). The queer activity of extreme male bodybuilding: gender dissidence, auto-eroticism and hysteria. *Social Semiotics* 14 (1): 49–65.

Roberts, S. A., S. L. Dibble, et al. (2003). Cardiovascular disease risk in lesbian women. *Women's Health Issues* 13 (4): 167–74.

Roberts, S. J. and L. Sorensen (1999). Health related behaviors and cancer screening of lesbians: results from the Boston Lesbian Health Project. *Women's Health* 28 (4): 1–12.

Robinson, F. and J. Keithley (2000). The impacts of crime on health and health services: a literature review. *Health, Risk and Society* 2 (3): 253–66.

Robinson, G. and M. Cohen (1996). Gay, lesbian and bisexual health care issues and medical curricula. *Canadian Medical Association Journal* 155 (6): 709–11.

Rogers, W. (2004). Evidence-based medicine and women: do the principles and practice of EBM further women's health? *Bioethics* 18 (1): 50–71.

Ross, A., L. Van der Paal, et al. (2004). HIV-1 disease progression and fertility: the incidence of recognized pregnancy and pregnancy outcome in Uganda. *AIDS* 18 (5): 799–804.

Rumm, P. D. and G. D. Johnson (2002). Key men's health issues in public health – women can help spread the word. *Wisconsin Medical Journal* 101 (4): 16–18.

Ruzek, S. (1978). *The Women's Health Movement: Feminist Alternatives to Medical Control*. New York: Praeger.

Ryan, H. et al. (2001). Smoking among lesbians, gays and bisexuals: a review of the literature. *American Journal of Preventative Medicine* 21 (2): 142–9.

Sabo, D. and D. Gordon (1995). *Men's Health and Illness: Gender, Power and the Body*. London: Sage.

Sadana, R., C. Mathers, et al. (2000). *Comparative Analyses of More than 50 Household Surveys on Health Status.* Geneva: EIP/GPE/EBD WHO.

Saltman, K. (2003). The strong arm of the law. *Body and Society* 9 (4): 49–67.

Saltonstall, R. (1993). Healthy bodies, social bodies: men's and women's concepts and practices of health in everyday life. *Social Science & Medicine* 36 (1): 7–14.

Sanders-Phillips, K. (2002). Factors influencing HIV/AIDS in women of color. *Public Health Reports* 117 (suppl. 1): S151–6.

Sandfort, T., R. de Graaf, et al. (2001). Same-sex sexual behavior and psychiatric disorders. *Archives of General Psychiatry* 58: 85–91.

Sandman, D., E. Soimantov, et al. (2000). *Out of Touch: American Men and the Health Care System.* New York: The Commonwealth Fund.

Sankaranarayanan, R., A. Madhukar Budukh, et al. (2001). Effective screening programmes for cervical cancer in low- and middle-income developing countries. *Bulletin of the World Health Organisation* 79 (10): 954–62.

Sargent, C. and C. Brettell (1996). *Gender and Health: An International Perspective.* New York: Prentice-Hall.

Sassatelli, R. (2002). Beyond health and beauty: a critical perspective on fitness culture. In G. Boswell and F. Poland (eds), *Women's Minds, Women's Bodies: Interdisciplinary Approaches to Women's Health.* Basingstoke: Palgrave Macmillan.

Save the Children (2004). *Children having Children: State of the World's Mothers.* London: Save the Children.

Sayers, J. (2002). Feeding the body. In M. Evans and E. Lee. (eds), *Real Bodies: A Sociological Introduction*, Basingstoke: Palgrave Macmillan.

Scarce, M. (1999). *Smearing the Queer: Medical Bias in the Health Care of Gay Men.* New York: Harrington Press.

Schiller, J. S. and L. Bernadel (2004). *Summary Health Statistics for the US Population: National Health Interview Survey.* Washington: National Centre for Health Statistics, Vital Health Stat Series 10 Number 220.

Schotanus, W. (1998). Older men's health – overcoming barriers to their care. *Journal of Medical Association Georgia* 87 (1): 37–8.

Schwarcz, R. and R. Fescina (2000). Maternal mortality in Latin America and the Caribbean. *The Lancet* 356: S11.

Schwartz, M. B. and K. D. Brownell (2004). Obesity and body image. *Body Image* 1 (1): 43–56.

Scully, D. (2003). Afterword. *Feminism & Psychology* 13 (1): 40–4.

Scully, D. and P. Bart (1978). A funny thing happened on the way to the orifice: Women in gynaecology textbooks. In J. Ehrenreich (ed.), *The Cultural Crisis of Modern Medicine.* New York: Monthly Review Press.

Seidler, V. J. (1997). *Man Enough: Embodying Masculinities.* London: Sage.

Seidman, S. N. and B. T. Walsh (1999). Testosterone and depression in aging men. *American Journal of Geriatric Psychiatry* 7 (1): 18–33.

Shaw, L., R. Hachamovitch, et al. (2000). Current evidence on diagnostic testing in women with suspected coronary heart disease: choosing the appropriate test. *Cardiology in Review* 8 (1): 65–74.

Shaw, S. (2002). Shifting conversations on girls' and women's self-injury: an analysis of the clinical literature in historical context. *Feminism & Psychology* 12 (2): 191–219.

Shelton, D. L. (1999). Men's health centers: not enough muscle. *American Medical News*, American Medical Association.

Shephard, R. J. and P. N. Shek (1998). Associations between physical activity and susceptibility to cancer – possible mechanisms. *Sports Medicine* 26 (5): 293–315.

Shields, P. G. (2002). Molecular epidemiology of smoking and lung cancer. *Oncogene* 21 (45): 6870–6.

Shinar, D., E. Schechtman, et al. (2001). Self-reports of safe driving behaviours in relationship to sex, age, education and income in the US adult driving population. *Accident Analysis and Prevention* 33: 111–16.

Showalter, E. (1987). *The Female Malady: Women, Madness and English Culture 1830–1980*. London: Virago.

Shriver, S., H. Bourdeau, et al. (2000). Sex-specific expression of gastric peptide receptor. *Journal of National Cancer Institute* 92 (1): 24–33.

Siddall, R. (1993). Time to screen for prostate cancer? Doctors in the Western world are beginning to question the lack of research into one of the most deadly diseases facing ageing men. *New Scientist* 137 (1859): 27.

Siefert, K., C. Heflin, et al. (2001). Food insuffiency and the physical and mental health of low income women. In M. Lennon (ed.), *Welfare, Work and Well-being*, New York: Haworth Press Inc.

Siever, M. D. (1994). Sexual orientation and gender as factors in socio-culturally acquired vulnerability to body dissatisfaction and eating disorders. *Journal of Consulting and Clinical Psychology* 62 (2): 252–60.

Simon, R. (2002). Revisiting the relationships among gender, marital status, and mental health. *American Journal of Sociology* 107 (4): 1065–96.

Singleton, N., R. Bumpstead, et al. (2001). *Psychiatric Morbidity of Adults Living in Private Households 2000*. London: The Stationery Office.

Siriwanarangsan, P., D. Liknapichtkul, et al. (2004). Thailand mental health country profile. *International Review of Psychiatry* 16 (1–2): 150–8.

Smith, C. and J. Allen (2004). *Violent Crime in England and Wales*. London: Office for National Statistics.

Smith, G., A. Bartlett, et al. (2004). Treatments of homosexuality in Britain since the 1950s – an oral history: the experience of patients. *British Medical Journal* 328: 427.

Smith-Rosenberg, C. (1974). Puberty to menopause: the cycle of femininity in nineteenth-century America. In M. S. Hartman and L. Banner (eds), *Clio's Consciousness Raised: New Perspectives on the History of Women*, New York: Harper & Row.

Solarz, A., ed. (1999). *Lesbian Health: Current Assessment and Directions for the Future*. Washington: National Academy Press.

Sproston, K., P. Primatesta, et al. (2002). *Health Survey for England*. London: The Stationery Office.

Stafford, M., S. Cummins, et al. (2005). Gender differences in the associations between health and neighbourhood environment. *Social Science & Medicine* 60: 1681–92.

Standing, H. (1997). Gender and equity in health sector reform programmes: a review. *Health Policy and Planning* 12 (1): 1–18.

Staples, R. (1995). Health amongst Afro-American males. In D. Sabo and D. Gordon (eds), *Men's Health and Illness: Gender, Power and the Body*, London: Sage.

Sternbach, H. (1998). Age-associated testosterone decline in men: clinical issues for psychiatry. *American Journal of Psychiatry* 155 (10): 1310–18.

Stewart, C. (2004). Chile mental health country profile. *International Review of Psychiatry* 16 (1–2): 73–82.

Stibbe, A. (2004). Health and the social construction of masculinity in Men's Health magazine. *Men and Masculinities* 7 (1): 31–51.

Stillion, J. (1995). Premature death among males: extending the bottom line of men's health. In D. Sabo and D. F. Gordon (eds), *Men's Health and Illness: Gender, Power and the Body*, London: Sage.

Stone, D., P. Chishti, et al. (2002). *Final Report of the European Review of Suicide and Violence Epidemiology (Eurosave) Project*. Glasgow: Paediatric Epidemiology and Community Health UN/ WHO.

Suba, E. J. and S. S. Raab (2004). Papanicolaou screening in developing countries: an idea whose time has come. *American Journal of Clinical Pathology* 121 (3): 315–20.

Sundari Ravindran, T. (2000). Engendering health. Seminar 489. <http://www.india-seminar.com/2000/489/489%zoravindran.htm>.

Sundari, T. (1994). The untold story: how the health care systems in developing countries contribute to maternal mortality. In E. Fee and N. Krieger (eds), *Women's Health, Politics and Power*, New York: Baywood Publishing.

Tang, H., G. L. Greenwood, et al. (2004). Cigarette smoking among lesbians, gays, and bisexuals: how serious a problem? (United States). *Cancer Causes Control* 15 (8): 797–803.

Tanner, M. and C. Vlassoff (1998). Treatment-seeking behaviour for malaria: a typology based on endemicity and gender. *Social Science & Medicine* 46 (4–5): 523–32.

Thara, R. and V. Patel (2001). Women's mental health: a public health concern. *Regional Health Forum* 5 (1): 24–33.

Thom, B. (2003). *Risk Taking Behaviour in Men: Substance Use and Gender*. London: Health Development Agency.

Thompson, N. and D. Bhugra (2000). Rates of deliberate self-harm in Asians: findings and models. *International Review of Psychiatry* 12: 37–43.

Thune, I. and E. Lund (1996). Physical activity and risk of colorectal cancer in men and women. *British Journal of Cancer* 73 (9): 1134–40.

Tolhurst, R. and F. K. Nyonator (2002). Developing a methodology for the analysis of gender equity in malaria. Special Programme for Research and Training in Tropical Disease (TDR) Report No 59, UNDP, UNICEF and WHO.

Tomlinson, R. (1997). China's smoking epidemic grows. *British Medical Journal* 315: 501–4.

Toner, B. B. and D. Akman (2000). Gender role and irritable bowel syndrome: literature review and hypothesis. *American Journal of Gastroenterology* 95 (1): 11–16.

Treaster, D. and D. Burr (2004). Gender differences in prevalence of upper extremity musculoskeletal disorders. *Ergonomics* 47 (5): 495–526.

Tulle-Winton, E. (1997). Happy in Castlemilk? Deprivation and depression in an urban community. *Health and Place* 3 (3): 161–70.

UNAIDS (2004). *2004 Report on the Global AIDS Epidemic: Fourth Global Report*. Geneva: UNAIDS.

UNAIDS/WHO (2003). *AIDS Epidemic Update*. Geneva: WHO.

United Nations (2003). *Indicators for Monitoring the Millennium Development Goals: Definitions, Rationale, Concepts and Sources.* New York: United Nations.

Ussher, J. (2003). I. Biology as destiny: the legacy of Victorian gynaecology in the 21st century. *Feminism & Psychology* 13 (1): 17–22.

Vandenbrinkmuinen, A., D. H. Debakker, et al. (1994). Consultations for women's health problems – factors influencing women's choice of sex of general-practitioner. *British Journal of General Practice* 44 (382): 205–10.

Vangen, S., C. Stoltenberg, et al. (1996). Ethnicity and use of obstetrical analgesia: do Pakistani women receive inadequate pain relief in labour? *Ethnicity and Health* 1 (2): 161–7.

Verbrugge, L. M. (1989). The twain meet: empirical explanations of sex differences in health and mortality. *Health and Social Behaviour* 30 (3): 282–304.

Vidaver, R. M., B. Lafleur, et al. (2000). Women subjects in NIH-funded clinical research literature: lack of progress in both representation and analysis by sex. *Journal of Women's Health & Gender-Based Medicine* 9 (5): 495–504.

Vlassoff, C. (1999). *Mainstreaming a Gender-Sensitive Agenda in Health Research: Perspective of International Organisations.* Geneva: Global Forum for Health Research.

Vlassoff, C. and E. Bonilla (1994). Gender-related differences in the impact of tropical diseases on women: what do we know? *Journal of Biosocial Science* 26 (37–53).

Waldron, I. (1991). Effects of labor force participation on sex differences in mortality and morbidity. In M. Frankenhaeuser, U. Lundberg and M. Chesney (eds), *Women's Work and Health: Stress and Opportunities*, New York: Plenum Press.

Waldron, I. (1995). Contributions of changing gender differences in behaviour and social roles to changing gender differences in mortality. In D. Sabo and D. F. Gordon (eds), *Men's Health and Illness: Gender, Power and the Body*, London: Sage.

Walker, J. and J. Carmody (1998). Experimental pain in healthy human subjects: gender differences in nociception and in response to ibuprofen. *Anesthesia & Analgesia* 86: 1257–62.

Waller, D. and A. McPherson (2003). *Women's Health*. Oxford: Oxford University Press.

Wang, Y. and Q. Zhang (2004). Socioeconomic inequality of obesity in the United States: do gender, age, and ethnicity matter? *Social Science & Medicine* 58 (6): 1171–80.

Watson, J. (2000). *Male Bodies: Health, Culture and Identity*. Buckingham: Open University Press.

Weich, S. and G. Lewis (1998). Material standard of living, social class and the prevalence of the common mental disorders in Great Britain. *Journal of Epidemiology and Community Health* 52: 8–14.

Weidner, G. (2000). Why do men get more heart disease than women? An international perspective. *Journal of American College Health* 48: 291–4.

Weiss, E. L., J. G. Longhurst, et al. (1999). Childhood sexual abuse as a risk factor for depression in women: psychosocial and neurobiological correlates. *American Journal of Psychiatry* 156: 816–28.

Wenger, N. K. (1997). Coronary heart disease: an older woman's health risk. *British Medical Journal* 315: 1085–90.

White, A. (2001). How men respond to illness. *Men's Health Journal* 1 (1): 18–19.

White, J. C. and V. T. Dull (1997). Health risk factors and health-seeking behavior in lesbians. *Journal of Women's Health* 6 (1): 103–12.

WHO (1997). *The Smoking Epidemic: A Fire in the Global Village*. Geneva: WHO.

WHO (1999). *The World Health Report 1999: Making a Difference*. Geneva: WHO.

WHO (2001). *The World Health Report 2001: Mental Health – New Understanding, New Hope*. Geneva: WHO.

WHO (2002a). *Gender and Road Traffic Injuries*. Geneva: WHO.

WHO (2002b). *Globalization, Diets and Non-communicable Diseases*. Geneva: WHO.

WHO (2002c). *Myths about Physical Activity*. Geneva: WHO.

WHO (2002d). *Tobacco Atlas*. Geneva: WHO.

WHO (2002e). *The World Health Report: Reducing Risks, Promoting Healthy Life*. Geneva: WHO.

WHO (2003a). *AIDS Epidemic Update*. Geneva: WHO.

WHO (2003b). *Gender, Health and Ageing*. Geneva: WHO.

WHO (2003c). *Integrating Gender into HIV/AIDS Programmes*. Geneva: WHO.

WHO (2003d). *Lives at Risk: Malaria in Pregnancy*. Geneva: WHO.

WHO (2003e). *Obesity and Overweight*. Geneva: WHO.

WHO (2003f). *Treat 3 by 5: Scaling Up Antiretroviral Therapy in Resource Limited Settings: Treatment Guidelines for a Public Health Approach*. Geneva: WHO.

WHO (2003g). *World Report on Violence and Health*. Geneva: WHO.

WHO (2004a). *Democratic Republic of Congo Country Profile*. Geneva: WHO.

WHO (2004b). *Making Pregnancy Safer*. Geneva: WHO.

WHO (2004c). *Neuroscience of Psychoactive Substance Use and Dependence*. Geneva: WHO.

WHO (2004d). *Suicide Rates per 100,000 by Country, Year and Sex*. Geneva: WHO.

WHO (2004e). *The World Health Report 2004: Changing History*. Geneva: WHO.

WHOSIS (2005). Table 1: Numbers and rates of registered deaths. Geneva: WHO Statistical Information System.

Wilkinson, R. (1997). *Unhealthy Societies: From Inequality to Well-being*. London: Routledge.

Williams, D. R. and T. D. Tucker (2000). Understanding and addressing racial disparities in health care. *Health Care Financing Reviews* 21 (4): 75–90.

Williamson, P. (1995). Men's health. Their own worst enemy. *Nursing Times* 91 (48): 24–6.

Wilson, M. (2001). Black women and mental health. *Feminist Review* 68: 34–51.

Winterich, J. A. (2003). Sex, menopause, and culture: sexual orientation and the meaning of menopause for women's sex lives. *Gender & Society* 17 (4): 627–42.

Wisnivesky, J. P., A. I. Mushlin, et al. (2003). The cost-effectiveness of low-dose CT screening for lung cancer: preliminary results of baseline screening. *Chest* 124 (2): 614–21.

Wizeman, T. and M. Pardue (2000). *Exploring the Biological Contributions to Human Health: Does Sex Matter*? Washington: National Academy Press.

Wunsch, F. V., J. E. Moncau, et al. (1998). Occupational risk factors of lung cancer in Sao Paulo, Brazil. *Scandinavian Journal of Work, Environment & Health* 24 (2): 118–24.

Wyatt, G., H. Myers, et al. (2002). Does a history of trauma contribute to HIV risk for women of colour? Implications for prevention and policy. *American Journal of Public Health* 92 (4): 660–5.

Wyke, S., K. Hunt, et al. (1998). Gender differences in consulting a general practitioner for common symptoms of minor illness. *Social Science & Medicine* 46 (7): 901–6.

Wynder, E. and J. Muscat (1995). The changing epidemiology of smoking and lung cancer histology. *Environmental Health Perspectives* 103 (suppl. 8): 143–7.

Xu, K. and T. Borders (2003). Gender, health and physician visits among adults in the United States. *American Journal of Public Health* 93 (7): 1076–79.

Yamey, G. (1999). Sexual and reproductive health: what about boys and men? *British Medical Journal* 319: 1315–16.

Yip, P., C. Callanan, et al. (2000). Urban. rural and gender differences in suicide rates: East and West. *Journal of Affective Disorders* 57: 99–106.

Yunus, M. B. (2002). Gender differences in fibromyalgia and other related syndromes. *Journal of Gender Specific Medicine* 5 (2): 42–7.

Yunus, M., F. Inanici, et al. (2000). Fibromyalgia in men: comparison of clinical features with women. *Journal of Rheumatology* 27 (2): 485–90.

Zierler, S. and N. Krieger (1997). Reframing women's risk: social inequalities and HIV infection. *Annual Review of Public Health* 18: 401–36.

Zinn, C. (1996). Australia targets men's health. *British Medical Journal* 312: 268.

Zitzmann, M. and E. Nieschlag (2001). Testosterone levels in healthy men and the relation to behavioural and physical characteristics: facts and constructs. *European Journal of Endocrinology* 144: 183–97.

Index